SHAKTI 25 YEARS ON

India's Nuclear Progression

SHAKTI 25 YEARS ON

India's Nuclear Progression

Editor

Rajiv Nayan

MANOHAR PARRIKAR INSTITUTE FOR DEFENCE STUDIES AND ANALYSES

PENTAGON PRESS LLP

First published in 2025 by
PENTAGON PRESS LLP
206, Peacock Lane, Shahpur Jat
New Delhi-110049, India
Contact: 011-26490600

Typeset in Palatino, 11 Point
Printed by Aegean Offset Printers, Noida

ISBN 978-81-982857-0-6 (HB)

Disclaimer: The views expressed in this book are those of the author and do not necessarily reflect those of the Manohar Parrikar Institute for Defence Studies and Analyses, or the Government of India.

www.pentagonpress.in

Contents

Abbreviations

AEC	Atomic Energy Commission
AERB	Atomic Energy Regulatory Board
AHWR	Advanced Heavy Water Reactor
AI	Artificial Intelligence
APLN	Asia Pacific Leadership Network
BARC	Bhabha Atomic Research Centre
BJP	Bhartiya Janta Party
BMD	Ballistic Missile Defence
BTWC	Biological and Toxin Weapon Convention
CAGR	Compound Annual Growth Rate
CBM	Confidence Building Mechanism
CCUS	Carbon Capture, Use, and Storage
CD	Conference on Disarmament
CEEW	Council on Energy, Environment and Water
CENTO	Central Treaty Organisation
CERN	Conseil Européen pour la Recherche Nucléaire (European Organi-sation for Nuclear Research)
CICIR	China Institutes of Contemporary International Relations
CIRUS	Canada-India Reactor Utility Services
CNS	Convention on Nuclear Safety
CO_2	Carbon dioxide
CPEC	China-Pakistan Economic Corridor
CPI (M)	Communist Party of India (Marxist)
CPNW	Convention on the Prohibition of the Use of Nuclear Weapons

CPPNM	Convention on the Physical Protection of Nuclear Materials
CSP	Concentrated Solar Power
CTBT	Comprehensive Test Ban Treaty
CWC	Chemical Weapons Convention
DAE	Department of Atomic Energy
DG-SPD	Director-General Strategic Plan Division
DISA	Disarmament and International Security Affairs
DSL	Defence Science Laboratory
EAM	External Affairs Minister
ENDC	Eighteen Nations Disarmament Committee
EU	European Union
FAO	Food and Agriculture Organisation
FBTR	Fast Breeder Test Reactor
FMCT	Fissile Material Cut-Off Treaty
FOAK	First Of A Kind
FSSAI	Food Safety and Standards Authority of India
GCNEP	Global Centre for Nuclear Energy Partnership
GHG	Green House Gas
GICNT	Global Initiative to Combat Nuclear Terrorism
GOI	Government of India
GW	Gigawatt
HDI	Human Development Index
HEU	Highly Enriched Uranium
IAEA	International Atomic Energy Agency
ICNND	International Commission on Non-proliferation and Disarmament
ICSANT	International Convention for the Suppression of Actions of Nuclear Terrorism
IEA	International Energy Agency
IISS	International Institute for International Studies
INF	Intermediate-Range Nuclear Forces
INPO	Institute of Nuclear Power Operations
INPRO	International Project on Innovative Reactors and Fuel Cycles
IRRS	Integrated Regulatory Review Service

ISR	Intelligence, Surveillance and Reconnaissance
ISRO	Indian Space Research Organisation
ITER	International Thermonuclear Experimental Reactor
J&K	Jammu & Kashmir
JCPOA	Joint Comprehensive Plan of Action
KWh	Kilowatt-hour
LAC	Line of Actual Control
LAWS	Lethal Autonomous Weapons System
LCOE	Levelized cost of energy
LOC	Line of Control
MEA	Ministry of External Affairs
MIRV	Multiple Independently-targetable Re-entry Vehicle
MOU	Memorandum of Understanding
MTCR	Missile Technology Control Regime
MTM	Mobile Transfer Machine
NAM	Non-Aligned Movement
NATO	North Atlantic Treaty Organisation
NCA	Nuclear Command Authority
NCBM	Nuclear Confidence Building Mechanism
NCG	National Cancer Grid
NDA	National Democratic Alliance
NFU	No-First-Use
NNWS	Non- Nuclear Weapons State
NOAK	Nth-of-a-kind
NPCIL	Nuclear Power Corporation of India Limited
NPT	Nuclear Non-Proliferation Treaty
NSAB	National Security Advisory Board
NSG	Nuclear Suppliers Group
NSS	Nuclear Security Summit
NSSP	Next Steps in Strategic Partnership
NWFW	Nuclear weapons free world
NWS	Nuclear Weapons States
OSRT	Operational Safety Review Team
PAROS	Prevention of Arms Race in Outer Space
PET	Positron Emission Tomography

PFBR	Prototype Fast Breeder Reactors
PHS	Pumped Hydro Storage systems
PHWR	Pressurized Heavy Water Reactor
PNE	Peaceful Nuclear Explosion
PRC	People's Republic of China
PRP	Personnel Reliability Programme
PTBT	Partial Test Ban Treaty
RDD	Radioactive Dispersal Device
RevCon	Review Conference
RO	Reverse Osmosis
RRCAT	Raja Ramanna Centre for Advanced Technology
SAARC	South Asian Association for Regional Cooperation
SCOMET	Special Chemicals, Organisms, Materials, Equipment and Technology
SEATO	Southeast Asia Treaty Organisation
SIPRI	Stockholm International Peace Research Institute
SLBM	Submarine-launched ballistic missiles
SMR	Small Modular Reactor
SPD	Strategic Plans Division
SRR	Strategic Restraint Regime
SSBN	Ship Submersible Ballistic Nuclear
START	Strategic Arms Reduction Treaty
TNWs	Tactical Nuclear Weapons
TPNW	Treaty on Prohibition of Nuclear Weapons
TWh	Terawatt-hours
UCIL	Uranium Corporation of India Limited
UK	United Kingdom
UN	United Nations
UNGA	United Nations General Assembly
US	United States
USDOE	United States Department of Energy
USSR	Union of Soviet Socialist Republics
VRE	Variable Renewable Energy
WANO	World Association of Nuclear Operators
WHO	World Health Organisation

List of Contributors

Dr RB Grover is an Emeritus Professor at the Homi Bhabha National Institute (HBNI) and a member of the Atomic Energy Commission. He worked at the Bhabha Atomic Research Center (BARC), the secretariat of the Department of Atomic Energy (DAE), and HBNI. Positions held by him include Director, Knowledge Management Group, BARC; Principal Advisor, Strategic Planning Group, DAE; and Vice-Chancellor, HBNI. Working in BARC, he specialized in nuclear reactor thermal hydraulics, process design and safety analysis. In recent years, he has been working on energy studies and the role of nuclear energy. He played a lead role in conceptualizing and setting up HBNI. He participated in negotiations with other countries and international agencies leading to the resumption of international civil nuclear trade. He was the Sous- Sherpa of the Government of India for all four Nuclear Security Summits. He is a fellow of the Indian National Academy of Engineering and a Padma Shri recipient.

Dr Roshan Khanijo is the Assistant Director (Research) at the Centre for Strategic Studies and Simulation (CS3), United Service Institution of India (USI), New Delhi. She is a strategic analyst. Her areas of focus are security, nuclear doctrines and nuclear force structure of Nuclear Weapon States especially China and Pakistan, disarmament and arms control, niche and disruptive technologies, etc. She has authored, edited books, Monographs and Occasional papers. Some of them are *Complexities and Challenges of Nuclear India, Hypersonic Glide Vehicles: Implications for India; China's Military Modernisation*, and *Does India Needs to Review its Nuclear Doctrines*. She has also written articles in Foreign /National Magazines. She has been a panellist in number of national and international workshops/Seminars. She has also worked in various 'Net Assessment studies like War Waging Potential of China, Net Assessment of Pakistan, SWOT Analysis Bangladesh etc. She was co guide for Ph.D. students and conducts regularly internship capsules for university students.

Air Marshal Rajesh Kumar retired in August 2021 after 39 years of distinguished service. He is a product of Mayo College, Ajmer and an alumnus of National Defence Academy, Khadakvasla. He is a graduate of Air Command and Staff College at Montgomery, Alabama as well as College of Defence Management, Secunderabad. He holds a Master's degree in Management Studies besides having been a Category A Flying Instructor and an Air Force Examiner. During his career he has held important assignments and has commanded both an operational IAF command as well as a Tri-service command. Besides operational roles, the Air Marshal has rich experience in the field defence production having been the Director of the Air Force Project Monitoring Team working on the prestigious Light Combat Aircraft Project as well as the Team Leader of the Air Force Project Management Team for Airborne Warning and Control System (AWACS) at Israel. For his distinguished service, he has been awarded the Param Vishisht Seva Medal and the Ati Vishisht Seva Medal. He is also the recipient of Vayu Sena Medal (gallantry) during Op Parakram.

Dr Rajesh Rajagopalan is Professor of International Politics at Jawaharlal Nehru University, New Delhi. His main areas of research are international relations theory, security studies and Indian foreign and security policies. His publications include three books, Nuclear South Asia: Keywords and Concepts [co-authored with Atul Mishra]; Fighting Like A Guerrilla: The Indian Army and Counterinsurgency; and Second Strike: Arguments about Nuclear War in South Asia. His research articles (some jointly authored) have appeared in a number of academic and policy journals such as International Affairs, The Washington Quarterly, Contemporary Security Policy, India Review, Contemporary South Asia, Small Wars and Insurgencies, South Asia, South Asian Survey, and Strategic Analysis.

Dr. Kanica Rakhra is currently an Assistant Professor at Kautilya School of Public Policy, Hyderabad and a Policy Advisor to the Civil20 India Secretariat, part of India's G20 Presidency. Prior to this, Dr. Rakhra was working with the Indian Ministry of External Affairs (2016-23). A former Fellow at Middlebury Institute for International Studies (2019), the Swedish South Asian Studies Network (2016) and the Harvard led-Arms Control Negotiation Academy (ACONA-2021), she holds a PhD from the Center for International Politics, Organization, and Disarmament (CIPOD) in Jawaharlal Nehru University. She has also participated in a number of Track 1.5 and Track 2 dialogues, written chapters for books, and published articles in various journals.

Dr Rajiv Nayan is Senior Research Associate at Manohar Parrikar Institute for Defence Studies and Analyses (MP-IDSA), New Delhi. He has been working with the Institute since 1993, where he specialises in international relations, security issues, especially the politics of nuclear disarmament, export control, non-proliferation, and arms control. He was Visiting Research Fellow at Japan Institute of International Affairs (JIIA), Tokyo, where he published his monograph "Non-Proliferation Issues in South Asia". He was also Senior Researcher at Peace Research Institute Oslo (PRIO), Senior Visiting Research Fellow at King's College, London and Visiting Fulbright Scholar at Center on International Cooperation (CIC), New York University. He holds a PhD and a Master of Philosophy in Disarmament Studies and a Master of Arts in International Relations from Jawaharlal Nehru University, New Delhi. In his doctoral dissertation, he studied the implications of Missile Technology Control Regime for Indian security and economy. Dr Nayan has published books as well as papers in academic journals and as chapters in books. His single-authored book *Global Strategic Trade Management* has been published by Springer in 2019. His edited book *The Nuclear Non-Proliferation Treaty and India* was published by Routledge in 2012.

Shri Niranjan Chandrashekhar Oak is a Research Analyst, Nuclear and Arms Control Centre, at Manohar Parrikar Institute for Defence Studies and Analyses (MP-IDSA), New Delhi. . He has completed his M.phil. from the School of International Studies (SIS), Jawaharlal

Nehru University (JNU), New Delhi and is currently pursuing PhD from Centre for Indo-Pacific Studies (CIPS), SIS, JNU. His research areas include nuclear and security issues, and emerging multilateralism in the Indo-Pacific region, and geopolitics of Southeast Asia, Oceania and the Indian Ocean Region. Previously, he has worked with the Maritime History Society (MHS), Mumbai, and the Centre for Land Warfare Studies (CLAWS), New Delhi. He is an alumnus of Mumbai University.

Shri M Ramanamurthi graduated from the 25th batch of the BARC training school. He then joined the analytical chemistry division, where he worked on the analysis of high-purity material. He was relocated to the human resource development division to coordinate the one-year training program for graduate and postgraduate candidates. He then moved on to the director's office, Bhabha Atomic Research Centre (BARC), to facilitate and coordinate various tasks of the Director of BARC with several wings of the Department of Atomic Energy (DAE) and BARC. He was also involved in the outreach activities of BARC, where he generated a large number of documentaries, video films and articles on the activities of BARC and DAE. He also made numerous presentations in various forums on the activities of DAE as part of the outreach programme.

Dr Manpreet Sethi, Distinguished Fellow at the Centre for Air Power Studies, New Delhi, leads the project on nuclear issues. She is also Senior Research Advisor, Asia Pacific Leadership Network. Expert on the entire range of nuclear issues, she has over 120 published papers and has authored, edited and co-authored nine books. She lectures regularly at National Defence College and other establishments of Indian Armed Forces, Police and Foreign Services. She has participated in all flagship nuclear policy conferences across the world. Member of Prime Minister's Informal Group on Disarmament in 2012, and of Executive Board of Indian Pugwash Society, she has been part of Track II initiatives. Currently on Board of Missile Dialogue Initiative, IISS, London, and Co-chair, Women in Nuclear India. She is member of International Group of Eminent Persons instituted by Prime Minister of Japan. She has been awarded K Subrahmanyam award

(2014) and commendations by Chief of the Air Staff (2020) and C-in-C, Strategic Forces Command (2022).

Dr Sheel Kant Sharma holds Ph.D. in High energy Physics (IIT Bombay). He was honoured with the Distinguished Alumnus Award by IIT, Bombay, in 2007 for his contribution to non-proliferation and nuclear policy. He joined the Indian Foreign Service (IFS) in 1973. He has served in Indian Missions in Kuwait, Saudi Arabia, Geneva, Algiers and Vienna. From 1981, beginning with a year's stint in the Institute for Defence Studies and Analyses, he has had an uninterrupted association with studies on disarmament, nuclear policy, security and cooperation, and strategic weapons development in various capacities, as scholar, diplomat, and an international civil servant. He has served in the capacity of Joint Secretary and Additional Secretary at Headquarters. He has been an Ambassador and Secretary General of the SAARC. He has worked in the IAEA Secretariat from 1994 to 2000 in the External Relations Division headed by Mohamed ElBaradei. From 2000 to 2004, he headed MEA's DISA Division as JS (DISA)/As (IO). He has been an ambassador to Austria and Permanent Representative to the UN in Vienna, the IAEA and UNIDO. He has served as an Indian Governor at the IAEA Board of Governors from 2004 to 2008. He has written copiously on issues on foreign affairs, especially nuclear matters, security and cooperation in South and South East Asia.

Ambassador D.B.Venkatesh Varma served in the Indian Foreign Service from 1988 to 2021. He has more than 12 years of experience in the field of multilateral non-proliferation and disarmament—nuclear, chemical, biological and conventional weapons, having served three postings in the Conference on Disarmament in Geneva. He also served as Joint Secretary in charge of Disarmament and International Security in the Ministry of External Affairs between 2010 and 2013. He was a member of the UN Group of Government Experts on Missiles and on Disarmament and Nuclear Non-Proliferation Education. He was also a Member of the Indian Delegation to the UNGA in 1998-1999, 2003-2005 and 2008-2016. He has attended 9 Sessions of the UN First Committee and 7 Sessions of the United

Nations Disarmament Commission. He has vast experience in India's Security and Defence policies and is the first Recipient of the S.K.Singh Award for Excellence in the Indian Foreign Service in 2011 for his contribution to the negotiations of the Civil Nuclear Initiative.

Shri Abhishek Verma is a Research Analyst at the Internal Security Centre at the Manohar Parrikar Institute for Defence Studies and Analyses (MP-IDSA), New Delhi. He has completed his Master's in International Studies from School of International Studies (SIS), Jawaharlal Nehru University (JNU), New Delhi. He is currently pursuing PhD from Centre for International Politics, Organisation and Disarmament (CIPOD), SIS, JNU. His doctoral thesis focuses on "Oligopoly in International Relations: A Study of 50 years of the Nuclear Non- Proliferation Treaty". His areas of research include International security, nuclear & arms control issues and US-China Great power rivalry. Shri Verma has done his internship in several IR think tanks like The Kootneeti, The Takshashila Institution (China Studies Program), Chennai Centre for China Studies (C3S) and Foreign Policy Research Centre. His publications include multiple research articles, occasional papers and monographs on China, great power rivalry and, arms control & nuclear issues. He has also reviewed several books for the Journals like Strategic Analysis, International Studies and Millennial Asia.

Shri K.N. Vyas is a mechanical engineer with an experience in the field of nuclear reactor engineering. This includes reactor core and fuel design involving thermal hydraulics and fuel performance analysis; design, analysis and manufacture of critical reactor equipment; design of reactor process systems; understanding of design and analysis of reactor safety systems, including engineered safety features. As Director, BARC, Shri Vyas had contributed for encouraging the use of nuclear science and technology for societal applications. Shri K.N. Vyas retired as Chairman, Atomic Energy Commission in 2023. As Chairman, Atomic Energy Commission, he has guided the activities of 30 different Units of the Department of Atomic Energy (DAE) which include R&D Institutes, Industrial Units and Aided Institutes. Presently Shri Vyas is working as a Homi Bhabha Chair Professor at the DAE.

Introduction

11 May 2023, marks a pivotal moment for India, commemorating 25 years since the nuclearization of the nation. It was on this date that India conducted significant nuclear tests, over a span of two days – 11-13 May 1998. These tests encompassed various types of nuclear devices, including fission, fusion, and low-yield. Through these tests and subsequent declarations, India unequivocally asserted its position as a Nuclear-Weapon State.

Remarkably, despite demonstrating its nuclear capabilities, the international community was reluctant to acknowledge as a nation with nuclear weapons. This reluctance underscored the intricate intersection of law, politics, and scientific realities. Intriguingly, attempts were made to bind a nation that had not been a signatory to such agreements into legal frameworks,, highlighting the complexities of navigating the global nuclear maze.

When India conducted its nuclear tests, the international system had transitioned into a post-Cold War phase. The Soviet Union and the socialist bloc had disintegrated, and the dominant bipolar world system, already strained, had shifted from multilateralism to a somewhat multipolar configuration by the 1960s. The détente period saw a relaxation of tensions, though not their absence. China had distanced itself from the socialist bloc and began engaging with the Western world. Supported by the West, China continued to modernize its military programmes, with the US and Europe relaxing technology transfer restrictions. Globalization, characterized by increasing interactions and interdependence, was seen as the new model for engaging China.

The academic community struggled to precisely define the post-Cold War international system, often describing it as unipolar. Scholars worldwide discussed the unipolar moment. While this appeared true at the macro level, at the micro or regional level, old tensions persisted. The lofty idea of a global village emerged, but in reality, nation-states, their territorial sovereignty, and their capabilities to solve their problems remained significant.

A new world order was to be projected not only through a broad macro system but also through its constituent elements. Francis Fukuyama proclaimed the "end of history" or the end of ideology in international relations, suggesting the conclusion of the ideological conflict that characterized the Cold War. However, this prediction had limited empirical evidence. One set of ideological conflicts was replaced by another in the post-Cold War world. The emergence of new actors in these conflicts had the potential to destabilize the international system and generate tension and anxiety globally, or at least in the affected regions.

At the regional level, wars continued. West Asia witnessed another round of tension and conflict when Iraq annexed Kuwait, leading to a war involving extra-regional powers. The US used force to liberate Kuwait, and both the region and the conflict saw developments related to WMD. Saddam Hussein threatened to use chemical weapons. Additionally, the Israel-Palestine conflict persisted, and many other countries in the region experienced tensions with Israel and among themselves.

In Europe, the world witnessed both hope and change. For centuries, Europe was the epicentre of global conflict and war. The twentieth century saw two World Wars and the Cold War, primarily involving European actors, with Japan and the US as extra-regional participants in the Second World War. Although the Cold War did not see direct warfare between the antagonistic powers, it was marked by high levels of tension and anxiety. A tense peace prevailed, with Europe remaining the principal theatre of the Cold War. After the Cold War, Europe underwent significant restructuring and realignment, bringing its own uncertainties, including concerns about the future of peace. Reactions ranged from euphoria to scepticism and caution.

Several new developments in Europe heralded a new era for the global order. The unification led to the emergence of a new Germany, which over the years has become Europe's powerhouse. Following the UK's exit from the EU, Germany assumed leadership of the EU. The demise of the Soviet Union and the socialist bloc erased the old East-West divide in Europe. East European countries began to move closer to Western Europe, gradually seeking membership in various Western institutions and groupings. Russia also engaged more deeply with other European countries, although old suspicions lingered.

The European order became stable after the Cold War and remained so for many years. Its security framework was predominantly shaped by the NATO. However, several European countries have still remained outside NATO. The organization expanded eastward, after initial resistance from Russia, which even engaged with NATO and was once on the verge of joining it. Many viewed this as a triumph of democracy and the liberal order, although sceptics questioned this perspective.

While the new global security order saw some changes, it did not eliminate nuclear weapons. Several countries renounced nuclear weapons for various reasons. South Africa dismantled its nuclear arsenal, and three former Soviet Republics—Ukraine, Belarus, and Kazakhstan—transferred ownership of the nuclear weapons in their territories to Russia. The US played a significant role in facilitating this transfer. Despite possessing nuclear weapons, Russia did not achieve the status of a superpower once held by the Soviet Union, as it lacked other sources of power necessary to sustain such a status.

The size of the nuclear arsenals of the former superpowers was reduced through bilateral arms control agreements, but even after the Cold War, over 92 per cent of the world's nuclear weapons remained in their possession. The importance of nuclear weapons in the doctrines and broader security policies of nuclear-armed States persisted. Nuclear deterrence continued to be the dominant doctrine, with no significant adoption of a NFU policy. The nuclear order was further stabilized by the indefinite extension of the NPT, which granted legitimacy to the five nuclear-armed States that had declared their arsenals before 1 January 1967. Israel, despite its undeclared but widely acknowledged nuclear arsenal, maintained its unofficial nuclear weapons status.

Non-proliferation took precedence over disarmament. India, a longstanding advocate of nuclear disarmament, consistently called for it. This demand emerged after the use of nuclear weapons during India's struggle for independence from British colonialism, upsetting the leaders of the Indian freedom movement who were appalled by the bombings in Japan. After gaining independence, nuclear disarmament became an official policy of the new government. The leaders of independent India were deeply concerned that advancements in science & technology could lead to the downfall of civilization and the extinction of humanity.[1] It highlighted the necessity for the world to curb the improper use and exploitation of the opportunities and benefits provided by science and technology. Dr. Rajendra Prasad, the first President of the Republic of India, made very touching remarks on this issue:

> "There is no known defence against a nuclear attack once it is launched. The only thing that the target country can do is to perfect a system of instant retaliation that would be able to function even when the rest of the country has been reduced to an atomic wreckage. It can however be poor consolation to the victim of a nuclear attack to know that after he has been wiped out of existence a similar fate would overtake the adversary."[2]

The lack of progress on nuclear disarmament made India restless. India consistently appealed to nuclear-armed countries to stop the arms race and pursue nuclear disarmament. By 1964, even China had conducted nuclear weapons tests, and no one paid attention to India's pleas. India continued to deplore nuclear tests and criticized the UN for its ineffectiveness on nuclear disarmament, even though it praised the UN for its impressive work on other fronts. The international organization was rendered ineffective by the veto-wielding nuclear-armed countries occupying the permanent seats on the UN Security Council.

Still, India did not shy away from supporting significant initiatives within the UN and beyond. It supported the January 1952 UNGA Resolution for establishing the UN Disarmament Commission under the Security Council. India was active in the Ten-Nation Disarmament Committee and its successors, such as the 1962 Eighteen-Nation Disarmament Committee and the 1969 Conference of the Committee on Disarmament. Since the creation of the current negotiating body, the CD, in 1978, India has been positively contributing to its meaningful agenda. India has always been supportive of the UN Special Sessions on Disarmament and the bodies created by them.

Outside the UN, India proposed the Rajiv Gandhi Disarmament Plan, which included phased steps towards nuclear disarmament. In 1988, Prime Minister Rajiv Gandhi introduced a comprehensive Action Plan to the UNGA, outlining a vision for a world free of nuclear weapons and marked by non-violence. Had it been executed, this plan would have eliminated nuclear weapons globally by 2008. India's subsequent proposals in the UNGA and the CD reflected its unwavering commitment to nuclear disarmament, aligning with the fundamental principles of Rajiv Gandhi's Action Plan, which sought to achieve nuclear disarmament within a specified timeframe.

Despite the frustrating behaviour of nuclear-armed countries, India remained engaged in nuclear disarmament efforts across various forums, including the NAM and the Six-Nation Initiative. On the NAM platform, India consistently reiterated the need for nuclear disarmament, emphasizing its potential to annihilate mankind. India often linked the quest for nuclear disarmament to development, reminding the world that newly liberated nations are meant to pursue development. However, until nuclear disarmament is achieved, developed countries may be restrained from transferring funds allocated for developing nuclear weapons to other critical areas.

The initial Appeal of the Six-Nation Five-Continent Peace Initiative was issued in May 1984, during a period when discussions among nuclear powers had broken down, resulting in accusations of distrust and mutual blame. By the time these nations convened in New Delhi in 1985, dialogue had just resumed. The meeting in Ixtapa offered a glimmer of hope. The Six-Nation initiative advocated for the elimination of warheads, emphasizing the need to separate the pursuit of peace from strategies of nuclear deterrence, with a universal rejection of such strategies. The initiative called for an end to the militarization of international relations and proposed the establishment of an international order based on peaceful co-existence. Their commitment was directed towards achieving a world completely free from all nuclear weapons.

India's endeavour for nuclear disarmament did not yield any encouraging results. On the contrary, the international community witnessed a completely different path taken by the countries designated as NWS under the NPT criteria. On 11 May 1995, the NPT RevCon granted an indefinite extension to the NPT, somewhat legitimizing the possession of nuclear weapons by these NPT-defined five NWS. In 1996, negotiations for the CTBT concluded, but the Treaty was drafted without any time-bound disarmament plan. The draft Treaty also had several issues that left India dissatisfied. A long-time champion of the CTBT changed its course and opposed the passage of the Treaty in the negotiating body—the CD. Consequently, the draft Treaty for the CTBT had to undergo revision and was ultimately approved by the General Assembly.

The post-Cold War period also witnessed a serious deterioration in India's strategic environment. Nuclear weapons and missile proliferation was rampant, and the international community seemed powerless to address it. A clandestine proliferation network facilitated the nuclear weapons programmes of countries like China and Pakistan, among others in Asia and beyond. While Pakistan pursued a uranium-based nuclear weapons programme through covert transactions after diverting from its original plutonium route, China also made significant advancements. Leveraging not only the proliferation network but also partnerships it had forged with the West in the 1960s, China expanded its nuclear capabilities. The deteriorating security environment compelled India to reassess its nuclear weapons policy.

Following its nuclear weapons tests, India issued statements aimed at engaging the international community. The primary objective was to alleviate concerns regarding its nuclear weapons acquisition. India reassured the world that its nuclear weapons were not intended for aggressive purposes but rather to deter the clandestine nuclear weapons development of certain aggressive countries. These statements also contributed to the evolution of India's nuclear doctrine. India outlined the broad contours of its nuclear doctrine/policy and engaged in proactive diplomacy, reaching out not only to State capitals but also to various international organizations and multilateral groupings.

The then Indian Prime Minister, Shri Atal Bihari Vajpayee, announced India's overarching nuclear weapons philosophy. Following China's lead, India adopted the doctrine of 'NFU' of nuclear weapons and declared a policy of no use of nuclear weapons against NNWS. The Government established a NSAB comprising non-governmental security experts, which submitted a Report known as the draft nuclear doctrine. Based on this Report, the Indian government formulated its nuclear weapons doctrine and disclosed certain aspects of it to the public. The doctrine underscored the importance of possessing a credible minimum nuclear deterrence. For India, nuclear weapons serve as a deterrent against adversaries, with no envisioned role in actual warfare unless necessitated by a nuclear attack, in which case it would be used in retaliation.

India is expected to develop its nuclear weapons stockpile in accordance with its nuclear doctrine. The philosophy of credible minimum nuclear deterrence sets a self-imposed limit on the size of the stockpile. As part of the NFU doctrine, India has tailored its nuclear force structure for retaliation and maintains a second strike capability. India has developed delivery vehicles to enhance the robustness of its nuclear deterrence and has established a robust command and control system. This system ensures that civilian political leadership maintains firm authority through the NCA, with the Executive Council, headed by the National Security Advisor, responsible for providing information to the political council for decision-making.

The Indian leadership remained committed to nuclear

disarmament, asserting that a world without nuclear weapons is the optimal environment for India's security. Subsequently, India produced a working paper outlining a time-bound nuclear disarmament plan. It emphasized the need for reducing the prominence of nuclear weapons in the doctrines of all nuclear-armed states. India also displayed a positive attitude toward nuclear testing and participated in negotiations for a FMCT. Over time, India engaged with various global non-proliferation initiatives and sought integration and accommodation in multilateral export control regimes.

The international response to India's nuclear weapons tests was mixed. Some countries strongly condemned the tests and imposed sanctions, which were later lifted as they recognized the security rationale behind India's nuclear weapons program and developed strategic partnerships accordingly. Countries like Russia and France demonstrated understanding from the outset, advocating for moderation in international forums despite not officially supporting India's nuclear weapons. The NAM countries, while not overtly endorsing the tests, criticized the hypocrisy of nuclear-armed states for their lack of seriousness regarding nuclear disarmament. Today, the world has come to accept India's nuclear status and treats it as a Nuclear Weapons State.

The book aims to evaluate various facets of nuclear India over the past twenty-five years, compiling contributions from scientists, diplomats, policy analysts, and research scholars. The scientists who have authored chapters have been integral to India's nuclear weapons programme. Dr. Ravi B. Grover, associated with the Strategic Planning Group of the DAE, and Dr. M. Ramanamurthi, working within the DAE, are among them. Dr. K.N. Vyas, who headed the DAE during the inception of the book project, retired a few months later.

Retired Indian diplomats who played key roles in dispelling misconceptions surrounding India's nuclear tests and elucidated the rationale behind India's nuclear pursuits, have also contributed chapters. Dr. Sheel Kant Sharma, the former head of the DISA division of the Ministry of External Affairs that negotiates nuclear issues and the former Indian ambassador to the IAEA, is one such contributor. Ambassador D. Bala Venkatesh Varma, who was part of the Indian delegation to the CD during that period, offers a first-hand account of the momentous events of the summer of 1998.

The book also features chapters by practitioners who served in various capacities within the Government of India. Air Marshal Rajesh Kumar, prior to retirement from the Indian Air Force, oversaw vital projects while managing both operational aspects of the Indian Air Force and Tri-service commands. Dr. Kanica Rakhra worked with the Indian MEA in the DISA Division, while Professor Rajesh Rajagopalan, before joining Jawaharlal Nehru University, worked for the National Security Council Secretariat, Government of India.

Additionally, contributors like Dr. Roshan Khanijo, Dr. Manpreet Sethi, Dr. Rajiv Nayan, Mr. Niranjan C. Oak, and Abhishek Verma, affiliated with different think tanks, have closely engaged with the Indian government on nuclear policy, strategy, and diplomacy. They actively participate in track 1.5 and track 2 dialogues on nuclear issues.

The book comprises eleven chapters, supplemented by an introduction and a conclusion. Dr. Rajiv Nayan, delves into the myths and realities of the Indian nuclear weapons programme. These myths predate 11 May 1998, and Dr. Nayan's aim is to dispel some of the prevailing misconceptions surrounding India's nuclearization. He notes that while some myths have dissipated over time, others persist. These enduring myths are perpetuated by both outdated notions within the policy community and entrenched anti-India sentiments in the international arena. Nevertheless, Dr. Nayan asserts that these myths are no longer widely embraced in the international community.

Ambassador D.B. Venkatesh Varma offers an overview of the circumstances in 1998 and emphasizes the strategic consistency and adept diplomacy that led to a significant shift in India's stance within the global nuclear framework over the subsequent twenty years. India safeguarded its military nuclear program while successfully engaging with the international community. Consequently, India's nuclear diplomacy liberated it from the constraints of nuclear isolation. For him, today, India is recognized as a crucial ally for advancing significant global endeavours in the nuclear domain. He wrote that after the commemoration of the 25th anniversary of the Pokhran II tests, it is crucial to reflect on the challenging journey undertaken thus far.

Dr. Sheel Kant Sharma, briefly reviews the significant events of more than 25 years since the Pokhran II tests. It then explores the rapidly evolving landscape of diplomacy in relation to the major technological trends of today, which also affect the nuclear context. He suggests how India should navigate new challenges. Dr. Sharma notes that the nuclear tests of May 1998 displayed a strong inner resolve, followed by a vigorous diplomatic campaign by India. He concludes that Indian diplomacy was successful on multiple fronts, highlighting India's strategic concerns and security policies, and enhancing acceptance from key states.

Air Marshal Rajesh Kumar asserts that India's nuclear force has expanded incrementally over three decades. He emphasizes that in the nuclear era, strategy has never solely dictated force architecture; technological advancements will continue to shape nuclear force structures, necessitating flexibility to adapt to these changes. Despite this, he notes that India's force structure has consistently adhered to the principle of minimum credible deterrence, ensuring survivability for a second strike capable of causing unacceptable damage to an adversary. This development aligns with the resource allocation deemed necessary by the political leadership to maintain the required level of deterrence.

Professor Rajesh Rajagopalan starts by explaining why India adopted its nuclear doctrine, emphasizing the strategic rationale behind a NFU policy and a credible minimum deterrent. He then examines some challenges India faces and their potential impact on its nuclear doctrine. He also argues that, despite these challenges, the strategic rationale of the current doctrine remains robust. Before delving into these issues, the chapter provides a brief overview of India's challenging journey to the 1998 tests and offers a short assessment of the past 25 years of India's nuclear weapons tests and policy.

Dr. Kanica Rakhra, provides a summary of significant advancements in the nuclear programmes of India and its two neighbouring countries, China and Pakistan. It describes the main features of their respective nuclear doctrines and examines the distinct bilateral relationships among these three states. The chapter also covers the Nuclear CBMs implemented in the region, detailing how India navigates its nuclear relationships within the context of regional security. Additionally, it highlights various Track-II diplomacy efforts and their influence on Nuclear CBMs between India and its nuclear-armed neighbours.

Dr. Manpreet Sethi, maps the contemporary nuclear reality, explains why it is in India's interest to pursue a NWFW and offers suggestions on possible pathways. She argues that despite the apparently low appeal for nuclear disarmament today, it is in India's interest to support and encourage relevant efforts. According to her, India's nuclear doctrine is illustrative of the kind of restraint that can foster an enabling environment for an NWFW.

Dr. R.B. Grover, discusses the role of nuclear energy in achieving net zero target. He maintains that on the energy front, India faces twin challenges: to decarbonise the energy sector, and to increase per capita energy consumption. For decarbonisation of the energy sector, massive electrification of energy at the point of end-use is necessary and that calls for a rapid increase in the generation of electricity. All low-carbon energy sources need to be deployed based on policies that are technology agnostic. India has mastered pressurised heavy water reactor as well as associated fuel cycle technologies. Several reactors are under construction. Advanced reactor technologies are under development. Overall, nuclear has to be a significant part of the energy mix to achieve a let zero and developed India by 2070.

Dr. K.N. Vyas and Dr. M. Ramanamurthi, explain how India, under the visionary leadership of Homi Jehangir Bhabha decided to embark on a nuclear energy programme soon after independence, believing firmly that the nation's requirements in energy, healthcare and food sectors can be positively impacted by a strong and robust nuclear energy and radiation technology research and development infrastructure in the country. It informs that the DAE has been successful in delivering the objectives set in a self-reliant manner over the last few decades in all the important sectors, benefiting all sections of the population in the true spirit *of Vasudhaiva Kutumbakam*.

Dr. Roshan Khanijo explains that India has come a long way from being an outlier to becoming a responsible NWS. Her non-proliferation credentials, her role in highlighting nuclear terrorism, and her becoming a major treaty partner, whether it the MTCR or Wassenaar agreement or her role the IAEA, the circle has been completed. Dr. Khanijo writes that security is a dynamic concept and new paradigms keep emerging and one such domain is the emergence of disruptive technology. These technological innovations are bound to create new challenges and the global architecture will require to adapt and change. India too will need to adjust her policies and become more proactive in highlighting the challenges, as also become a part of the solution.

Mr. Niranjan C. Oak and Mr. Abhishek Verma examine India's relationship with the non-proliferation regime. They describe India's nuclear journey as progressing through distinct phases. The phase of estrangement was marked by sanctions and a moratorium on international aid. This was followed by the engagement phase, characterized by the lifting of sanctions and diplomatic efforts. Subsequently, India entered the integration phase, highlighted by the politically and diplomatically challenging India-US Civil Nuclear Cooperation Agreement, which ultimately led to an India-specific NSG waiver. Finally, the accommodation phase saw New Delhi gaining membership in several non-proliferation and nuclear security groups.

The concluding chapter outlines the broad trends emerging from the various chapters of the book. It highlights the principal issues that have defined nuclear India for over 25 years. Given the book's diverse themes, these trends reflect the multidimensional nature of India's nuclear existence, policy, doctrine, and global engagement.

NOTES

1 Rajendra Prasad, "The Case for Unilateral Disarmament: Inaugural speech at the Anti-Nuclear Arms Convention, New Delhi 16. June 1962," Ministry of External Affairs, https://meaindia.nic.in/cdgeneva/?pdf0597?000

2 Ibid.

1

Myths and Realities of India's Nuclear Weapons

Rajiv Nayan

Introduction

Myth has a role to play in statecraft, especially in relation to diplomacy. It played a role in ancient times, too. The old States, especially Greece, used myths and legends in diplomacy.[1] Their descendants have not shunned the use of myths and mythmaking in modern diplomacy. As an instrument of statecraft, it forces an entity to focus attention on one aspect of the phenomenon, diverting attention from recognizing the complete picture, as constructing a comprehensible plot is generally considered useful for sustaining a myth in the long run. The synergy between academics and policy is the most viable arrangement for the purpose. Mythmaking uses all the tools to appear logical and accurate, ranging from law to morality to security.

One of the writers on the subject opines: "Myths are part and parcel of contemporary international politics, and they are all around us. From the invocation of 'the international community' to talk of Afghanistan as a 'graveyard of empires' or home of 'warlords', and from ideas of 'antiseptic battlefields' in modern warfare to concepts of 'coordination', 'participation' and 'effectiveness' in the work of international organisations – international politics is replete with powerful narratives and commonly held beliefs that qualify as myths."[2] The scholarship on the subject also acknowledges: "Myths can certainly be created for strategic purposes."[3] Myths about nuclear weapon policy are also floated from time to time.

In 1998, India's decision to test its nuclear device and to declare its intention of becoming a nuclear weapons state received diverse reactions. The cover over Pakistan's nuclear status was blown and through its nuclear weapons tests it claimed to become a nuclear weapons state as well. The Western world in general reacted adversely to the Indian nuclear tests. Yet some division did surface in the group in the initial years, which gave the impression that even the Western world was divided on India's nuclear status. In the then G-8 meeting, France and Germany along with Russia, did not take the strong stand against India unlike other members, and appeared to appreciate the circumstances which forced India to become a nuclear weapon country.

On the one hand, the countries and the groups opposed to the Indian nuclear test initiated several measures, including the imposition of sanctions on India; on the other, some countries and other entities hostile to India, indulged in a propaganda war against it. The spreading of myths regarding the Indian nuclear bomb and its nuclear weapons policy was part of the propaganda. The forces created myths about Indian nuclear weapons to tarnish and delegitimise the arsenal and the decision for nuclearisation. This ran parallel to the Indian official statement and other outreach activities to explain the rationale of going nuclear.

Myths were also resorted to after realising that the official explanation appeared logical to the comity of nations and as a result, started making an impact on the global public opinion in favour of the Indian decision to go nuclear. When mythmaking is not based on facts or on proper research, its impact starts waning. This was the case with the Indian bomb as well. Some myths disappeared because of the intellectual onslaught by the Indian State/government and civil society, but some persisted because of the support of the powerful forces misinterpreting facts and developing imaginary patterns to influence the minds of the policy-makers; or as Chiara Botticci describes it, hatching of 'a more or less coherent plot'.[4] Although several myths were created before and after the 1998 Indian nuclear tests, the chapter focuses on five dominant myths regarding India's nuclear weapons and its policy.

Violation of the NPT

When India tested its nuclear devices, a section of the international community, including the media opposed it vehemently. The test was seen as a violation of the NPT. Some of those who called the Indian nuclear test a violation of the Treaty did not understand that the violation of the Treaty is relevant only to the country that is a party to the Treaty and has to accept its obligations. A non-member is not expected to commit to the Treaty. Admittedly, some people who called the test a violation of the NPT were bitter and perpetual opponents of India and India's nuclear weapons programme.

Seemingly, this act and resulting action may have created an impression in a section of the international community that India is a violator of the NPT since the world is divided into NWS and NNWS by the member states of the NPT on the basis of the cut-off date (1 January 1967) stipulated by the NPT. The Glenn Amendment requires the President of the US to impose sanctions against a NNWS for conducting tests of nuclear devices.[5] Under this Amendment, the US government imposed sanctions against India and Pakistan. Interestingly, some US Congressmen also held the view that by conducting nuclear weapons tests India had violated the NPT.[6]

With the passage of time, it began to be clear that India, which is not a member of the NPT, cannot be called a violator. Admittedly, some Western non-proliferation ideologues keep spreading the false narrative that India is a violator of the NPT. However, predominantly, the Western policy-making community now holds the correct perspective that India, as a non-member state cannot be a violator of the Treaty. In different statements and writings, Western scholars and policymakers are acknowledging it.

The Indian political leadership and officials have been underlining, from the very beginning, that India is not a member of the NPT; so, the NPT was not violated in the 1998 tests. Although in the initial reactions after the tests, India highlighted the discriminatory nature of the Treaty or the non-compliance of the Article VI of the NPT by its member states. It also highlighted the proliferation behaviour of some of the member states. Gradually, it began to highlight the fact that it did not violate the NPT because it was "never a signatory to the NPT."[7]

Some called the tests a violation of the Non-proliferation Regime, if not the NPT. One American official stated, "India's decision to conduct these nuclear test explosions is a serious violation of international non-proliferation norms, and a repudiation of international efforts to contain the further spread of nuclear weapons and pursue nuclear disarmament. This action constitutes a dangerous precedent for the international nuclear non-proliferation regime."[8] Similar views were expressed by others in the initial years after the tests.

However, even those who appreciated the rationale of India going nuclear, saw India as an opponent of the nuclear regime whose mainstay is the NPT.[9] This section, which had been positive towards India, viewed the Indian test in terms of revising the asymmetrical and unfair power structure supported by the then-existing nuclear regime, including the NPT. The Indian government maintained that, "At no stage did we support irresponsible theories that projected nuclear proliferation as a new version of balance of power."[10]

Another myth: "Since the 1998 nuclear tests, it has been India's objective to circumvent the NPT by persuading a dominant power to recognize it as a nuclear weapons state." In fact, India has been a supporter of the idea of non-proliferation and the non-proliferation regime even if it stayed away from the NPT. India does not want to weaken the NPT.

The Indian government maintains: "India is a nuclear weapon state. Though not a party to the NPT, India's policies have been consistent with the key provisions of NPT that apply to nuclear weapon states. These provisions are contained in Articles I, III and VI. Article I obliges a nuclear weapon state not to transfer nuclear weapons to any other country or assist any other country to acquire them and India's record on non-proliferation has been impeccable.

Article III requires a party to the Treaty to provide nuclear materials and related equipment to any other country only under safeguards; India's exports of such materials have always been under safeguards. Article VI commits the parties to pursue negotiations to bring about eventual global nuclear disarmament. It needs to be emphasised that India today is the only NWS that remains committed to commencing negotiations for a Nuclear Weapons Convention, in order to bring about a nuclear-weapon-free-world, the very objective envisaged in Article VI of the NPT."[11]

Finally, as a legal opinion underlines, "It can therefore be argued that India is not merely a non-signatory to the NPT, but is also a persistent objector to any customary international law norms that may 'mirror' the provisions of that treaty."[12] This legal opinion, to a great extent, has influenced the global academic community and effectively busted the myth that India had violated the NPT.

De facto or De jure

After India conducted its nuclear tests and declared itself a nuclear weapon country, a new phrase was used for India—a 'de facto NWS'.[13] Except a few countries, most others have joined the NPT, where the predominant narrative is that only a country that had tested its nuclear weapons before 1 January 1967 as per the NPT criteria, may be recognized as an NWS. Under the NPT, only the US, Russia (the then Soviet Union), France, the UK, and China are qualified to be called NWS; others despite possessing nuclear weapons will be called NNWS. A former IAEA Chief once explained, "It is worth noting that countries that master uranium enrichment and plutonium separation become de facto nuclear weapons capable states."[14] There are several countries with such capabilities but they are not called 'de facto nuclear weapons state'.

However, when a nuclear weapon country possesses nuclear weapons or it announces its decision to possess the nuclear weapon, or demonstrates the existence of its nuclear weapons, it becomes difficult to deny the objective reality. In such a situation the myth of a de facto nuclear weapons state is presented, contrasting it with de jure nuclear weapons countries. This categorization considers the NWS defined so under the criteria of the NPT de jure NWS.

As discussed, the reality of India's possession and even acknowledgment of nuclear weapons has complicated the NPT yardstick. Stuck in this complexity, it seems many preferred to call India a de facto nuclear weapons state. However, this status did not help it in nuclear commerce. The NPT members and bodies like the NSG considered India a NNWS. In fact, before the clean exemptions given to India in the NSG guidelines, several countries were using the so-called de facto status to stem or block the flow of nuclear commerce. For example, someone from Australia's Uranium Information Centre stated, "If India was acknowledged as a de facto NPT member by global authorities, Australia might reconsider its export ban."[15] This statement, too, underscores the disparity in thinking within the NPT member countries. The denial of the reality was creating more complexity.

Gradually, the international community began to understand the futility of the term. Even before the NSG Guidelines waiver for India, a section of the Western world started rethinking. In fact, once Mohamed ElBaradei, the former IAEA chief remarked: "For me India, Pakistan, and Israel are weapons states, at least two of them have declared to be weapons states, and as I said a couple of years ago, the idea that they are de jure or de facto to me is totally irrelevant."[16] He further underlined, "If there is a war, a nuclear war, between India and Pakistan, we are not going to say this is not a nuclear war because we do not recognize them (as nuclear powers)."[17]

The Indian government in a different context stated, "So while we are not recognized as a nuclear weapons state under the NPT, there is a recognition that India has a military program and a civilian programme, and whatever safeguards are finally agreed upon with the IAEA will have to take this factor into account, and there will be, therefore, appropriate safeguards."[18] However, Shri Atal Bihari Vajpayee, the then Prime Minister of India, had already made the most profound statement in 1998, when he rightly asserted: "India is a NWS. This is a reality that cannot be denied. It is not a conferment that we seek; nor is it a status for others to grant."[19] The same sentiment echoed in the statements and positions taken by the subsequent Governments of India.

One of the legal writings on the issue maintains that, "Ultimately India retains a legal right to possess its nuclear weapons under both treaty law and customary international law."[20] Any investigation, as per the law, has to take into account "the hard fact that India is in possession of nuclear weapons and is understandably determined to keep hold of them."[21] The law also considers 'India's continued persistent objection, both de jure and de facto',[22] that this makes the entire division or classification into the de facto and de jure status of India's nuclear status irrelevant.

Status or Security

That the Indian nuclear bomb was a tool for India's status enhancement was yet another myth pedalled just after the nuclear tests in 1998. Admittedly, this myth still keeps surfacing. Some view that India's glorious past was to be revived by nuclear weapons. It is true that India is an ancient civilisation, and it did have a glorious past with accomplishments in many areas, including science and technology. It was, and to an extent, is still known for spreading ideas and philosophy of *Vasudhaiv Kutumbakam* (one family for one earth). But ancient India did not use its science and technology for hegemonic purposes.

Moreover, ancient India imposed ethical constraints on the use of those weapons which may have devastating consequences. Nuclear science, a modern technology had already been acquired by several countries by the time India successfully tested its nuclear weapons. In fact, India contended that if others claim right to possess and use this science, India too has its rights. It has nothing to do with its ancient past. It may be lauded as an accomplishment of Indian scientists in a country that was termed a developing country because of centuries of colonial subjugation. Undoubtedly, despite curbs and sanctions, the Indian scientific and technological establishment accomplished the task of nuclear weapon development by mastering the entire nuclear fuel cycle. It is a matter of honour for this community which worked hard against heavy odds. However, it ought not to be linked to the prestige/status rationale.

Another group argues that, by exploding nuclear weapons, the government tries to instil a sense of prestige and status among its citizens. The objective could be electoral, civilizational or nation-building. This rationale is applied not only to the 1998 tests but also to the 1974 PNE. Such projections are never empirically grounded. Neither the immediate nor the long-term fact so far has indicated that citizens are mobilised for these narrow goals. As mentioned, a nation and its citizens celebrate the scientific accomplishments of the country, which are achieved under tremendous resistance and pressure. This helps in motivating the new generation to undertake science and technology projects and programmes to strengthen the capability of a country to deliver goods to its citizens. Quite significantly, the celebration of nuclear weapons tests, by some elements in India, should not be taken as an indicator that nuclear weapons have been acquired for national prestige.

Some argue as a matter of habit that the Indian nuclear weapons programme is to be for prestige, nothing else. Such a thinking originates and is shaped by some established and abstract international relations theories. Such theories generalise on limited facts. Such contextual theories and ideas emanating from them may not be the appropriate tool to analyse the Indian nuclear bomb. Although a number of writers[23] seriously disagree with the prestige angle given to the Indian nuclear weapons programme they blame the lack of transparency of the Indian government as being responsible for the creation of this myth. Paradoxically, secrecy around the Indian nuclear weapons programme is held responsible; however, the statement issued by the Government of India regarding the objective of the nuclear weapons is not taken into account as an act of transparency and as a positive move.

The understanding of the successive Indian governments has been that nuclear technology has transformed the nature of global security. For years, India strived for a world without nuclear weapons, and after being unsuccessful in its endeavour, India opted for the nuclear option. Had prestige been the objective, it would have acquired nuclear weapons, not campaigned for nuclear disarmament. The Indian government has been repeatedly emphasising: "Nuclear weapons are an integral part of India's national security and will remain so, pending non-discriminatory and global nuclear disarmament."[24] India maintains this position because it views that nuclear weapons are ingrained in the security policies of a few countries. India is also of the view that as long as these countries possess nuclear weapons, it will be difficult for India to renounce its nuclear weapons. The Vajpayee government explicitly stated, "We subscribe to the principle of equal and legitimate security interests of nations and consider it a sovereign right."[25]

Hindu Bomb or Domestic Political Consensus

Closely related to the status/prestige myth was the myth that the 1998 nuclear test was a Hindu bomb driven by Hindu nationalism.[26] On the one hand, as discussed, myth makers argued that building the nuclear bomb was aimed at galvanising Indian masses for electoral gains by instilling in them a sense of false pride. On the other, civilizational moorings were traced for exploding the bomb as discussed in the previous section. The argument goes that no other political party except BJP and its predecessor Jan Sangh openly advocated for a nuclear weapon. Other parties talked about either keeping the option open or aggressively advocating for nuclear disarmament.

Admittedly, the test for the Indian nuclear bomb was conducted by the NDA government, headed by Mr Atal Bihari Vajpayee. The BJP was not the only constituent of the NDA; there were other parties too, in the NDA. Some of the parties believed in the socialist ideology. Moreover, all of them, including the BJP were committed to the Indian Constitution whose Preamble is 'solemnly resolved to constitute India into a sovereign socialist democratic republic.' There may be some Hindu reverberations on the streets but the leadership always maintained that it is a bomb with no religious connotation. Its only objective is securing India by deterring its adversary.

As for domestic politics or as discussed in the previous section, the prestige dimension of the nuclear bomb, even Mrs Indira Gandhi was accused of conducting the PNE to 'circumvent the domestic crisis'.[27] Quite surprisingly, the Hindu nuclear bomb was discussed in the works of some writers in relation to the Chinese nuclear invasion.[28] In fact, like the prestige issue, the issue of domestic political division is highlighted to project the parochial character of the nuclear bomb. As evident and as mentioned in the previous section, it was done or is being done, not only against BJP for conducting the 1998 tests but also against the Congress for conducting the PNE. An authoritarian and Islamic Republic like Pakistan always sees India as a Hindu nation, and its bomb a Hindu bomb notwithstanding whether BJP or the Congress is in power.

In reality, the Indian nuclear bomb is quite broad based. The foundation stone of the nuclear weapons programme had been laid during the Congress regime. The Congress Party had the dilemma of exercising the nuclear option but it prepared the country for building the bomb scientifically and technologically. In fact, a section of the Congress Party supported building the bomb since at least the 1960s. It has also come to be known that Nehru supported the military option being kept open for the development of the nuclear science and technology programme. When the NDA government conducted the tests in 1998, at that time, the Congress party did hold some demonstrations against it.

Yet, the Manmohan Singh government reposed its faith in nuclear weapons and considered it necessary for Indian security. On 13 August 2007, in a debate in the Indian Parliament, he categorically stated, "Despite changes in Government and changes in political leadership we have always tempered the exercise of our strategic autonomy with a sense of global responsibility and with a commitment to the ideals of general and complete disarmament, including global nuclear disarmament. This Government believes that our commitment to these ideals and our efforts to realize them must continue, and continue with even greater vigour, now that we are a nuclear weapon state. The possession of nuclear weapons only increases our sense of responsibility and does not diminish it."[29]

Some of the writings highlighted political differences, especially the Left parties on the nuclearisation in India.[30] The Left parties, which had a different position on nuclear weapons, gradually recognised their relevance when the world had failed to negotiate a nuclear weapons convention. In a statement, the CPI (M) leadership expressed its displeasure on the India-US civil nuclear agreement, "that India has not been recognised as a nuclear weapons state, implicitly or otherwise."[31] It was also apprehensive that when India conducts its nuclear test, the agreement might collapse.[32] In other words, it implicitly saw a need for a possible test of the nuclear weapons and the consequences of the test for the deal. The entire approach of the CPI(M) demonstrated that a nuclear weapons test is more important than the deal.

Pakistan or General Security

That India developed its nuclear weapons for fighting a war with Pakistan has been a myth basically generated by South Asian scholars based in the Western and in a few Asian countries. Pakistan's government and its policy makers have also been campaigning to limit India to South Asia and to fixing the Indian nuclear bomb in the India-Pakistan binary for a long period. Strangely, the line – that the Indian nuclear bomb had only a South Asian dimension – had existed even before India conducted nuclear tests. Indian and Pakistani nuclear bombs are boxed in the South Asian region. It does not stop here. Those who project the thinking that the Indian nuclear weapon is Pakistan-centric construct the scenario of a nuclear arms race in South Asia. This fictional scenario is without much foundation as both the countries do not declare the size of their arsenals. Yet, a tit-for-tat arms race is projected on the basis of developments in ballistic missiles and other potential nuclear delivery vehicles. On a different plane, some analysts in the US hold the view that American inaction over the Pakistani missile tests led a disappointed India to conduct nuclear tests.[33] Though this view may be sympathetic to India's test, it still is not able to appreciate and conceptualise the Indian decision beyond Pakistan. Quite interestingly, those who build this theory most likely overlook the Pakistani nuclear policy pronouncement and its nuclear doctrine. Pakistan officially maintains that its nuclear weapons have been acquired to deter India's conventional superiority. This clearly denotes that it is Pakistan that needs nuclear weapons to deal with a conventionally superior India and not vice-versa. Going by the

Pakistani version, India will be well placed to deal with Pakistan even with its conventional weapons. Still Pakistani officials and some non-Pakistani writers keep writing about instability caused by South Asia's nuclearisation, potential India-Pakistan conflict, and so on. The real idea is to scare the world, accept Pakistan's importance and its terror design.

Although, in the initial years, Pakistan was envisaged as the sole objective of India's nuclear weapons by the Western world and Pakistan itself, yet gradually, the China factor in India's security calculus is being recognised worldwide. But before this understanding steeped in the thinking of the larger part of the world, the solution to the perceived 'crisis' or 'instability' after the Pakistani nuclear tests was offered by reigning-in only India and Pakistan in a control framework. Both the countries were advised to undertake risk/crisis mitigating decisions.[34] Admittedly, some of the commentators continue to push for 'sustained nuclear risk-reduction' talks between India and Pakistan despite recognising the China factor in India's nuclearisation.[35] India is advised to make all the concessions.

Although, officially, India never articulates that its nuclear weapon is country-specific, yet the Indian strategic community has been quite vocal in pronouncing the Chinese angle for the Indian nuclear weapons programme. In fact, several Western scholars have also acknowledged that the perception of an India-Pakistan nuclear contest is misplaced. And it is the China factor that really moved India to turn nuclear.[36] Quite interestingly, the UK government's briefing for its MPs maintains, "India's nuclear policies are motivated by regional threats, notably Pakistan, but also increasingly China."[37]

The Indian government informs, "we believe that the security concerns of States extend beyond narrowly defined regions. Consequently, the notion of preservation of a balance in defence capabilities in the regional or sub-regional context is unrealistic and unacceptable"[38] This applies certainly to the South Asian situation and possibly, applicable to even the newly drawn India-Pakistan-China triangle. This triangle to an extent does fall within the Indian security region. Yet, it is also relevant to understand that India maintains that nuclear weapons with their delivery systems have a global reach and therefore, only a global solution in nuclear disarmament needs to be achieved.

Yet another myth relating to implications of the nuclearisation of India and Pakistan emanates from the belief that nuclear India is Pakistan-focused. South Asia was prognosticated as the new centre of regional instability. Kashmir was projected as the nuclear flashpoint. Both the countries were feared to have 'a capability of waging a nuclear war.'[39] One of the American government agencies predicted, a "full-scale nuclear exchange between the two rivals could kill up to 12 million people immediately and injure up to 7 million."[40] The same assessment also noted that if the two countries do not have a full exchange, both may have at least a limited nuclear war.

The Indian government has been countering this narrative, which was quite vigorous in the early years. After the attack on the Indian Parliament, the Indian government mobilised its troops. At that time, once again the myth of an India-Pakistan nuclear war was adapted. The then Indian defence minister, George Fernandes, in an interview to *The New York Times* clarified,

> "I don't agree with the idea that India and Pakistan are so imprudent and excitable that they'll forget what nuclear weapons can do. India's nuclear doctrine says that it will never be the first to use a nuclear weapon and will never use one against a non-nuclear state. We look at our nuclear weapons purely as a deterrent.
>
> Pakistan's President General Pervez Musharraf did say recently, in trying to raise the stakes, that he could use his nuclear weapons if India attacked. I made the point at the time that no man in his senses would ever mean this. I also said in response to his saber rattling that if he should finally take that kind of step, perhaps out of desperation, he should realize that India can survive a nuclear attack, but Pakistan cannot."[41]

The doomsayers maintained that the two South Asian countries had fought the wars in the past and the absence of redlines between the two countries may lead the two war-prone countries to fight another war in the nuclear mode. Its devastating consequences are likely to extend beyond the immediate region. In the extended region, a humanitarian crisis was prophesised. Radioactive contamination, famine, disease, etc. were projected to be the new challenges because of the use of nuclear weapons.

This myth was busted soon. India and Pakistan fought a war in Kargil in 1999. The war was fought without nuclear weapons. This war also busted the long-held myth that the war between two nuclear weapons countries would compulsorily be nuclear in nature. In a way, the nuclearisation of India and to an extent, of even Pakistan, rewrote the old nuclear theology. It should have silenced the theoreticians of nuclear holocaust in South Asia, but after a few years, the irrational imagination resurfaced. Pakistan's nuclear policy is primarily responsible for this kind of occasional and sporadic illusion. Pakistan does not have a 'NFU' doctrine and very often talks about the use of nuclear weapons not only on the battlefield, but also in general; it tries to use nuclear weapons as a shield to promote terror in India and the region.

Pakistan would occasionally carry forward the threat to use nuclear weapons if India uses conventional intervention. Even this myth was shattered when India struck inside the territory controlled by Pakistan after the Uri and Balakot terror incidents. The world, which feared a nuclear exchange, witnessed a trembling and sulking Pakistan knowing fully well the consequences of initiating a nuclear strike against a nuclear weapon country. The Pakistani bluff was called.

On 5 August 2019, the Indian Parliament initiated action on the long pending abrogation of Article 370. The change heralded a new beginning for Jammu, Kashmir and Ladakh. The state was divided into two union territories, with Legislative Assemblies. The Indian Home Minister stated, "Pakistan has misused the presence of Article 370 to sow the seeds of separatism and terrorism in J&K. I appeal to all those who favour Article 370, to ponder what benefits the provision brought to the state. It only prevented development and facilitated terrorism there. Only by repealing this provision, we can bring the people to the mainstream and embrace them with open arms. J&K is the heaven on earth and I assure everyone that it would continue to remain so when all the laws of Union of India become applicable to the state...."[42] No one witnessed a nuclear flashpoint in Kashmir. The phrase has almost disappeared from the global strategic nuclear discourse.

As a result, the international community appears assured that a South Asian nuclear exchange was a bad dream and theory. Gradually, writers and experts on the subject have started moderating their views and analyses. Interestingly, the Western governments had long realised the futility of this projection. Even the media has started writing about the fallacious setting constructed by a section of the policy-making community. For example, a leading Western newspaper noted, "The risk of a major war between India and Pakistan has probably gone down now that both are NWSs. But the fact that Pakistan is so unstable still makes the countries bomb much more worrying than, say, China's."[43]

Conclusion

The reality is that nuclear India celebrated the silver jubilee of its existence. During this time, it has augmented and magnified its positive image in the world. Today India is not merely called a responsible country but also a responsible nuclear state. The 25 years of nuclear India could be a lesson for other nuclear weapons countries, including those designated as the NWS under the NPT. This also busted many myths created erroneously or deliberately by the policy-makers. The misrepresentation of ideas and the situation may have persisted in some of the myths among some sections. However, any serious examination will destroy such persisting myths.

In the international community, no one talks of India as a violator of the NPT. Predominantly, the belief or understanding is that the NPT is not relevant in the Indian case. Even for India's membership of the NSG, all other members except China want to go beyond the NPT criteria. India is engaged with a broad non-proliferation regime that is facing a crisis in perpetuity, if it has not already collapsed.

Likewise, the prestige of the Indian nuclear bomb is hardly discussed except by those who speak or write on the basis of old notes or outdated writings. The security dimension has become more pronounced and prominent, more so, in light of new security developments in the world, in Asia and in the Indian neighbourhood. China's military, including its nuclear challenge, is globally recognised. Pakistan is exposed for raising the South Asia bogey with some of its partners in the non-proliferation community. One of the motives is providing a shield to China, its time-tested friend. The South Asia angle is being replaced by the Southern Asia angle that is oriented towards China as well.

Nuclear India is domestically grounded with the consensus in the political class that India will remain nuclear till there is global nuclear disarmament. India's unilateral disarmament will face the toughest resistance from those quarters known for opposing India's nuclearisation. The gradual broadening of the nuclear weapons support base has further strengthened the security narrative of the Indian nuclear weapons programme. Different contours of India's nuclear policy have been properly discussed and a consensus has also emerged on the nuclear doctrine and the management of atomic institutions.

NOTES

1 Dragana Radoviæ, "Greek Mythology and Gods", *Diplomacy & Commerce*, 8 November 2020 at https://www.diplomacyandcommerce.rs/greek-mythology-and-gods/ (Accessed on 22 September 2023).

2 Berit Bliesemann de Guevara, "Introduction: Myth and Narrative in International Politics", in Berit Bliesemann de Guevara (ed.), *Myth and Narrative in International Politics: Interpretive Approaches to the Study of IR*, Palgrave Macmillan, London, 2016, p. 1.

3 Dvora Yanow, "Foreword", in Berit Bliesemann de Guevara Ibid., p. vi.

4 Chiara Botticci, "A Philosophy of Political Myth", in Berit Bliesemann de Guevara, *Myth and Narrative in International Politics: Interpretive Approaches to the Study of IR*, Cambridge University Press, Cambridge, 2007.

5 Jeanne J. Grimmett, "Nuclear Sanctions: Section 102(b) of the Arms Export Control Act and Its Application to India and Pakistan", *CRS Report for Congress*, Order Code 98-486 A, 5 October 2001 at https://apps.dtic.mil/sti/pdfs/ADA477888.pdf (Accessed on 22 September 2023).

6 For example, the testimony of Karl Inderfurth, "Situation in India", US State Department Archive, 13 May 1998 at https://1997-2001.state.gov/policy_remarks/1998/980513_inderfurth_india.html (Accessed on 22 September 2023).

7 "Interview of Prime Minister Dr. Manmohan Singh with CNN, July 20, 2005", *India's Foreign Relations – 2005: Documents*, p. 202, Ministry of External Affairs, Government of India at https://www.mea.gov.in/Uploads/PublicationDocs/186_foreign-relations-2005.pdf, (Accessed 5 January 2024).

8 The testimony of Karl Inderfurth, no. 6.
9 T.V. Paul, "The Systemic Bases of India's Challenge to the Global Nuclear Order", *The Nonproliferation Review*, Fall 1998 at https://www.nonproliferation.org/wp-content/uploads/npr/paul61.pdf (Accessed 5 January 2024).
10 Government of India, Ministry of External Affairs, "Lecture by Foreign Secretary on 'Nuclear Non-Proliferation and International Security' at the Institute for Defence Studies and Analyses", *India's Foreign Relations – 2005: Documents*, p. 222 at https://www.mea.gov.in/Uploads/PublicationDocs/186_foreign-relations-2005.pdf (Accessed 5 January 2024).
11 Unstarred Question Number 2647, "Nuclear Non-proliferation treaty", Rajya Sabha, 16 August 2001 at https://fsi.mea.gov.in/rajya-sabha.htm?dtl/9150/Q_2647__Nuclear _Nonproliferation_treaty, (Accessed 5 January 2024).
12 James A. Green, "India's Status as a Nuclear Weapons Power under Customary International Law", *National Law School of India Review*, 24 (1), 2012 at https://repository.nls.ac.in/cgi/viewcontent.cgi?article=1229&context=nlsir (Accessed 5 January 2024).
13 "Tenth NPT Review Conference: Nuclear Weapons Threat at an All-time High", Brief, European Parliamentary Research Service, European Parliament, 2022 at https://www.europarl.europa.eu/RegData/etudes/BRIE/2022/733594/EPRS_BRI (2022) 733594_EN.pdf, (Accessed 5 January 2024).
14 Mohamed ElBaradei, "Statement to the Sixty-Third Regular Session of the United Nations General Assembly", International Atomic Energy Agency, 28 October 2008, News Center at https://www.iaea.org/newscenter/statements/statement-sixty-third-regular-session-united-nations-general-assembly (Accessed 5 January 2024).
15 Sandeep Tucker, "Canberra to keep ban on nuclear sales to India", *Financial Times*, 3 March 2006 at https://www.ft.com/content/124c4742-aa91-11da-8a68-0000779e 2340 (Accessed 5 January 2024).
16 Aziz Haniffa, "El Baradei backs India-US N-deal", Rediff.com, 7 November 2005 at https://www.rediff.com/news/2005/nov/07aziz.htm (Accessed 5 January 2024)
17 Ibid.
18 "Address of Foreign Secretary Shyam Saran at the Carnegie Endowment for International Peace on 'Transforming U.S.-India Relations: Forging a Strategic Partnership' WashingtonDC, 21 December 2005"; *India's Foreign Relations – 2005: Documents*, Government of India, Ministry of External Affairs at https://www.mea.gov.in/Uploads/PublicationDocs/186_foreign-relations-2005.pdf P.1505 (Accessed 5 January 2024).
19 https://fsi.mea.gov.in/rajya-sabha.htm?dtl/9547/Q_2968__Recognition_Of_India_As_ A_ Nuclear_Power;
20 James A. Green, no. 12.
21 Ibid.
22 Ibid.
23 Gaurav Kampani, "Why India's Post-1998 Evolution as a Conventional Nuclear Weapons Power Evokes Surprise", *Journal for Peace and Nuclear Disarmament*, 2 (1), 2019, pp.170-183 at https://www.tandfonline.com/doi/epdf/10.1080/25751654.2019.1620434?needAccess=true&role=button (Accessed 5 January 2024).
24 "India's Explanations of Votes on Resolutions at the UNGA First Committee, 2015" Permanent Mission of the Government of India to the Conference on Disarmament, Government of India at https://pmindiaun.gov.in/Cdgeneva/statement_content/MjA3 (Accessed 5 January 2024).

25 "Shri Atal Bihari Vajpayee, 'Evolution of India's Nuclear Policy', Indian Parliament Library at https://eparlib.nic.in/bitstream/123456789/756733/1/249.pdf (Accessed 5 January 2024).

26 Paul Williams, *Race, Ethnicity and Nuclear War: Representations of Nuclear Weapons and Post-Apocalyptic Worlds,* Liverpool University Press, 2011; Zafar Nawaz Jaspal, "India's Nuclear Weapons in the Control of Hindu Supremacists" at https://www.hilal.gov.pk/eng-article/detail/MzY1NQ==.html (Accessed 5 January 2024); Bill Drexel, "Hindu Nuclear Politics and the Logic of Realism," *The Review of Faith & International Affairs,* 20 (1), 2022; Sumit Sarkar, "The BJP Bomb and Aspects of Nationalism", *Economic and Political Weekly,* 4 July 1998, pp.1725-1730.
Andrea Malji, "The Rise of Hindu Nationalism and Its Regional and Global Ramifications", *Education About Asia,* 23 (1), Spring 2018, p. 42.

27 Scott Curtice, "Why Do States Build Nuclear Weapons? Proliferation Models as Concurrent Pressures on a State", Wright Flyer Paper No. 82, March 2021, Air University Press at https://www.airuniversity.af.edu/Portals/10/AUPress/Papers/WF_82_ CURTICE_ WHY _DO_STATES_BUILD_NUCLEAR_ WEAPONS_PROLIFERATION_MODELS_AS_CONCURRENT_PRESSURES_ON_A_STATE.PDF (Accessed 5 January 2024).

28 Neville Maxwell, "China's Aggression in 1962 and the 'Hindu Bomb'", *World Policy Journal,* 16 (2), Summer, 1999, pp. 111-118; Frank E. Couper, "Indian Party Conflict on the Issue of Atomic Weapons", *The Journal of Developing Areas* 3 (2), January 1969, pp. 191-206.

29 "Prime Minister Manmohan Singh : Civil Nuclear Energy Cooperation with United States", Lok Sabha, Parliament of India, 13 August 2007 at https://sansad.in/ls/knowledge-centre/speeches, (Accessed 5 January 2024).

30 Carsten Rauch, "Hushed Hope - India, the Nuclear Deal, and Nonproliferation", PRIF Working Paper No. 7, December 2010 at https://www.hsfk.de/fileadmin/HSFK/hsfk_downloads/PRIF_WP_07.pdf, (Accessed on 5 January, 2024).

31 Communist Party of India (Marxist), *Left Stand on the Nuclear Deal: Notes Exchanged in the UPA-Left Committee on India-US Civil Nuclear Cooperation,* Progressive Printers, July 2008 at https://cpim.org/upa/2008_nuclear-notes.pdf (Accessed 5 January 2024)

32 Ibid.

33 Tim Weiner, "Nuclear Anxiety: the Blunders; U.S. Blundered on Intelligence, Officials Admit", *The New York Times,* 13 May 1998 at https://www.nytimes.com/1998/05/13/world/nuclear-anxiety-the-blunders-us-blundered-on-intelligence-officials-admit.html (Accessed 5 January 2024).

34 John F. Burns, "Nuclear Anxiety: The Overview; Leaders in India and in Pakistan Tone Down Crisis", *The New York Times,* 30 May 1998 at https://www.nytimes.com/1998/05/30/world/nuclear-anxiety-the-overview-leaders-in-india-and-in-pakistan-tone-down-crisis.html?searchResultPosition=13 (Accessed 5 January 2024).

35 Michael Krepon, Nuclear Race on the Subcontinent", *The New York Times,* 4 April 2013 at https://www.nytimes.com/2013/04/05/opinion/global/nuclear-race- on-the-subcontinent.html?action=click&module=RelatedCoverage&pgtype=Article&region=Footer (Accessed 5 January 2024).

36 J. Mohan Malik, "India Goes Nuclear: Rationale, Benefits, Costs and Implications", *Contemporary Southeast Asia,* 20 (2), August 1998, p. 193.

37 Claire Mills, "Nuclear Weapons at a Glance: India and Pakistan", Research Briefing, Number 9070, The House of Commons Library at https://researchbriefings.files.parliament.uk/documents/CBP-9070/CBP-9070.pdf (Accessed 5 January 2024).

38 "India's Explanations of Votes on Resolutions at the UNGA First Committee, 2015", Permanent Mission of India to the Conference on Disarmament at https://pmindiaun. gov.in/Cdgeneva/statement_content/MjA3, (Accessed 5 January 2024)

39 Thom Shanker, "12 Million Could Die at Once in an India-Pakistan Nuclear War", *The New York Times,* 27 May 2002 at https://www.nytimes.com/2002/05/27/world/12-million-could-die-at-once-in-an-india-pakistan-nuclear-war.html?searchResultPosition=30 (Accessed 5 January 2024).

40 Ibid.

41 Michael Richardson, "Q&A / George Fernandes : India and Pakistan are not 'imprudent' on nuclear option", *The New York Times,* 3 June 2002 at https://www.nytimes.com/2002/06/03/news/qa-george-fernandes-india-and-pakistan-are-not-imprudent-on-nuclear.html?searchResultPosition=10 (Accessed 5 January 2024).

42 "Parliament approves Resolution to repeal Article 370, paves way to truly integrate J&K with Indian Union", Press Information Bureau, Ministry of Home Affairs, Government of India, 6 August 2019 at https://pib.gov.in/newsite/PrintRelease.aspx? relid=192505 (Accessed 5 January 2024).

43 Gideon Rachman, "A Nuclear-Free World? No Thanks",*The Financial Times,* 4 May 2010 at https://www.ft.com/content/a30e936e-56dd-11df-aa89-00144feab49a (Accessed 5 January 2024).

2

Pokhran Fall Out at the Conference on Disarmament: How India's Nuclear Diplomacy Turned Multilateral Pressure to Its Advantage

DB Venkatesh Varma

It was only to be expected that before long, the diplomatic whirlwinds unleashed by India's nuclear tests of 11 and 13 May 1998 in Pokhran would reach the shores of Lake Leman in Geneva – the seat of the CD. The impact of Pakistan's nuclear tests of late May would follow soon thereafter. Containing the diplomatic fallout of the Pokhran Il tests in the Geneva-based CD was an important reference point in the subsequent evolution of India's nuclear diplomacy as a nuclear weapon State. This chapter provides a snapshot of issues during 1998 and highlights the policy coherence and diplomatic deftness, which allowed for a major turnaround in India's position in the global nuclear order over the next two decades. India's military nuclear programme has been protected while its engagement with the international community has been accomplished. India's nuclear diplomacy therefore enabled India to break the chains of nuclear apartheid.

Pokhran II Tests

It was the week of Buddha Purnima. Pokhran II coincided with the opening week of the spring session of the Conference. Plenary meetings of the CD are held in the historic and ornate Council Chamber – venue of important meetings. It was here that important meetings of the League of Nations took place; it was the seat of the Eighteen-Nation Disarmament Committee which negotiated the NPT. After 1980, it became the CD, created by the First Special Session of the UNGA on Disarmament held in 1978, as the world's single multilateral disarmament negotiating forum, consisting of militarily significant States, working by consensus on an agenda whose priority items related to the cessation of the nuclear arms race and nuclear disarmament.

By 1998, the CD had just emerged from a bitterly contested negotiation of the CTBT in 1995-96. Under the redoubtable Ambassador Arundhati Ghose, India had opposed the CTBT because it did not contribute to the goal of nuclear disarmament. Despite India's opposition and contrary to the CD's rules of procedure, the text of the Treaty was tabled in the UNGA by Australia, adopted by majority vote, and was opened for signature in September 1996. By the summer of 1998, it had been adhered to by over 140 countries but had not entered into force given the ill-advised insertion by the UK delegation in the Treaty of Annex II States whose ratification was a necessary condition. India figured on that list. Though this provision was questionable in international law, several countries had begun viewing the CTBT as establishing an 'international norm' against nuclear testing, even without its entry into force. There was pressure on India to join. India's refusal to sign signalled its resolve to protect its national security interests in a nuclearized international security environment, especially after the 1995 indefinite extension of the NPT and the series of nuclear tests conducted by three nuclear weapon States – France, China, and UK – just prior to the conclusion of the CTBT negotiations. This was the setting for the Pokhran II nuclear tests in 1998.

Against this background, India's nuclear tests did not surprise serious international observers, in particular the CD's seasoned diplomats. There was a clear message on exercising the nuclear option in the election manifesto of the BJP, which had come to power within a larger NDA coalition of parties under Prime Minister Atal Behari Vajpayee. It was expected that India's national resilience and its pursuit of strategic autonomy would manifest itself in some form, breaking through the self-restraint exercised in nuclear weaponization after 1974. Several CD diplomats followed India's statements very closely. The Chinese diplomats tried hard to discern India's evolving position. Though the actual tests took CD diplomats by surprise, many of them said that given the pressure on India the tests were not wholly unexpected. Following Pokhran II nuclear tests, India reluctantly became an open nuclear weapon State, though outside the NPT.

The CD had a well-deserved reputation as body of high professionals, very formal in its demeanour with representatives of the world's most powerful countries. Thursdays is plenary day in the CD. After the tests of 11 and 13 May, the first Thursday fell on 14May. It was a day of high drama. Emotion and anger against India were high but also admiration for India's defiant assertion of its national interests by conducting the nuclear tests against heavy international odds.

The CD Debate

The Plenary began at 1030 am on 14 May, under the Presidency of Syria which was holding the monthly rotating Presidency of the Conference. The Council Chamber was full; so was the visitors' gallery, along with the entire international press corps based in Geneva. The Indian delegation headed by its Permanent Representative, Ambassador Savitri Kunadi, was seated with the focus of a thousand eyes in the room and the world media. Tension in the room was palpable. Normal diplomatic courtesies were absent. The gravity of the occasion was not lost on anyone. But not for a moment did this affect the poise or demeanour of the unflappable Indian Ambassador and her delegation, which included Counsellor Hamid Ali Rao. For the next four- and-a-half hours, 40 countries spoke on India 's nuclear tests, with many of them belonging to the Western group, nuclear weapon States and their allies. Ambassador Munir Akram of Pakistan was the first speaker and it was not a surprise, given his own record and his country's position, that his speech was replete with venomous anti-India rhetoric. Of the 40 delegations which spoke, a few expressed outright condemnation, most expressed concern; a few others saw the tests as being a wakeup call for nuclear disarmament. Many of them also urged Pakistan not to conduct tests of its own. From the G-21, the CD group belonging to developing countries, only a handful spoke. India's statement was short but unapologetic– it set out the rationale for the tests but reaffirmed India's commitment to nuclear disarmament. There was close coordination between the Indian delegation to the CD and Joint Secretary (JS) DISA in the MEA, Rakesh Sood, who was the key person coordinating India's international stance after the nuclear tests.[1]

The plenary concluded at 4.30 pm. In contrast to the tense atmosphere in the Conference chamber, diplomats from several countries – one from a nuclear power, and many from developing countries, especially from the Arab group – approached the Indian delegation to convey, not so much by word as by touch and gesture, that whatever may have been said on the floor of the CD, their personal respect and admiration for India remained high. Many diplomats from the developing world privately conveyed that though their national statements said otherwise, they had high personal regard for the Indian delegation for showing great dignity and poise in representing India's interests. One diplomat told the author that he was witness 'to a day of judgement of the cosmic nuclear order, with India bravely pitted against the nuclear weapon states and their allies.'

Pak Nuclear Tests

The diplomatic ground shifted considerably following Pakistan's nuclear tests on 28 and 30 May. The Plenary held on 2 June, witnessed the Western Group speak in full strength. But unlike the previous Plenaries, several delegations belonging to the G21 also spoke. New Zealand, which was now warming up to a leading role in opposing the nuclear tests, issued a statement on behalf of 47 members of the

CD, condemning the tests, stating that peace in Asia was a global concern and called on both countries to sign and ratify the CTBT and accede to the NPT as non-nuclear weapon States and support the FMCT negotiations in the CD. Another 46 statements were made during the day. While most statements did not differentiate between the Indian and the Pakistani tests, there were a few notable exceptions. China fully endorsed the Pakistani line that the tests conducted by India were a provocation to which Pakistan had reacted. There were some notable statements that looked at the broader significance for nuclear disarmament. Ambassador Iftekar Chowdhury of Bangladesh noted that the subcontinent, historically subject to colonial domination, now had the means to redefine its relationship with the rest of the world. There was understanding and sympathy in the statement by Ambassador Hewa Palihakkara of Sri Lanka as well, who said that the security of South Asia cannot be considered in isolation, while stressing the need for global nuclear disarmament.

After its own nuclear tests, there was a change in Pakistan's approach as it sought international mediation on South Asia, including on Jammu and Kashmir. Significantly, some of the other demands made by Pakistan on nuclear stabilization in South Asia and conventional imbalance, found resonance in the P-5 Foreign Ministers' meeting held in Geneva two days later, which put in place the key elements for UN Security Council Resolution 1172, adopted in New York on 6 June 1998.[2] The first week of June – the meetings in Geneva and New York – showed tactical convergence between the US and China, in which Pakistani interests were reflected, though this convergence did not last for long. It can be said in retrospect that the first week of June was the high point of India's international isolation after the nuclear tests. But this situation did not last long as it contained within itself a fundamental contradiction between tactical solidarity of the nuclear weapon States, particularly the US and China, and their differing geopolitical imperatives. India sensed these differing perceptions and set about to exploit them diplomatically.

Impact of Nuclear Tests

CD proceedings also had a significant long-term impact on the debate within the NPT driven non-proliferation regime. The non-nuclear weapon States became more vocal on the weak global disarmament commitments of the nuclear weapon States following the indefinite extension of the NPT and the inadvisability of pushing a country like India into a corner on CTBT. Such questions led to the formation of new groups such as the 'New Agenda Coalition'[3] and reinforced focus within the NPT on nuclear disarmament leading to pathbreaking commitments in the 2000 NPT RevCon. It is another matter that implementation fell far short of expectations, in turn triggering breakaway initiatives, which led eventually to the adoption of the TPNW, which has attracted adherents only from the non-nuclear weapon States under the NPT, thus creating a competing legal argument within the NPT. India's tests of 1998 did not create fissures in the non-proliferation regime as much as they cast light on existing ones.

India used the CD to explain[4] the statements made by its leaders – in and outside Parliament. The main points were the following: the rationale for the nuclear tests after 24 years of restraint, its doctrinal and diplomatic policies as a NWS, including NFU of nuclear weapons, strict export controls of sensitive technologies, voluntary moratorium on nuclear explosive testing, and readiness to engage in FMCT negotiations, while calling for, but not linking it, to support for a Nuclear Weapons Convention. India's statements also rejected Pakistan's allegation of provocations (while leaving open the possibility of expanding CBMs, which were subsequently taken forward in the Lahore Declaration) or call for compartmentalized approaches on South Asia or international mediation on Jammu and Kashmir. More broadly, India began to engage on doctrinal issues as a nuclear weapon State – proposing measures to prevent nuclear war, nuclear restraint to reduce chances of accidental or unauthorised use of nuclear weapons and in providing security assurances to non-nuclear weapon States and to established nuclear weapon free zones. The traditional conceptual link with time-bound elimination of nuclear weapons through a Nuclear Weapons Convention was retained. Thus, India maintained its long-standing principled position on nuclear disarmament and retained its leadership position on nuclear issues within NAM in the First Committee in New York and in the G-21 in the CD, even after the Pokhran II tests.[5] This was a major diplomatic achievement.

At the CD, India's willingness to engage in FMCT negotiations was of high significance. This created an effective lightening rod to dispel international concern and compelled Pakistan to fall in line. A decision to appoint an Ad hoc Committee on FMCT was adopted on 11 August 1998.[6] This Committee held two meetings before close of the CD's annual session in September 1998. It was everyone's expectation that the Ad hoc Committee on FMCT would be re-established when the CD reconvened in January for its 1999 session. It was not to be.

First Committee Resolution

With the closure of the CD's annual session in September, the scene of action shifted to the UNGA's First Committee in October. New Zealand, Canada and Australia tabled a Resolution on 'Nuclear Testing' which 'expressed grave concern over and strongly deplored the nuclear tests conducted in South Asia.' Its Preamble recalled UN Security Council Resolution 1172 and called on all States to adhere to the NPT and to sign and ratify the CTBT. This Resolution became a major test of will – for India to beat back the nuclear powers by mobilizing the NAM and moderates in the Western Group (for which India tabled a new Resolution on 'Reducing Nuclear Danger', an initiative that portrayed India's confidence and defiance in the face of daunting odds) and for the nuclear powers and their allies, an opportunity to isolate India and showcase UNGA support for UN Security Council Resolution 1172. By October, the G8 and EU had condemned South Asian nuclear tests. More significantly, at the NAM Summit in Durban (29 Aug - 3 Sept), Indian diplomacy of the highest order and the global stature of its leadership – Prime Minister Vajpayee, ensured that the Final Document of the Durban Summit contained only a reference to the 'complexities arising from the nuclear tests', with no words critical of India, let alone condemnation. The negative tide against India had started to turn.

Pakistan saw the writing on the wall and instead of confronting India, choose to work with India in the UNGA, though for the brief period of the duration of the First Committee. A few South Asian countries pitched in with varying degrees of support. Amendments were tabled by India and Pakistan separately and jointly as well as amendments on behalf of SAARC group of countries. Though the Latin American group was largely in favour of the Nuclear Testing Resolution, there were several countries in the African group who were willing to stand up, in particular Zimbabwe, Nigeria and Zambia stood up against western pressure and tabled amendments that sought to dilute the exclusive focus on South Asia. Had any of these amendments been adopted, it would have become difficult for the co-sponsors of the original Resolution to have taken it forward. These cleverly drafted amendments were the subject of intense lobbying in New York and in capitals. In the event, no-action motions were carried through with the slimmest margins, in one case 63 votes for with 60 against; in another case, 59 votes for to 57 votes against. Though the Resolution was adopted without amendment, with 98 votes for with 31 abstentions, 4 brave countries joined India (and Pakistan) in voting against – Benin, Bhutan, Zambia and Zimbabwe. These countries merit special mention for standing up for India at a time when intense pressure was applied on them.

While the Nuclear Testing Resolution was passed successfully, its political bottom had fallen off, providing only a hollow victory for its main sponsors.[7] It was clear that the wave of diplomatic opposition to India's nuclear tests, sought to be fashioned in various foras including in the CD, had started to ebb by the time of the First Committee vote in November 1998. This created a substantive need for all sides to look for areas of engagement bilaterally, and in multilateral fora. India's expressed willingness to engage on FMCT negotiations in the CD, assumed significance as a key indicator of not only the moderate nature of India's nuclear ambitions, its readiness for engagement but also its credibility as an interlocutor.

India's Policy as a Nuclear Power

India's nuclear policy was characterised both by restraint and responsibility. These elements fed into the India-US bilateral dialogue that commenced in late 1998 until 2000 (Jaswant Singh-Strobe Talbot Dialogue), the NSSP dialogue between 2002 and 2004, a key precursor of the India-US Civil Nuclear Initiative (based on the 18 July 2005 Joint Statement), India's engagement with the NSG and its bilateral agreements with several countries, between 2005 and 2008.

The changing fortunes of FMCT negotiations have had long-term consequences. By late 1998, while the public focus was on the nuclear tests of India and Pakistan, China began to back pedal on FMCT negotiations by establishing a linkage with PAROS, while also calling for the CD to adopt a comprehensive and balanced programme of work. Though the US held the Presidency of CD in January 1999, it was unable to put forward a Programme of Work that allowed commencement of FMCT negotiations. In the meantime, India worked within the G-21 to put forward CD/1570 and CD/1571 to keep up the profile of nuclear disarmament in the CD's Programme at Work, but short of linkage between core issues.

Pakistan's Negative Role

Thereafter, a combination of factors – growing P-5 disunity, (exacerbated by US attack on the Chinese Embassy in Belgrade), wavering US focus leading to Senate rejection of the CTBT in late 1999, growing mobilization within non-nuclear weapon States on nuclear disarmament– compelled the Nuclear Weapon States to gain time by agreeing to the 13 Practical Steps at the 2000 NPT RevCon to compensate for lack of progress in the CD. While lip service was paid to FMCT, negotiations in the CD were stalled due to China's opposition and after 2002, the lukewarm interest of the Bush Administration in a verifiable FMCT. Despite several efforts, the stalemate continued until the advent of the Obama Administration, which reverted to US support for an FMCT with verification. During the Algerian Presidency in 2009, the CD adopted a decision to again establish an Ad Hoc Committee on FMCT on 29 May 2009, which

Pakistan initially agreed to, but soon backtracked from it, and with China's help, stalled negotiations. Citing the India-US Civil Nuclear Initiative as affecting its national security interests, Pakistan has blocked FMCT negotiations since 2010. With Pakistan paying almost no punitive costs for blocking the CD, the stalemate persists till date. The minimum necessary common ground amongst the nuclear powers to allow for the CD to commence substantive negotiations has almost disappeared in recent years. This has added to the deep malaise that now afflicts the multilateral disarmament agenda. However, the CD has been one of the more important platforms for India's international engagement for relieving international pressure, exploiting opportunities, utilising avenues for constructive engagement and finding common ground consistent with its national security interests as a nuclear weapon State. India's policy of international engagement has succeeded in fulfilling its national security interests.

India's Diplomatic Success

There was a coherent compatibility between the commitment to negotiate FMCT in the CD, as a treaty banning future production of fissile material for nuclear weapons, and the other commitments as part of the Separation Plan which affected some portions of India's unsafeguarded nuclear programme. India's position on FMCT negotiations in the CD was an important reference point around which other international commitments impacting on its nuclear programme were put in place. It is significant that despite many challenges – both internal and external – India was able to maintain a balance between its commitment to negotiate a multilateral FMCT in the CD, its opposition to a moratorium on the prohibition of production of fissile material for weapons purposes, the logic of the separation plan and its impact on its unsafeguarded reactors, its opposition to legally binding commitments on nuclear explosive testing, on the one hand and on the other, the material requirements for a robust nuclear weapon programme outside international constraints or commitments. This balance finally resulted in the international mainstreaming of a nuclear-armed India despite not being a party to the NPT, with no constraints on international cooperation for its civilian nuclear programme – a diplomatic achievement of very high significance.

In the two decades since 1998, there has been a sea change in India's position in the global nuclear order. As a result of broad-based engagement, the success of the Civil Nuclear Initiative has mainstreamed India in the nuclear order – previous NSG restrictions have been lifted; numerous bilateral and multilateral nuclear cooperation agreements have been concluded and major progress has been made through membership of key export control bodies. While India has successfully joined the MTCR, the Australia Group and the Wassenaar Arrangement, due to Chinese perfidy and US backtracking, India's diplomatic engagement on its membership of the NSG did not yield the expected results. Apart from this gap, India's nuclear diplomacy since 1998 has largely achieved its stated objectives.

India today is considered an essential partner for the success of key international initiatives in the nuclear field. At the same time, it has maintained conceptual coherence and displayed consummate diplomatic skill in navigating the strategic crosscurrents of the global nuclear order. India has preserved and protected both the policy and material basis for its strategic autonomy and its nuclear doctrine. India is thus well positioned to address current and emerging international security challenges. On the 25th anniversary of the Pokhran II tests, it is important to recall the difficult road traversed so far, but also the success achieved in breaking the chains of nuclear apartheid – due to the sagacity of our leaders and the deftness of our diplomacy which has brought laurels for India as a nuclear power.

NOTES

1 For details see Plenary records CD/PV 792 and 795, Conference on Disarmament, 1998.

2 UN Security Council S/RES/1172, 1998.

3 The 'New Agenda Coalition' initially consisted of Brazil, Egypt, Ireland, Mexico, New Zealand, South Africa, Sweden, and Slovenia. The latter two left the coalition soon thereafter.

4 See statements by Ambassador Kunadi CD/PV 795, pp. 42-46.

5 India's Working Paper on Nuclear Disarmament issued in the CD as an official document – CD/1816, combines its traditional support for nuclear disarmament

while combining new elements on nuclear risk reduction consistent with its nuclear doctrine of 2003.

6 See Conference on Disarmament document – CD/1547 of 11 August 1998, which established an ad hoc committee on FMCT negotiations.

7 See UNGA First Committee Official Records 12 November 1998A/C.1/PV.29. Ambassador Satyabrata Pal – DPR in the Indian Mission to the UN, spoke eloquently in the First Committee debate in defence of India's position.

3

Indian Diplomacy and the Nuclear India

Sheel Kant Sharma

India's diplomatic profile in the past 25 years has been considerably enhanced and elevated in overall terms. The nuclear weapon tests of May 1998 demonstrated an inner strength and resolve. These were followed by a concerted diplomatic offensive by India. Diplomacy succeeded on several fronts, bringing Indian strategic concerns and security policies to the fore and yielded significant results in raising acceptability by key States. India's doctrine of credible nuclear deterrence, its technological prowess in nuclear, Space and related fields, and its mainstreaming with global nuclear trade as well as all export control regimes, fructified India as a stabilizing force. Nuclear India today does not evoke negative reactions. India's atomic energy establishment has important bilateral cooperation agreements with major nuclear powers, sharing the vision of nuclear energy as integral to a clean, green and sustainable energy future. The ISRO, which was among the entities placed under restrictions by the US in 1998, is today a global player and has established itself as a dependable provider of Space launch services. India's economic progress has been marked by the most rapid growth, and in the face of global headwinds, India throws up sound macro-economic indices. It remains committed, however, first and foremost to addressing domestic pressures of a 1.4 billion strong population.

This is how nuclear India can be succinctly described in circa 2023 in the global diplomatic setting. To begin with, this chapter takes a quick look back at the milestones over these past 25 years since the Pokhran II tests. Then the rapidly changed perspective of diplomacy is discussed in conjunction with the predominant technological themes of today, which impact the nuclear context as well. The chapter then attempts to draw inferences as to how India ought to chart its course amidst new challenges.

India has emerged as a responsible member of the comity of nations armed with nuclear weapons, through systematic diplomatic engagement with its key partners and through its actions – actions taken in responding to challenges thrown by the enveloping security environment, which are widely acceptable to an overwhelming majority of nations. India is a responsible State, because it is bound to act in pursuance of its constitutional duties, its transparent legal systems, the restraints that it has accepted to observe and its historical experience with such restraints, the manner in which it conducts international relations, its adherence to the UN Charter and to the statutes of UN bodies like the International Court of Justice, WHO, The United Nations Educational, Scientific and Cultural Organization, International Telecommunication Union, and International Atomic Energy Association, just to name a few. A responsible State is sensitive and responsive to the opinions of other States. There is a great deal to do for each State to earn the qualification of "responsible". It is rooted in tangible demonstrable actions and actions that are in the works and/or binding. This applies to nuclear weapon States as well as other powers with nuclear prowess and all frontiers of technology.

India stood by its commitments made during security dialogues that commenced after the tests in 1998, with the US, France, the UK, Russia, Germany, the EU, Japan, South Korea, Australia and other members of the NSG. One culmination of this process was in the spectacular prognosis of the historic India-US Joint Statement of 18 July 2005 at Washington DC. This comprised affirmation of India as a State advanced in nuclear technology and the entry into force of nuclear cooperation agreements not only with the US, but also with Australia, Japan and Canada. While the process in the US went through systemic and step-by-step legal track, Japan's responses were rooted in its historically held moral reservation against nuclear weapons – it being the only nation that suffered the horrors of Hiroshima and Nagasaki. Japan has long had the technological competence to cross the Rubicon. In giving approval to the India-Japan nuclear cooperation agreement, the Japanese Diet validated India's record of being averse to nuclear weapons for almost a quarter century despite a demonstrated capability to go ahead and acquire nuclear weapons – an aversion which has been duly reflected in India's nuclear doctrine: India has made a unique commitment to working multilaterally towards the goal of a nuclear weapon-free world as integral to its security doctrine. That India continues to stand by its commitments made to the international community for nearly twenty years, has weighed in its favour in conclusion of the agreement for cooperation. This is in addition to the weighty argument underlining sustainable energy needs of the fastest growing among the emerging economies. Likewise, there has been vindication of India's record in agreements with Australia and Canada, who attach the highest importance to the nonproliferation ethos.

Nuclear cooperation coherently fits into the much larger domain of strategic partnership with these countries. This partnership embraces the frontiers of science and technology, germane to the latest round of the industrial revolution. The agreements pave the way for, and catalyze, multi-dimensional cooperation, for mutual benefit by sustaining and upgrading human resource to advances in fuel cycle, metallurgy, software, cyber domain and AI, as well as diverse interconnected fields.

This broad-based diplomatic matrix is in harmony with the most far-reaching and steadily growing relationship with the US, a relationship for which the nuclear agreements between India and the US have given the maximum thrust. The India-US nuclear cooperation agreement and the exemption for India by the NSG have been building blocks for bringing India into international nuclear commerce as a country with 'advanced nuclear technology'. India's Safeguards Agreement with the IAEA concluded in 2008, was also integral to this process. India's record since the 2008 NSG exemption and the safeguards agreement with the IAEA contextualizes India's long-held support for nuclear nonproliferation in spirit more than in letter. India as a nuclear-armed State fully complies with NPT's prohibitions, which are applicable to a nuclear weapon State. The US Administration's appreciation of India's tangible cooperation with the global nonproliferation order reached its climax when, in 2016, President Barack Obama actively initiated full membership for India in the NSG, an initiative that brought immense credit to India and called into question the credentials of the country which blocked India's entry. That country, China, was exposed by coming out to link India's entry to that of Pakistan in the face of the latter's dismal and deceitful record on nuclear proliferation as was borne out by revelations in 2003-04 of the clandestine nuclear walmart run from Islamabad. In these past six years since Chinese obstruction to India's NSG membership, India has emerged stronger while its detractors have only appeared inglorious in their cussedness.

Meanwhile nuclear energy planning in India has moved on with determined pace and tangible achievements, providing heft to its nuclear diplomacy. India's quest remains focused on nuclear power for its sustainable development needs. It plans to build nuclear reactors to attain 63000 MW of capacity by 2032. What merits particular mention in India's quest is the AHWR. A 700 MW reactor indigenously built by India went critical in 2019 and demonstrated the competence and skills of Indian scientists and engineers. The concept and design of the AHWR evolved at the BARC, in collaboration with diverse capabilities of the Indian nuclear enterprise. Among other things, the introduction of Thorium bundles has been actively promoted in the AHWR. It has been a considered view of top Indian scientists that an AHWR 'has robust safety strengths of unprecedented magnitude' and requires lower level of technological infrastructure, which may be particularly relevant to developing countries. In the construction of the AHWR, there can be a perfect response to safety and security requirements for a much bigger role of nuclear power that lies ahead.

In quite a few countries, nuclear power's fortunes may appear to be presently declining but that is nothing new, as a similar decline has been witnessed more than once in the past half a century. While entirely reasonable, the present full-throttle thrust for new and renewable energy options still leaves enough space for nuclear energy in the energy mix, considering all factors. Nuclear power will remain emissions-free, renewable and essential for meeting base load requirements in the present century. Nuclear power plants are now designed for much longer lifetimes and for capacity factors that can cope with management of "load following" in electricity grids comprising solar, wind and hydro. It is an extraordinary pace with which technology for renewables has evolved and costs come down, which challenges the nuclear option on economic grounds. The cost of solar panels, for instance, has come down drastically between 2002 and 2022. However, for surface transport and aviation, the solution is seen in green hydrogen, for production of which, nuclear power can be a viable route. In addition, the role of nuclear power reactors in shipping may be an important factor.

Nuclear power prospects did suffer a severe blow on account of safety and its appeal took a nosedive in the immediate aftermath of Fukushima. But that has been gradually offset by several developments, including the categorical imperative for clean and sustainable energy, pressures on growing economies, for independence from fossil fuel and domestic reassessment of nuclear power's positive contribution even in many European countries apart from continued reliance in China, Japan and India. Japan has not completely ruled it out. Japan, as also South Korea, retains the edge in advanced stages in nuclear technology development and has competence in its diverse facets. (even though the Fukushima ordeal has shown some disagreeable features with regard to management of reactor safety).

The global situation concerning nuclear weapons as it exists today is qualitatively very different from how it appeared in 1998. It is vastly transformed in relation to even how it could be visualized at that point of time. In 1998, a global nuclear order did prevail – albeit not favourable nor sensitive to India's legitimate security and developmental needs. That order was much less uncertain than what has become of it today. The five NPT NWSs then appeared broadly on the same page; which does not appear conceivable today. So many facets have unravelled rapidly and utterly muddied the perspective. It is necessary to dwell on this malaise and describe the facets. These are:

1. The global nuclear order of 1998 no longer appears viable. To quote from W.B. Yeats's famous poem, "The Second Coming", the words in it ring true once again as they did more than hundred years ago, during the period between the World Wars:

   "Turning and turning in the widening gyre
   The falcon cannot hear the falconer;
   Things fall apart; the centre cannot hold;
   Mere anarchy is loosed upon the world, the blood-dimmed tide is loosed, and everywhere
   The ceremony of innocence is drowned;
   The best lack all conviction, while the worst
   Are full of passionate intensity."

   A global order, howsoever imperfect, is founded on idealism and is sustained by sincere conviction, not cynicism. Cynical maneouvres by some of the powerful, are centre stage in the present scenario.

2. Nuclear weapons are viewed from almost entirely different prism today than how they were perceived in 1998. These weapons today engender greater doubts and uncertainty within the strategic edifice of nuclear deterrence. Today they evoke contrasting reactions even among those who seemed sanguine about managing to live with nuclear weapons. On the other hand, those who are convinced against nuclear weapons have grown stronger in conviction that these weapons are for nothing good while the peril they can trigger

can be closer than ever before. The 140-plus States, adherents to the Ban Treaty, the concerted anti-nuclear movements and the vast majority in the UN – except nine nuclear armed States – are much more opposed to nuclear weapons, and much more stridently against their use or threat of use. India too has been firm and forthright against use or threat of use of nuclear weapons, even as it has longstanding reservations against unilateral nuclear disarmament. India's role in the G20 Summit in Indonesia in 2022 was important, as the Summit statement stressed clearly the inadmissibility of the use or threat of use of nuclear weapons.

3. Diplomacy among the most powerful NWSs has by now perfected the art of drawing global attention by the scary talk about nuclear weapons, ballistic missiles and attendant dangers – though beneath the scary talk might lie a political motive, about which adversaries play to their advantage. If one side holds the reigns of the global economy and may spawn sweeping sanctions and maximum pressure, for the other, it reinforces national consolidation, prestige, and redressal of long-held grievances, no matter what it may cost to lives, economy and well-being of people, home and abroad. Under the nuclear scare spawned by the great powers, flourishes a fevered arms competition in an ever-rising spiral. Asymmetric strategies, which are adopted today by the weaker powers, comprise menacing dimensions.

4. For the wider world, concern about nuclear peril is heightened whenever great power relations nosedive, just as they have since the onset of the war in Ukraine.[1] There is an underlying leitmotif in the eruption of the tragic denouement which prevails between Russia and Ukraine – which is that, despite the past decades of tumult and massive transformations, rise and falls, in the global settings – nuclear weapons, even while seen as a singular peril, might in the final analysis, fail in shaping relations among panicky great powers, or between great powers and their adversaries. Therefore, in times of such crises as bedevil Russia's relations with the West, voices for

addressing the nuclear peril are drowned in risky geopolitical games. The US, Russia and China comprise a formidable triumvirate under whose disjointed helm, a nuclear disarmament agenda lies in a hopeless charade.

There is a transitional international order being shaped by right- wing ascendancy worldwide with inflated notions of national sovereignty and protectionism.

The burning question is, whether the painstaking work of drafting disarmament type minutiae (such as those that figured the last time, as recently as 2014, in the JCPOA) should become less relevant than the sparse texts that tend to emerge from great powers or contemporary high-level meetings of bilateral or multilateral or regional forums. The US and Russia have forfeited the gains of nuclear disarmament fostered by President Ronald Reagan and Mikhail Gorbachev, throwing the disarmament campaigners worldwide into panic.

Skepticism informs diverse facets of US-China relations where grave misgivings abound. The US wants China to join the process of nuclear disarmament alongside Russia. However, there is deep mistrust in America about any and every aspect of the "cooperative" dimension of ties with China, including Chinese participation in American stock markets, Chinese academics, contracts for infrastructure with Chinese companies and China's inroads made in American social media. These tendencies in the US are reciprocated by the Chinese with increasingly severe, North-Korea-like, rhetoric as well as active steps to assert power. So, the potential has diminished immensely for pursuit of negotiations towards any goals, be they in regard to disarmament or climate change or pandemics. The G-7 Summit in Japan in May 2023, had tried to improve the situation but it remains fluid due to positions taken by China, Russia and North Korea.

5. Conventional armaments and advanced dual-capable weapon systems have emerged to dominate the scenarios of war. Cyber threats to nuclear command, control and surveillance are much

more sinister than they were in 1998. Cyber security concerns have grown almost exponentially in the past two decades, especially when seen in sync with extraordinary developments in AI and quantum computing. There is a new global contest about advanced technology for weapons use. Space-based systems are dual-use and far more sophisticated than before. The net impact of these developments has been to throw into a hopeless flux, the clear hierarchy of ultimate threat perceptions in the nuclear age, i.e., the highest priority to addressing humanity's peril in nuclear weapons use or threat of use; conventional war involving great powers; proxy wars and regional armed conflicts below the nuclear threshold, including State-sponsored non-State actors. In place of an unequivocal commitment to banning nuclear weapons and forswearing their use, the agenda of disarmament today is replete with whataboutery.

6. Advance technology controls have made a comeback in this decade in a new avatar. Critical new materials are being viciously contested for control, rather than in cooperation – which had a brief window during post-Cold War globalization. Semiconductor chips, for instance, are on the frontiers of technology, where fervent attempts are under- way to enforce controls. On the offensive side, such chips are critical to strategic weapons systems, advance missiles, diverse kind of drones as well as conventional systems, like military aircraft for future wars, ships and submarines and their control and guidance systems involving radars, sensors and interceptors. Agreements related to nuclear weapons in the past drew upon advance technology for verification, compliance and confidence- building. Even the Iran nuclear deal incorporated in the JCPOA entails considerable use of sensors, real-time communications, surveillance and monitoring and analysis, that rests on high technology, which in turn requires chips as central and critical components. Today, it becomes hard to visualize a verification system that could substitute the elaborate and now almost defunct systems, which were

integral to the INF Treaty the START and New START treaties for instance.

The situation briefly described above makes for new boundary conditions for diplomacy today. The world today is really at the cusp of complete transformation in civilizational terms. As the Chief Editor of the *Bulletin of the Atomic Scientists* stated "AI will be the new nuclear weapon". According to a one-sentence statement that the Center for AI Safety, a nonprofit organization has issued,

> "Mitigating the risk of extinction from A.I. should be a global priority alongside other societal-scale risks, such as pandemics and nuclear war,"

The Center for AI Safety's statement bears signatures of 350-plus top "executives, researchers and engineers working in A.I." as reported by *The New York Times* on 1 June 2023. *The New York Times* report by Kevin Roose needs to be quoted in some detail to elucidate the issues at stake.

> "Eventually, some believe, A.I. could become powerful enough that it could create societal-scale disruptions within a few years if nothing is done to slow it down, though researchers sometimes stop short of explaining how that would happen.
>
> These fears are shared by numerous industry leaders, putting them in the unusual position of arguing that a technology they are building – and, in many cases, are furiously racing to build faster than their competitors – poses grave risks and should be regulated more tightly."[2]

We are thus at the threshold of a big international drive to forge laws and regulations for AI research and innovation, and possibly to create another international authority like what the IAEA has been for the nuclear realm. Some top executives are reported to have proposed several ways that powerful A.I. systems could be responsibly managed and have emphasized "cooperation among the leading A.I. makers, more technical research into large language models and the formation of an international A.I. safety organization, similar to the IAEA, which seeks to control the use of nuclear weapons."[3] It is useful to recall that in March this year too, a letter signed by several hundred top AI researchers and big industry leaders including Elon Musk, had called for a six-month pause on whatever the corporations are doing with regard to AI.

This is in a way reminiscent of the years immediately after the advent of the atom bomb in 1945. Top scientists and eminent philosophers were in the forefront then too, in appealing to the governments concerned to stop further development of nuclear weapons and to stop further testing. AI's risks appear to be far more immediate and sweeping as pointed out above and suggestions of a pause or for regulation and control should alert humankind to learn from the mistakes made in not blocking in time, the path taken by nuclear weapon States towards a runaway arms race and ever-deadlier weapons.

The foregoing mention of AI-related risks is but a very brief pointer to the global scenario which is unfolding. A full discussion would require at least another chapter, which might however detract from the nuclear focus.

In this global setting, India has to chart its path carefully even as it is uniquely placed to pursue a vision of how it would like the nuclear world – as indeed the future world order – to be. India is unique because as a NWS it has displayed prowess, consistency, responsibility, unwavering maturity of judgment and a comprehensive outlook wedded to peace and stability. India has demonstrated through this past quarter century that its transition to becoming a NWS has not been gung-ho or a negative development at all, regardless of the exaggerated apprehensions voiced by prejudiced parties. On the contrary, India as a nuclear power and an emerging fast-growing economy, has made a positive impact in arresting the deterioration in the security environment. As the world's most populous country, India's solemn promise comprises an open democratic system to peacefully harness the enormous human resource.

The contours of India's diplomacy in this utterly complicated international situation are shaped with utmost care and fortitude. The leverages at hand to deal with challenges that lurk and loom are much more, compared to the late 1990s. It is pertinent to quote the remark of the Australian Professor Brian P Schmidt, that, "India's ability to do world-class science has become an order of magnitude higher". There is a coherent thrust towards "Atmanirbharta" from the Government's side, and the corporate system's response shows determination. Pursuit of strength in the domestic realm concerning all spheres of advanced technology, will be integral to diplomacy in the coming decades. As the pace of technology is quite rapid, a clear emphasis on urgency of action is the *sine qua non*.

Action on climate change will be in harmony with the pursuit of futuristic dual-use technology. And while failure on the climate front is assessed today as a certainty towards catastrophe, nuclear peril has intimations of calamity of a more immediate nature, even though couched in probabilistic terms. Moreover, the State that will hold sway on solar panels may have tangible controls in immediate terms, on a global economy, which should be geared to net zero emissions. Nuclear weapons only raise the spectre of a global demise and offer nothing for the immediate. The race for technology controls is becoming more and more potent with time. AI infuses multiple critical dimensions to humanity's collective and individualistic advancement. Indian diplomacy will need to be *de rigueur* about all that the present situation warrants on AI. Like in the case of controls on nuclear weapons, any international endeavour to regulate and control AI will bank upon countries with demonstrable prowess. India's challenge will be to strive to attain capabilities that would lend strength to its voice. There is a horrendous jumble to resolve: ranging from semiconductor chips, to critical minerals, quantum supremacy, biogenetics, Space, Science &Technology and AI. Human resource requirements in these fields are stupendous and resilience of supply chain comprises human resource in a critical manner.

Therefore, challenges for diplomacy today belong to a much wider universe than was conceivable 25 years ago, when India transitioned to an overt nuclear-armed status. Confluence of interests will be the key in the world that is unfolding today. Indian diplomacy has shown remarkable practical understanding in recent years in charting a path committed to India's needs and aspirations and crystal clarity about the present era not being an era of war. This trajectory will need to be fortified by active pursuits in every interconnected domain.

NOTES

1 US and NATO restraint in helping Ukraine in its war against Russia as reported in Western media generally is due to fear of escalation to a nuclear war. Contrast this with long-held US position in regard to Protocol 1 of the 1949 Geneva Convention that it did not apply to nuclear weapons' use in times of war, particularly in relation to reprisals (as revealed in US National Archives recently). This is the short message that Russia is conveying.

2 Kevin Roose, "A.I. Poses 'Risk of Extinction,' Industry Leaders Warn", The New York Times, 30 May 2023 at https://www.nytimes.com/2023/05/30/technology/ai-threat-warning.html (Accessed 23 July 2023).

3 Ibid.

4

The Evolution of Nuclear Force Structure and Doctrine

Rajesh Kumar

While India's nuclear journey started with Dr Homi J. Bhabha soon after Independence, there was always the spectre of China's impending nuclear test that would firmly park India in a nuclear neighbourhood, with the resultant effects on its security as a nascent nation state. It is worth recalling that in the post-1962 environment, when China tested its nuclear device in October 1964, the PTBT of 1963, which banned atmosphere testing, was in vogue. Despite this geopolitical environment, China continued such testing until 1980. Further, when China tested its nuclear device in 1964, it was not even a member of the UN and at that time, China expected other countries to become nuclear powers because it wanted others to join it and support its stand. Official Chinese statements in October 1964 stated:

> "(China) proposes to the governments of the world that a Summit Conference of all the countries of the world be convened ... and that as the first step, the Summit conference conclude an agreement to the effect that the nuclear powers and those countries which may soon become nuclear powers undertake not to use nuclear weapons either against non-nuclear countries and nuclear free zones or against each other" and "There is no such term as de

> jure or de facto nuclear weapon state. I suppose, you explode an atomic bomb and presto you are a nuclear weapon state...period!"[1]

India's ambitions as a nuclear power therefore were in response to the security environment post the 1962 war and geopolitical developments such as Pakistan's dalliance with SEATO and CENTO, along with the Chinese nuclear test. The primacy of India's nuclear posture stems from the desire to deal with the threat from across its northern borders. While the nuclear force structure and doctrine have been worked through various geopolitical pressures of the NPT, the CTBT and the NSG, a distinctive thread of consistency that runs through their evolution is that nuclear weapons are political weapons meant primarily for deterrence. In that respect, Indian nuclear thought was remarkably similar to the Chinese concepts on nuclear deterrence, until at least the last decade.

Even though Indian strategic thought has evolved over the years, geopolitical realities and the prevailing security environment of India's neighbourhood and borders have influenced its evolution. It is therefore useful to recount some of the significant points in India's nuclear history. The post-1965 period up to and until the 1971 war as well as the oil crisis of 1973, shifted India's focus from China to Pakistan. All strategic dialogue focused on the threat from the West. Despite the adoption of the NPT on 01 July 1968 and the writing on the wall post- 1965, India could not accelerate its attempts to carry out an early nuclear test, having suffered setbacks due to the deaths of Prime Minister Lal Bahadur Shastri and Dr Homi J. Bhabha.

Post-1971 India accelerated its efforts for a PNE by interpreting Article IV of the NPT in its favour. PNEs were not unknown at that time with the US and USSR having programmes for using nuclear explosions for developmental work. Even the IAEA discussed PNEs within the framework of peaceful uses of nuclear energy.[2] The PNE brought the complete attention and wrath of the NPT proponents on India. It had the effect of slowing down India's programme, while it gave a fillip to Pakistan's nuclear programme propelled by Zulfiqar Ali Bhutto's famous quote: "We will eat grass, even go hungry, but we will have our own". Despite the PNE, India's march towards weaponization was slow and there was considerable strategic restraint as was evident by Prime Minister Rajiv Gandhi's presentation of a comprehensive Action Plan for Ushering in a Nuclear Weapon Free and Non-violent World Order to the third Special Session on Disarmament at the UN in 1988.

Pakistan in the meantime seemed to have a free pass from the West that benignly saw Dr. A.Q. Khan smuggle centrifuges from the Netherlands and obtain weapon designs from China. By this time, it had also become clear that Pakistan was close to weaponization. India's nuclear posture and planning had to then cater for the geopolitical realities of two nuclear-armed neighbours. Events that led India to conduct nuclear weapon tests in 1998 were the indefinite extension of the NPT in 1995 and the adoption of the CTBT. The CTBT had *emerged* with the narrow objective of stopping new countries from developing nuclear weapons despite its title of comprehensive. The existing NWS could continue to modernize their arsenals through computer simulations and non-explosive testing. India had strong misgivings about this discriminatory stance, as well as the treaty's entry-into-force provision, which, contrary to customary practice, identified a list of 44 countries to sign the treaty mandatorily. India was one of them. As a result, India blocked the treaty at the CD, where it was being negotiated. However, the draft text of the CTBT was placed before the UNGA by Australia, where it was adopted by Resolution A/RES/50/245 and opened for signature. Countries had only until October 1999 to sign the CTBT.[3]

The nuclear stranglehold was tightening around India. By this time, China had already conducted as many as 45 nuclear tests and had developed solid-fuelled, road-mobile, medium-range missiles and the first-generation SSBNs. China had also conducted a nuclear test for Pakistan, and the latter was fomenting insurgencies in J&K and Punjab, its confidence boosted by its nuclear weapons capability. Caught in a security and non-proliferation bind, India was compelled to develop its own nuclear weapons to establish credible deterrence against nuclear coercion or blackmail by countries that held claims on Indian territories.[4] Having committed to weaponization India had to evolve a doctrine and force structure in order to back its claims of being a responsible nuclear power.

The first real test of India's nuclear doctrine came during the Kargil conflict in 1999. President Clinton's statement that South Asia was "the most dangerous place in the world" is reflective of how the world viewed the region at the time. It was therefore critical that India's resolute stand to restore status quo ante without crossing the LoC and non-signaling of any nuclear intent despite some noises from the Pakistani side about the dangers of a conflict between nuclear-armed States led to India's image as a responsible nuclear power. Therefore, when the draft nuclear doctrine was introduced in the public domain on 17 August 1999, it was studied with much more seriousness by experts than would normally have been the case.

The draft doctrine was a well thought out move by the government. Facing a barrage of criticism from the international community as well as significant sanctions, the NSAB, set up in December 1998, was tasked with the preparation of a nuclear doctrine. The Board had Mr K. Subrahmanyam as its convener along with retired military and civilian officials and academics. The objective of putting it in the public domain was four-fold.

Firstly, it signaled India's resolve to retain its nuclear weapons programme despite international condemnation of its tests. The act of declaring a nuclear doctrine underscored India's serious consideration of the role and requirements of its nuclear deterrence and that it was not going to cap, roll back or eliminate the programme.

Secondly, it projected India as a 'responsible' nuclear State that had voluntarily placed its nuclear cards on the table.[5] Thirdly, it established India's overall deterrent posture as a political declaration of intent directed at potential adversaries. The aim of this posture was to establish deterrence and influence the calculus of the adversary's leadership, that if nuclear aggression was to be considered by them, it would not go unpunished.

Lastly, it also demonstrated to the public that the government is committed to safeguarding national security and is able to provide guidance to the officials who would be expected to act in the event of a crisis. This is perhaps what Prime Minister Vajpayee wished to convey when he said: "We want that document to be properly studied before it attains finality."[6]

If a secondary objective of placing the draft doctrine in public domain was to test the waters for a reaction from international community, it did not receive a reaction that would gladden an Indian's heart. The US State Department statement read: "We don't find it an encouraging document. We find it a document that describes the desire to develop a nuclear arsenal and that is something that we think is not in the security interests of India, the subcontinent, or the United States, or the world."[7] Other countries too followed suit in a similar vein. Japan, as the only country to have been at the receiving end of a nuclear strike, was also severely critical of the doctrine. It took another two years of diplomacy and persuasion to restore aid from Japan in the aftermath of the nuclear tests. Eventually though, India was able to project itself as a responsible nuclear power through diplomacy. The elements of restraint in the doctrine as well as a commitment to universal disarmament as a part of the doctrine played their parts in no small measure.

The draft doctrine was followed by the issuance of a press note on the operationalization of the nuclear doctrine on 4 January 2003, by the Cabinet Committee on Security. There are small differences between the draft and the official doctrine but the doctrine rests on three major pillars – *credible minimum deterrent, NFU, and massive retaliation in case of attack by nuclear weapons.* In addition, there are other elements. Nuclear retaliatory attacks can only be authorized by the civilian political leadership through the NCA; non-use of nuclear weapons against non-nuclear weapon States, and in the event of a major attack against India, or Indian forces anywhere, by biological or chemical weapons, India will retain the option of retaliating with nuclear weapons. There is also continued commitment to the goal of a nuclear weapon-free world, through global, verifiable and non-discriminatory nuclear disarmament.

While drafting the doctrine India has not only had to keep an eye on the doctrines practiced by its potential adversaries Pakistan and

China but also contemporary international thought on the subject. Fortunately, India has learnt from the arms race between the US and the USSR and the responses of the countries during every development in the arms race. Indian strategic thinkers had seen the futility of nuclear war fighting and put forward their suggestions for India's nuclear doctrine keeping in mind the Reagan-Gorbachev formula: "A nuclear war cannot be won and must never be fought." The doctrine therefore eschews the notion of a pre-emptive strike to destroy the enemy's nuclear weapons. It also recognizes that there will be no bolt-out- of–the-blue attacks and therefore there is no need to build a force that remains permanently on alert. As a sidelight, it took eight years and many crashes of the B-52 (with nuclear weapons) for the US to stop their Strategic Air Forces to remain on airborne alert.

Reading and internalizing the nuclear doctrine of Pakistan and China – against whom India's deterrence is primarily directed – has been more complicated, as there are no written doctrines in public domain. In 1999 as a response to India's draft doctrine, Pakistan had remarked that it was an attempt "to score points and present itself as a more responsible nuclear power in the region." There were also some indications from the Pakistani establishment that Pakistan was giving finishing touches to its own nuclear doctrine.[8] The promised Pakistani doctrine has never been placed in the public domain. Instead, India has had to rely on statements such as "[Nuclear weapons will be used only] if the very existence of Pakistan is at stake.... Nuclear weapons are aimed solely at India. In case deterrence fails, they will be used if; India attacks Pakistan and conquers a large part of its territory(space threshold): or India destroys a large part either of its land or air forces (military threshold): or India proceeds to the economic strangling of Pakistan (economic threshold); or India pushed Pakistan into political destabilization or creates a large-scale internal subversion in Pakistan (domestic destabilization)" articulated by Lt Gen Khalid Kidwai (Retd), DG SPD in 2001, to comprehend the nature of the deterrence practiced by its adversary.

While the doctrine at that time envisaged using nuclear weapons in the defensive mode, the situation turned on its head in 2018, when the General now NCA Advisor, stated in 2018: "Over the years Pakistan's nuclear policy has transited to the concept of Full Spectrum Deterrence while remaining within the larger philosophy of Credible Minimum Deterrence as a response to the evolving nature of the threat". Clearly, this was in the context of stopping a conventional attack with TNWs. China's doctrine is also opaque and glimpses of its nuclear policy are visible only through official statements and White Papers. Some pillars of China's policy are summarized as "China undertakes not to use or threaten to use nuclear weapons against non-nuclear-weapon States or nuclear-weapon-free zones at any time or under any circumstances"[9] and "Chinese public policy has always been one of the "NFU" while maintaining a deterrent retaliatory force targeted for counter value targets."[10]

China's nuclear policy always assumed a stronger enemy, but in recent years China has taken a muscular tone militarily. Open source satellite imagery indicates a significant expansion of missiles silos in the hinterland. Some experts estimate that at the current rate of expansion, China might triple its nuclear warheads from an estimated figure of 350 to about 1000 by 2030 because of its strategic competition with the US. China's nuclear policy according to one White Paper, "upholds a nuclear strategy of active defense, and will not use or threaten to use nuclear weapons against non-nuclear-weapon states or nuclear-weapon-free zones unconditionally." However, the Paper also states that China will "resolutely safeguard national sovereignty, security, and development interests," which suggests that it may consider using nuclear weapons in certain circumstances.

In addition, Chinese official and non-official sources seek to remove China from any descriptions of a South Asian nuclear triangle. According to Dr. Lora Saalman, a Senior Researcher within SIPRI's Armament and Disarmament and Conflict, Peace and Security vertical, *"for many years, China has considered South Asian nuclear issues to factor only India and Pakistan – but its reluctance to involve itself has strengthened over the past decade. In 2011, when this author hosted a China–India nuclear dialogue that generated an edited volume, one Chinese general expressed surprise at the extent of Indian strategic concerns over China. A 2019 global nuclear review by the CICIR devoted a single short paragraph to South Asia without any discussion of spill-over effects. Indeed, when preparing for the current project in 2019, a Chinese expert cautioned that a proposed trilateral event with Chinese, Indian and Pakistani experts in Beijing would be poorly perceived in China."*[11]

India's doctrine has had to evolve through these significant security changes in the neighbourhood as well as the perceived deterrence postures of its two principal adversaries. In the period prior to the adoption of the doctrine, there had been furious debate about the NFU aspect of the doctrine. Many commentators, frustrated by the impunity of terrorist attacks by elements originating from Pakistan, have called it a weak response to the prevailing security environment. India however adopted the NFU in keeping with its understanding that nuclear weapons are primarily for deterrence. In recent times, analysts have also pointed out the stated policy of Pakistan to use TNWs to stop Indian armoured formations in case of a conventional conflict with India. This development has reignited the debate on the doctrine of NFU. The *Nasr* missile provides Pakistan with "flexible deterrent options" in order to have "full spectrum deterrence" against India.

Therefore, the argument is that India needs to 'keep its options open and not commit itself to NFU'. The extensive public debate that preceded the signing of the 123 Agreement sparked off a free and frank airing of views by experts and academia on nuclear issues – something that had been lacking earlier. A healthy debate on the NFU has also been taking place since then. Many experts on nuclear issues advocated very strongly for a revision of the NFU policy. When asked to comment on the subject, the Defence Minister on 21 August 2019 while on a visit to Pokhran for paying homage to the former Prime Minister Atal Bihari Vajpayee on his first death anniversary, made a statement on NFU. He said that NFU is not a binding commitment, while India has strictly adhered to that position. 'What happens in future depends on the circumstances.'[12] This statement has been construed by thinkers outside India to be the harbinger of a more offensive nuclear doctrine. Despite these developments, there are more proponents for the NFU policy than there are opponents. The

NFU policy is firmly in place and there are no official indications that it will be revoked anytime soon. Review and debate will continue as an internal mechanism to meet and update security needs but if and when the NFU policy is reversed, it will also be naturally followed by a change in posture and force structure.

The second aspect of the doctrine that has been called into question by some experts is the notion of massive retaliation. Some critics have argued that to retaliate in this manner forecloses the option of a graduated response. India might then encourage its adversary to employ its own arsenal in the fear that it may be disarmed by India's massive retaliation. Thus, India might invite greater nuclear use upon itself. It would also rob India of the opportunity of escalation dominance. Secondly, with regard to China, given its existing nuclear superiority and higher survivability quotient, the doctrine does not seem credible.[13] Lastly, the policy of massive retaliation fails the test of proportionality.

Proportionality is a criterion not associated with weapons of mass destruction when the survival of the State is at stake and a defence of last resort is invoked. It is however relevant when conflict short of that existential exigency is involved.[14] These postulates give rise to a view that this makes India's doctrine seem less credible especially in the eyes of Pakistan. Reading India's doctrine as threatening massive retaliation, Lieutenant General Khalid Kidwai, the longtime director of Pakistan's SPD, for example, has dismissed it as "very unrealistic" and one that has "not been thought through.[15] Critics who state that massive retaliation is not credible have failed to take into account the NFU issue. Having committed itself to absorbing the first strike, however large or small it may be, India can hardly be expected to formulate a graduated response. A graduated response could then be required to target enemy nuclear weapons leading to a counterforce strategy – something India has eschewed from the beginning by bedding its doctrine to the central notion that nuclear weapons are for deterrence and not war-fighting. In any case, most studies, simulations and war games have concluded that a single nuclear exchange would eventually end in a full-fledged nuclear war between the adversaries.

Therefore, the doctrine is justified in ensuring deterrence as its first step. As Shyam Saran, former Indian foreign secretary, stated: "India will not be the first to use nuclear weapons, but ... if it is attacked with such weapons, it would engage in nuclear retaliation which will be massive and designed to inflict unacceptable damage on its adversary. As I have pointed out earlier, the label on a nuclear weapon used for attacking India, strategic or tactical, is irrelevant from the Indian perspective. A limited nuclear war is a contradiction in terms. Any nuclear exchange, once initiated, would swiftly and inexorably escalate to the strategic level. Pakistan would be prudent not to assume otherwise as it sometimes appears to do, most recently by developing and perhaps deploying theatre nuclear weapons. It would be far better for Pakistan to finally and irreversibly abandon the long-standing policy of using cross-border terrorism as an instrument of state policy and pursue nuclear and conventional confidence building measures with India which are already on the bilateral agenda."[16]

With the current force structure that has evolved over the years the idea of massive retaliation is definitely credible for Pakistan and to a limited extent for China too (given its own NFU policy). It can be said that the aspect of massive retaliation was forward looking at the time of its conception and has in reality has stood the test of time despite its many sceptics. The real danger however is of continued scepticism by adversaries leading to miscalculation during a time of crisis. Adversaries would be well advised to read the portion of the draft doctrine that states: "deterrence requires that India maintain ... the will to employ nuclear forces and weapons."[17]

The force structure also has evolved from the guidance in the draft doctrine that states that: "*India's nuclear forces will be effective, enduring, diverse, flexible, and responsive to the requirements in accordance with the concept of minimum credible deterrence. These forces will be based on a triad of aircraft, mobile land based missiles and sea-based assets in keeping with the objectives outlined above. Survivability of the forces will be enhanced by a combination of multiple redundant systems, mobility, dispersion and deception."*[18] The force structure therefore rests on one pillar of survivability (obvious fallout of the NFU policy) as well as the other pillar of a triad of forces. The triad of India's nuclear force structure is based on *Prithvi* short-range ballistic missiles and various versions of the *Agni* intermediate-range ballistic missile manned by the missile groups of the Indian Army; nuclear bombs carried on aircraft of the IAF; and SLBMs deployed on SSBNs with the Indian Navy. *INS Arihant*, the first indigenously designed SSBN, is reported to be operational and a second SSBN is reported to be undergoing sea trials. India has willingly abjured the use of battlefield or TNWs, which lower the threshold of use due to the proclivity to use them or lose them. Tactical weapons also require complex command and control mechanisms, enhance the risk of unauthorized and accidental launches, are difficult to manufacture, and are costly to maintain.[19]

India also continues to develop strategic delivery systems based on the triad with longer ranges and trajectories that are more effective in order to increase survivability as well as bring hitherto uncovered areas of the adversaries within striking range to increase the credibility of its deterrence. Indian analysts hold a variety of different views on the number of nuclear warheads that India needs for credible minimum deterrence. The figures vary from the low double digits at the lower end to just over 400 at the upper end. Suggestions for weapons yield range from fission weapons with 15 to 20 kiloton yields to thermonuclear weapons in the megaton range. The recommended delivery vehicles embrace the entire range of the triad, including ICBMs and cruise missiles. As discussed earlier, the sole purpose of India's nuclear weapons is to deter the use of nuclear weapons and the threat thereof. Minimum deterrence is not a numbers game. Its ends areserved if the adversary is deterred from crossing the nuclear rubicon and from threatening to do so. As Kenneth Waltz famously said, "More is not better if less is enough."[20]

The current nuclear forces available to India as estimated by the *Bulletin of Atomic Scientists* in 2020 are as under:

Indian Nuclear Forces 2020

Type	*NATO designation*	*Number of launchers*	*Year deployed*	*Range[a] (kilometers)*	*Warhead × kilotons yield*	*Number of warheads*
Aircraft						
Vajra	Mirage 2000H	32	1985	1,850	1 × bomb	32
Shamsher	Jaguar IS	16	1981	1,600	1 × bomb	16
Subtotal		48				48
Land-based Ballistic Missiles						
Prithvi-II	n.a.	30	2003	350	1 × 12	30
Agni-I	n.a.	20	2007[d]	700+	1 × 40	20
Agni-II	n.a.	12	2011[e]	2,000+	1 × 40	12
Agni-III	n.a.	8	2014?	3,200+	1 × 40	8
Agni-IV	n.a.	n.a.	(2020)	3,500+	1 × 40	n.a.
Agni-V	n.a.	n.a.	(2025)	5,200+	1 × 40	n.a.
Subtotal		70				70[f]
Sea-based Ballistic Missiles						
Dhanush	n.a.	2	2013	400	1 x 12	4
K-15	(Sagarika)	1/12	(2018)	700	1 x 12	12
K-4	n.a.	n.a.	?	3,500	1 x ?	0
Subtotal		16				16
Total		**134**				**150**

Source: https://doi.org/10.1080/00963402.2020.1778378 Accessed on July 15, 2023.

Given India's deterrence requirements and nuclear resources it is reasonable to assume that India's nuclear force has been enlarged in phases over three decades. In the nuclear era, strategy has never been the sole determinant of force architecture. This, according to Rajesh Rajagopalan, is exemplified by the US decision to deploy MIRVed missiles when the technology became available in order to help the US circumvent nuclear-arms-reduction negotiations. The trajectory of technology will continue to drive nuclear force structures, so force structures must be made flexible enough to adapt to changing technology.[21] India's force structure has evolved around the concept of minimum credible deterrence and has always been mindful of survivability in order to conduct a second strike that would inflict unacceptable damage on the adversary. It has also been influenced by the resource allocation that the political leadership has deemed necessary for maintaining the requisite level of deterrence.

A question that is often asked is "how much is enough?' As long as India's nuclear deterrent is sized in ways that permit it to maintain the smallest secure second-strike force capable of inflicting unacceptable punishment on an aggressor, its nuclear deterrent would, by definition be both minimum and credible. As Lt Gen B.S. Nagal has rightly noted, India's force size and structure will inevitably be "dynamic because the adversaries' arsenals are increasing by the year."[22] This conclusion only echoes the early judgment offered by Jaswant Singh in the aftermath of the 1998 nuclear tests when, in response to US demands that India quantify in "concrete terms" the size and character of its minimum deterrent, he declared that New Delhi's force levels were "not a fixity."[23] Since the notion of a minimum deterrent is thus inherently elastic with respect to the number of nuclear weapons, the force structure will continue to evolve around the developments in the neighbourhood.

While the evolution of force structure would continue along the guidelines in the doctrines and the numbers would be commensurate with the arsenals of the adversaries some disruptive events could call for a complete change of nuclear policy and forces. These disruptive events could be firstly, development of BMD on a scale to be effective over the entire country and secondly development of high-resolution real-time ISR capability so as to be able to track nuclear forces of the adversary in real time whether static or mobile. These capabilities if acquired by the adversary – especially China – could lead India to be vulnerable to nuclear coercion or nuclear blackmail. This would have a serious effect on India's deterrence posture as well as national security. The answer would then perhaps be to find better methods to improve survivability, increase numbers and foster technologies that enable penetration of BMD. Indian policy makers would be well advised to keep an eye on developments in these areas.

In conclusion, the evolution of India's nuclear doctrine and force structure indicates that its initial conceptions of deterrence that were articulated early in the aftermath of the 1998 tests have survived quite robustly more than two decades later. The commitment to no first use still endures despite endless debates because it comports well with the extant balance of capabilities vis-à-vis Pakistan and China and fits India's interests.[24] The force structure needed for a minimum credible deterrent continues to evolve as more modern delivery systems continue to be developed. As missile ranges increase and delivery platforms proliferate, the survivability aspect ensures credibility of this deterrent posture. The threat of massive retaliation in case of a nuclear attack has been retained at the doctrinal level, as required by the end objective of deterrence. Despite some doubts about the capability to carry out massive retaliation, the new delivery systems and capabilities are indeed competent to accomplish the goal of unacceptable damage to the adversary in all currently probable scenarios.

Overall, the strategic restraint shown by India in the expansion of its warheads despite the developments in the neighbourhood have emphasized the confidence that India's policy makers have in the deterrence quality that has been generated by its force structure and doctrine. A remarkable thread of consistency runs through the developments in force structure through the last two decades. The doctrinal aspects have stood the test of time reasonably well and indicate the foresight and maturity of Indian strategic thought right from its inception. India has also withstood the external pressures to roll back its weaponization programme in a resolute manner. This has been possible largely due to a clear articulation of its deterrence posture as well as its security needs. While India's nuclear doctrine has worked well until now, future disruptive technologies have the potential to force changes to the steady path that India has chosen. India needs to stay abreast of such developments in these disruptive technologies as well as intensify its own research efforts in these areas so as not lose ground in the deterrence matrix of the neighbourhood.

NOTES

1 P.K. Singh, Paper presented at the workshop on "China and India: Nuclear Doctrine and Dynamics", Tsinghua University, Beijing.

2 Georges Delcoigne, "A Review of IAEA Activities Relating to PNE", *IAEA Bulletin*, 17 (5), October 1975 at https://www.iaea.org/sites/default/files/publications/magazines/bulletin/bull17-5/17505082628.pdf. (Accessed 15 July 2023)

3 Manpreet Sethi, "Why Did India go Nuclear", NuClearly Put, No.1, 31 January 2023 at https://capsindia.org/wp-content/uploads/2023/01/CAPS_NuClearlyPut_MS_31_01-_23.pdf (Accessed 15 July 2023)

4 Ibid.

5 Manpreet Sethi, "The Making of India's Nuclear Doctrine", NuClearly Put, No.3, 31 March 2023 at https://capsindia.org/wp-content/uploads/2023/03/CAPS_NuClearly-Put_MS_31_03_23-1.pdf (Accessed 15 July 2023)

6 Ibid.

7 Ibid.

8 Ibid.

9 "Statement on security assurances issued on 5 April 1995 by the People's Republic of China", United Nations, 6 April 1995, S/1995/265.

10 "China Publishes White Paper on Arms Control" at http://www.china.org.cn/english/2005/Aug/140343.htm (Accessed 15 July 2023).

11 Lora Saalman, "China's detachment from the South Asian nuclear triangle" at https://www.sipri.org/commentary/blog/2020/chinas-detachment-south-asian-nuclear-triangle (Accessed 1 July 2023).

12 Sreemoy Talukdar, "Rajnath Singh's Remarks on 'No First Use' of Nukes Indicate Ambiguity in Nuclear Policy in India's Interest." *Firstpost*, 21 August 2019 at https://www.firstpost.com/ india/nfu-has-outlived-its-purpose-rajnath-singhs-remarks-on-shift-in-indias-nuclearpolicy-indicate-ambiguity-in-doctrine-essential-7191381.html (Accessed 15 July 2023).

13 Manpreet Sethi, *Nuclear Strategy* , Knowledge World, New Delhi, 2009, pp. 143.

14 Antoine Levesques, Desmond Bowen and John H. Gill, "Nuclear Deterrence and Stability in South Asia: Perceptions and Realities", *IISS Primer*, May 2021.

15 Khalid Kidwai and Peter Lavoy, "A Conversation With General Khalid Kidwai." Carnegie Endowment for International Peace, 23 March 2015 at https://carnegieendowment.org/files/03-230315carnegieKIDWAI. pdf, 4–5, 8–9, As cited in Ashley Tellis, *Striking Asymmetries : Nuclear Transitions in South Asia*, Carnegie Endowment for International Peace, Washington, DC, 2022, p .91.

16 Ajai Shukla, "After a Pakistani TNW Strike, India Can Go for Pakistan's Nuclear Arsenal: Former NSA Shivshankar Menon,", *Business Standard*, 18 March 2017 at http://ajaishukla.blogspot.com/2017/03/afterpakistani-tnw-strike-india-will.html as quoted in Ashley Tellis, Ibid., p. 94.

17 "Draft Report of NSAB on Indian Nuclear Doctrine" at http://meaindia.nic.in , (Accessed 15 July 2023).

18 Ibid.

19 Gurmeet Kanwal, "India's Nuclear Force Structure 2025" at https://carnegieendowment.org/2016/06/30/india-s-nuclear-force-structure-2025-pub-63988 (Accessed 15 July 2023).

20 Ibid.

21 Ibid.

22 B.S. Nagal, "Perception and Reality: An In-Depth Analysis of India's Credible Minimum Deterrent," *Force*, October 2014 at https://forceindia.net/guest-column/guest-column-b-s-nagal/ perception-and-reality/ (Accessed 15 July 2023)

23 "India Dismisses US Demand on Minimum Nuclear Deterrence," *Hindustan Times*, 6 January 1999 as cited in Ashley Tellis, no. 15, p. 86.

24 Ashley Tellis, no. 15, p. 133.

5

Nuclear No First Use as Restraint: India's Nuclear Strategy

Rajesh Rajagopalan

Introduction

India's nuclear test in 1998 ushered in India's formal nuclear weaponization. The Atal Behari Vajpayee government not only declared that India meant to maintain India's nuclear weapons status but moved quickly to institutionalize this by proposing a formal doctrine and outlining its elements of in the Indian parliament. India's actual weaponization likely took place at least a decade earlier, but there remains little clarity about India's capabilities and intention during this decade prior to formal declaration of weaponization in 1998. Though India maintained some restraint subsequent to formal weaponization – especially in its nuclear doctrine – the conduct of further nuclear tests and in its missile development, it was clear that the weaponization decision itself would not be reversed. A quarter century later, there is little doubt that India made the right decision. Indeed, if anything, India was three decades too late in moving forward with its weaponization decision.

India's nuclear tests were greeted with jubilation in India but considerable anxiety elsewhere. There was a constant drumbeat of speculation about the dangerous consequences of weaponization, accompanied by exploration of the pathways to nuclear escalation and war between India and Pakistan. Despite India's relatively restrained nuclear doctrine that included both a NFU pledge as well as clear limits about the size and shape of the arsenal in the form of a credible minimum deterrent, the expectation was that weaponization opened the doorway to nuclear excesses and potential nuclear war. On the other hand, among some Indian strategists, the Indian doctrine was considered too passive and inadequate to meet India's needs. Some of these debates continue, but a quarter century later, it is difficult to argue that India's nuclear doctrine has not been successful.

Still, new challenges require a constant reassessment of the doctrine. India's strategic circumstances are changing in at least two important ways that are relevant to the nuclear doctrine. First, China's dramatic nuclear expansion will massively alter the nuclear India's thinking. Second, India's nuclear challenge is acquiring a trilateral dimension from what was largely two bilateral relationships until now. In other words, what was traditionally a relatively exclusive India-Pakistan and India-China relationship, is now becoming an India-Pakistan-China relationship. Finally, the level of strategic collaboration between China and Pakistan is likely to put greater pressure on India's nuclear doctrine. For example, if Pakistan and China were to collaborate in some manner in a conventional two-front war against India, India may feel greater pressure to escalate to the nuclear level, a contingency it never had to worry about earlier.

To consider these multiple issues facing India's nuclear doctrine, this brief chapter will begin by outlining why India adopted the nuclear doctrine it did, focusing on the strategic logic of NFU and credible minimum deterrent. Next, it considers some of the challenges that India faces and how they might affect its nuclear doctrine. The subsequent section argues that despite these challenges, the strategic logic of the current doctrine remains strong. But before getting into these concerns, the chapter begins with a brief overview of India's troubled path to the 1998 tests and then briefly attempts a quarter century assessment of both India's nuclear weapons tests and its nuclear policy.

India's Uncertain Path to the 1998 Nuclear Tests

India's nuclear tests in 1998 came almost a quarter century after the first Indian test in 1974. This test itself was considerably delayed. By the mid-1960s, India's nuclear condition was getting progressively worse. Though India had begun developing a nuclear programme that was broad enough to build nuclear weapons too, India dithered about taking the actual decision to build a nuclear arsenal. China's nuclear test in 1964 should have forced India to reconsider its stance because India had suffered a grievous military defeat at the hands of China in the border war in late 1962. Indeed, India was aware that China was making progress towards a nuclear weapons programme well before its nuclear test in 1964 because China's nuclear progress was no great secret.[1] The US had discussed with India the progress that the Chinese nuclear weapons programme was making before 1964. One of the reasons for the US and the Soviets concluding the PTBT in 1963 was concern about China potentially conducting its first nuclear test. This was expected to be an atmospheric test, which the PTBT would ban. Though India enthusiastically joined the PTBT, China (and France, which also expected to continue atmospheric nuclear tests) refused, understanding that the PTBT was at least in part designed to constrain its nuclear weapons programme. As a recent analysis pointed out, for China, these were "discriminatory attempts by the superpowers to consolidate their nuclear monopoly and constrain China's nuclear development."[2]

Nevertheless, India did not pursue nuclear weapons in the 1960s, mainly because Indian leaders, particularly Prime Minister Lal Bahadur Shastri was deeply opposed to the idea of India building and becoming a nuclear weapon armed power. Indeed, so deep was his opposition to India building these weapons that he sought British help in countering the claims of the leader of India's nuclear programme that India could afford nuclear weapons. The British government were happy to provide Shastri with the estimates he needed, though they knowingly exaggerated these estimates because Britain had little interest in India building nuclear weapons.[3]

India put its faith instead in nuclear security guarantees from the great powers, though whether these were worth much is open to question.[4] Recall that this was at around the same time that France was withdrawing from NATO military structure because President Charles de Gaulle was unwilling to trust even its NATO allies with French nuclear arms. But for Indian leaders even after Shastri, the nuclear guarantee seemed a compromise worth making to avoid building Indian nuclear arms.

In addition, India also put its faith in multilateral arms control negotiations. Prime Minister Nehru had proposed a CTBT in the mid-1950s, and India signed up for the PTBT partly in the hope that this would halt the progress of Chinese nuclear weapons. When this failed, India put its energies into the NPT. India's hopes were obviously unwise because the interests of the great powers determined multilateral arms control negotiations, not any abstract notions of justice or equity. Thus, the CTBT was twisted into something that served the interests of the US and the Soviet Union, which was, preventing China's nuclear progress. That this was also in India's interest was entirely fortuitous. But India would not be lucky twice: as the NPT negotiations progressed, it became clear that this was not going to lead to nuclear disarmament but to an unequal division of the world into nuclear-armed 'haves' and those who were not, or the 'have-nots'. India's expectation that it could be otherwise was itself foolish, and there was strong support within the Indian establishment for acceding to the treaty. Prime Minister Indira Gandhi, however, decided at the last minute to stay out, thus leaving India with the option of building nuclear weapons later. This was not a comfortable option because this would leave India permanently out of the NPT, which closed the door on nuclear entry by 1 January 1967. India was not legally bound by a treaty it did not sign, especially as far as building nuclear weapons was concerned, but this legalism was not particularly beneficial beyond this, because India did pay a price (and continues to pay it) for being left out of the NPT order.

The only way this situation could have been rectified was if India had conducted its first test before January 1, 1967. But Indian leaders were unwilling to take this step. Of course, it is unclear whether India had the capacity, both in terms of fissile material as well as the rest of the technologies and material, for conducting a nuclear test before this date. But the critical point is that India's leaders did not even attempt to pursue this path, thus condemning India to an expensive outsider status in the NPT for the last six decades. Though they faced a powerful, nuclear-armed adversary in China, which should have forced India to reconsider its non-nuclear status, a number of factors helped sway India away from pursuing nuclear weapons in a much more determined manner. For one, the threat from China was largely seen as a conventional war threat, and India was building an elaborate conventional military force to handle the Tibet border.[5] India, in other words, could afford to build such a force to counter China because India was not particularly weak relative to China now. Second, India did seek nuclear security guarantees against China, which it thought would be honoured. Finally, India also put an inordinate amount of hope on nuclear arms control. Clearly, the latter two reasons were indicators that ideological factors, namely, the deep aversion that India's leadership held regarding nuclear weapons may have played an unusually large role in determining India's security policy, but it must be remembered that this was made possible by India's comfortable security situation and its material equality with China.

This situation was only marginally rectified by the 1974 test. The rationale behind the test remains unclear because there appear to be no written records of any prior discussions regarding this test. Prime Minister Indira Gandhi also did not take the logical next step of building a nuclear arsenal, which makes the decision to test even more puzzling. In any case, testing several years after the NPT cut-off date made little difference to India's status under the non-proliferation regime.

Pakistan's rapid progress in building its nuclear weapons clearly concerned the Indian government and a decision to restart the nuclear weapon programme was apparently taken in 1979 under the Janata Party government, but unrelated political troubles further delayed this. By the mid-1980s, further clear evidence of Pakistan's potential weaponization appear to have finally forced India's hand. By the time India conducted the 1998 nuclear tests, it had already built at least some nuclear weapons, though details remain unclear. India's slow and hesitating path to building a nuclear arsenal clearly cost it. First, and most seriously, it placed India outside of the NPT system. Second, it placed great pressure on India – especially after the Soviet Union collapsed– when India had to deal with not only demands that it join the NPT as a non-weapon State but also the CTBT.

Quarter Century Assessment: Nuclear Tests and Nuclear Policy

India's nuclear tests were both unavoidable and necessary. Some analysts argued that the tests would harm India's security interests.[6] While it did not solve all of India's security problems, not becoming an overt nuclear weapons power would have created considerable subsequent problems for India.

Early assessments suggested that the tests would make South Asia much more dangerous.[7] India and Pakistan did go through several crises. Within months of the tests, Pakistan attempted to use nuclear weapons as a shield from behind which, it sought to take mountain heights near Kargil, setting off weeks of fighting before the intruders were expelled. About two years later, another crisis followed after Pakistani-sponsored terrorists attacked the Indian parliament. This time, there was large-scale military mobilization, which lasted for months. Several years later, the terrorist attack on Mumbai raised fears of another escalation. But none of these crises escalated beyond the conventional confrontation – the Mumbai attack did not even lead to that – which points to the fact that escalation is not automatic, as suggested in much of the alarmist literature on South Asian nuclear issues, and that political leaders were able to keep tight control over nuclear weapons.

A decade later, India's surgical strike in 2016 in response to a terrorist attack in Uri, and an even stronger air attack on Balakot in response to a terrorist attack on Indian forces in Pulwama, also illustrated that the nuclear threshold was much higher than had been assumed. The point was that small nuclear forces such as India's and Pakistan's are not set up to respond on a hair-trigger, as was the case in the US-Soviet Cold War contest. But because much of the nuclear theology was based on the latter case, there was an exaggeration of the danger of nuclear escalation.[8]

More importantly, it is becoming clearer than ever before that, exercising India's option to build nuclear weapons was the right step, even if it was delayed by several decades. While the delay did cost India dearly – and continues to cost it – not exercising the option would have been even more damaging. Nuclear weapons have only limited utility in that they are useless for most purposes other than deterring other nuclear weapons. This has two components. First, nuclear weapons cannot be used to compensate for conventional military power, nor can they provide a shield for compellence. Pakistan's experience, as well as India's, demonstrate this. Pakistan attempted to use nuclear weapons to seize territory in Kargil, but it could do little when India used its conventional military power to attack and expel the intruders. India did impose some limitations on itself, such as not crossing the LOC in conducting its military operations. But even if India had been less restrained, it is difficult to imagine that the war would have escalated (especially if it was limited to the territory in contention). Pakistan's hope that the fear of nuclear escalation would work in either preventing an Indian military response or that it would bring in external pressure to do this, were both mistaken. Though both types of pressures existed, they did not constrain India as much as Rawalpindi hoped.

But the second is the more important point: nuclear weapons can only be deterred with nuclear weapons. In a world in which many countries already have nuclear weapons, acquiring these become an essential security imperative. This is an even greater imperative for countries that fear potential existential threats even outside of a nuclear confrontation. Countries such as Israel, Ukraine and Taiwan – and indeed, even Pakistan fit within this category. Ukraine gave up nuclear weapons on guarantees made jointly by both Russia and the West, but as we can see, these guarantees have been meaningless.[9] It is little wonder that now many smaller and relatively weaker countries are rethinking their choice of giving up nuclear weapons, including South Korea, Japan – and even Australia.[10]

If it is imperative that States that fear for their survival build nuclear weapons, the need for other States to have nuclear weapons still exists, in a world in which nuclear weapons cannot be eliminated. India has campaigned for nuclear disarmament for decades, ever since it became independent. But this has been diplomatic energy wasted because the world is no closer to nuclear disarmament today than it was in the early 1950s, when only the two superpowers had nuclear weapons. In an era in which great power competition is intensifying, the prospects for nuclear disarmament is even less likely. Thus, we have to simply learn to live with nuclear weapons, focusing instead on reducing the dangers associated with them. But a nuclearized world also means that States that do not have nuclear weapons will be permanently handicapped. It is of course quite possible that a non-nuclear armed State will never face such a contingency where its lack of nuclear arms will not be exploited. But this is not something that States will generally leave to chance or hope. To the extent that States are able to, they will pursue every means of security that they have. India's somewhat uncertain path to building nuclear weapons reflect some of the favourable structural circumstances as well as some ideological propensities, as pointed out earlier. Ultimately, even if rather late, India was forced to face up to the reality that it could not avoid building nuclear weapons.

Restraint and the Logic of NFU

Once India made the decision that it had to build nuclear weapons, it also needed to make decisions about how its nuclear weapons would be employed. This was a task originally given to the NSAB, headed by the doyen of the Indian strategic community, K. Subrahmanyam. They produced the draft Indian nuclear doctrine, which was the basis of the subsequent official Indian doctrine that was announced in January 2003, though there were some important changes between the draft doctrine and the one officially announced.

The draft nuclear doctrine set out some of the key elements of India's nuclear policy, including NFU as the broad condition under which India would use nuclear weapons and credible minimum deterrent as the determinant of India's nuclear force structure. These elements were not much of a surprise to those who followed India's nuclear debate. George Perkovich, for example, accurately predicted what he expected to be some of the key elements of the Indian doctrine well before the draft nuclear doctrine was released.[11] Indeed, the Indian government itself had outlined some of its views before the Indian parliament in the months after the 1998 nuclear test, including its idea about both minimum credible deterrent and the NFU.[12]

Thus, elements of Indian thinking about nuclear weapons were visible well before the draft nuclear doctrine was proposed. Nevertheless, India was also deeply interested in engaging diplomatically with global powers, especially the US, and this made it imperative that India put its best foot forward as a 'responsible nuclear power'. In pursuit of this, India declared a moratorium on nuclear tests and its commitment to ensuring that its nuclear technology will not be transferred to any other State. India also started a dialogue with the US, with India's EAM Jaswant Singh and US Deputy Secretary of State Strobe Talbott engaging in extended discussions over India's nuclear policy and US-India relations.[13] India's nuclear doctrine was at least a part of this because India wanted to leverage this into illustrating its credentials as a responsible nuclear power. The NFU helped considerably in this, especially because Pakistan was unwilling to accept NFU as its nuclear doctrine. This comparison was particularly beneficial to India in outlining the difference between the two new nuclear powers.

Nevertheless, India's nuclear doctrine was also based on strategic logic.[14] The central reason behind India's NFU was the recognition that nuclear weapons served only a very limited purpose, that of ensuring national survival. The only real threat to such survival was a nuclear attack. Nuclear weapons are unique because unlike any other weapon, they could wreak so much destruction in such a short time that they could potentially end an entire society in an afternoon. The only way to prevent such destruction is to threaten similar destruction on any potential adversary, thus deterring them from pursuing such a course of action. Threatening retaliation is the only solution because there is no defence against these weapons. Though there were attempts by deterrence theorists in other parts of the world to consider the use of nuclear weapons for more limited tactical purposes than national survival, most Indian nuclear strategists were rightly sceptical of such possibilities. This drove some of the strongest proponents of India's nuclear weapon programme to be also deeply critical of the kind of elaborate nuclear doctrines and arsenals being developed by other countries, especially the two Cold War superpowers. It was not a logic that they wanted India to follow, because it made little sense for anyone, and definitely not for India.

NFU was the outcome of this strategic logic. (The other corollary was a limited nuclear arsenal). If the primary purpose – indeed, the only purpose – of nuclear weapons was deterrence of other nuclear weapons, then threatening retaliation was the only manner in which these weapons could be used. The threat of retaliation is of course the essence of deterrence: preventing someone from taking an action by threatening to punish them if they did. Retaliation, by definition, could only be for an action that was already taken, in this case, a nuclear attack that has already happened. Deterrence and retaliation automatically meant that there was no logic to using nuclear weapons first: hence, NFU. Additional benefits also accrue from NFU: tighter political command over nuclear weapons, a much more relaxed command and control regime and a much safer nuclear arsenal.

India's NFU doctrine was thus the consequence of well-thought-out strategic considerations. That this also helped India in illustrating its credibility as a responsible nuclear power, was an added bonus, but it was not the driving force behind the framing of the NFU doctrine. One indication of this is that the doctrine, especially the NFU pledge, has now survived unscathed for two decades, since it was first officially stated in January 2003. That does not mean that the doctrine faced no challenges. Indeed, there have always been doubts in some quarters of the Indian strategic community about the advisability of the NFU doctrine. Moreover, India's international political and security circumstances have also changed considerably since the early days after the 1998 nuclear tests. These changes represent another set of challenges. I turn to these challenges now.

Challenges for NFU

Both sets of challenges to NFU – the traditional opposition to the logic of NFU as well as the changed strategic circumstances that India faces today – need to be taken seriously. The first has been with India from the very beginning, indeed even in the debates about the framing of the doctrine in the NSAB in 1999.[15]

The original criticism of the Indian nuclear doctrine was broader than just criticism over the NFU, but the NFU was a significant part of it. Some of these critics of the NFU argued that an NFU posture is only possible for a country that has "extreme confidence not only in the survivability of its national nuclear forces sufficient to muster a devastating retaliatory strike, but also in the efficacy of its crisis management system," which are both wanting in the Indian context.[16] There is also criticism about the fact that NFU is only a declaratory policy, though, of course, this can go both ways: those defending NFU can also claim that the NFU does not really constrain India.[17] Others have pointed to recent changes in India's security condition to call for changes in India's NFU policy.[18] These concerns have been joined by occasional statements from senior Indian officials, who have suggested that the NFU needs to be rethought. For example, former Defence Minister Manohar Parrikar publicly mused about whether India should bind itself to the NFU, even though he stated this was his personal view rather than the view of the government.[19] A couple of years later, the current Indian Defence Minister, Rajnath Singh, also made comments about NFU that were not entirely categorical, though this was about the future policy rather than current one.[20] Neither of these represented any change in India's NFU policy, but these were decidedly unnecessary formulations that suggested some level of unhappiness with the NFU policy. Subsequent Indian reiterations of NFU policy officially were helpful but did not entirely undo the damage.[21]

The changed security circumstances that India faces today have added to the traditional concerns about NFU. In brief, this changed strategic condition relates to the growing security competitiveness with China and China's own changing nuclear policies. China's spectacular economic growth over the last several decades has made the country a peer competitor to the US, but has also led it to engage in aggressive behaviour and military confrontations all along its borders, from the East China Sea to the South China Sea and the Sino-Indian border. Over the last decade, China's has repeatedly attempted to probe Indian defences along the LAC that divides Indian and Chinese military forces at the India-Tibet border. In addition, in 2017, China also created a crisis at the Sino-Indian-Bhutan trijunction, near Doklam. Another confrontation in Ladakh at the Galwan River Valley in 2020 led to Indian and Chinese forces massing along the LAC. This continues, with little sign of any progress despite many rounds of talks between the military commanders on both sides. The massive disparity in power between India and China, and China's aggressiveness, are new factors that created concerns in New Delhi.

More specifically, China also appears to be engaged in a large-scale expansion of its nuclear forces.[22] The reasons are unclear. China has some concerns that the US may expand its defensive missile shield in a manner that would erode China's retaliatory nuclear forces. However, the sudden increase in China's missile silo-building activities appear unrelated to any specific actions by the US in missile defences. In other words, no specific trigger is visible for these Chinese actions. A more likely possibility is that China has decided that it wants nuclear parity with the US, and intends to match US and Russian nuclear force strengths. However, why China would deploy its new missiles in silos which are easily detectable holes in the ground, is also unclear. China has been moving towards mobile missiles, which would make silo deployment something of a technological and strategic retreat.

These questions aside, the expansion of the Chinese nuclear arsenal cannot but be a source of concern to India. India has so far been admirably relaxed about the balance in terms of numbers of nuclear warheads and missiles. For example, India has not made any comment about the fact that Pakistan has more nuclear warheads, as per credible published reports. Nor has Indian nuclear force structuring indicated any change in responding to Pakistan's nuclear superiority. Similarly, India has so far not indicated any concern with the existing imbalance between Indian and Chinese nuclear forces nor any commitment to matching China's forces. Whether this will continue in the face of a nuclear balance that will tend towards 1:10 (if China builds about 1500 warheads), remains to be seen. Definitely, there can be some pressure on the Indian government to reconsider its NFU along with other aspects of its nuclear policy.

Indeed, some of these pressures would grow if there is any indication of military coordination between China and Pakistan. India has been concerned about a two-front problem for some time, with India's Army Chief expressing these concerns as far back as 2009.[23] A collusive threat from China and Pakistan acting in concert remains a serious concern for Indian defence planners.[24] This would put India at a serious conventional military disadvantage, and it would be possible for Indian defence planners to consider giving up the NFU to strengthen India's deterrence by adding an additional layer of uncertainty.

Conclusion: The Continuing Strategic Utility of NFU

Thus, India's NFU policy, which has been the essential basis of India's deterrence policy for well over two decades, now does face some headwinds. The NFU policy was based on the assumption of India's conventional superiority vis-à-vis Pakistan and at least defensive sufficiency vis-à-vis China. If that basic strategic premise no longer holds, can NFU continue to make sense?

In short, yes. Giving up the NFU makes sense if India intends to use nuclear weapons first. Though the conventional military balance has definitely swung against India in the last couple of decades – particularly with China – India still faces no existential threats in any conventional war. Even the worst possible outcome imaginable in a war with China (or even China and Pakistan together) pale in comparison with the consequences of a nuclear war. Thus, it makes little sense to choose nuclear war and the destruction it would entail, to escape a conventional military defeat, however bad such a defeat might be. Proponents of giving up the NFU would need to explain under what specific circumstances it would make sense for India to escalate to the nuclear level.

Would threatening to use nuclear weapons help to offset a conventional military imbalance? Pakistan has done this repeatedly. But this works only if the adversary is deterred by such threats. India has repeatedly called Pakistan's nuclear bluff, for example in the Kargil War, in the surgical strikes and in the Balakot attack. In each instance, Pakistan proved unwilling to escalate, thus illustrating that Pakistan's threats were hollow, and were degrading its deterrent threats in the future. This is a risky gamble for India because if Indian forces were not set up for a first strike (as they are not currently) and if the stake is not high enough, an adversary may be willing to call India's bluff.

Alternatively, India's NFU continues to have strategic utility because of all the reasons mentioned earlier: India is a large and powerful country that faces no (conventional) existential threats; and its nuclear weapons are essentially to deter other nuclear weapons. Beyond this, India's nuclear weapons have no role to play. Framed thus, the NFU is perfectly suited to India's needs even in the context of a gross imbalance in both conventional and nuclear balance with China.

NOTES

1 George Perkovich, *India's Nuclear Bomb: The Impact on Global Proliferation*, University of California Press, Berkeley, 1999, p. 64.

2 Nicola Horsburgh, *China and Global Nuclear Order: From Estrangement to Active Engagement*, Oxford University Press, Oxford, 2015, p. 50.

3 Susanna Schrafstetter, "Preventing the 'Smiling Buddha': British-Indian nuclear relations and the Commonwealth Nuclear force, 1964–68," *Security Studies*, 25(3), 2002, pp. 87-108.

4 Andrew B. Kennedy, "India's Nuclear Odyssey: Implicit Umbrellas, Diplomatic Disappointments, and the Bomb," *International Security*, 36 (2), Fall 2011, pp. 120-53.

5 Yogesh Joshi, "Perceptions and Purpose of the Bomb: Explaining India's Nuclear Restraint Against China", *Modern Asian Studies*, 56(4), July 2022, pp. 1083-1124.

6 Kanti Bajpai, "The Fallacy of an Indian Deterrent," in Amitabh Mattoo (ed.), *India's Nuclear Deterrent: Pokhran II and Beyond*, Har-Anand Publications, New Delhi,1999, pp. 150-88.

7 Stephen P. Cohen, "Nuclear Weapons and Conflict in South Asia," Brookings Institution, 23 November 1998 at https://www.brookings.edu/articles/nuclear-weapons-and-conflict-in-south-asia/ (Accessed 7 July 2023); Scott D. Sagan, "The Perils of Proliferation in South Asia," *Asian Survey*, 41(6), 2001, pp. 1064-86.

8 Rajesh Rajagopalan, *Second Strike: Arguments About Nuclear War in South Asia*, Viking, New Delhi, 2005.

9 William J. Broad, "Ukraine Gave Up a Giant Nuclear Arsenal 30 Years Ago. Today There Are Regrets," *New York Times*, 5 February 2022 at https://www.nytimes.com/2022/02/05/science/ukraine-nuclear-weapons.html (Accessed 7 July 2023).

10 Robert E. Kelly, "US Should Get Out of the Way in East Asia's Nuclear Debates," *Foreign Policy*, 15 July 2022 at https://foreignpolicy.com/2022/07/15/us-south-korea-japan-east-asia-nuclear-debates-nonproliferation/, (Accessed 7 July 2023). On the Australian debate, see Heiko Timmers, "Nuclear Weapons? Australia Has No Way to Build Them, Even If We Wanted To," *The Conversation*, 9 July 2019 at https://theconversation.com/nuclear-weapons-australia-has-no-way-to-build-them-even-if-we-wanted-to-120075. (Accessed 7 July 2023)

11 George Perkovich, no. 1, p. 4.

12 "Statement by Ambassador Savitri Kunadi in the Plenary Meeting of the Conference on Disarmament in Geneva, 6 August", as reproduced at http://www.acronym.org.uk/old/archive/spindcd.html (Accessed 7 July 2023); Ministry of External Affairs, "Prime Minister's Statement in Parliament on 'Bilateral Talks with United States' (15th December 1998)", *Foreign Affairs Record*, 44 (12), December 1998, pp. 193-95.

13 "Interview with Jaswant Singh, Minister of External Affairs, *The Hindu*, 29 November 1999", as reproduced in http://www.acronym.org.uk/old/archive/spsingh.htm, (Accessed 7 July 2023).

14 The following is borrowed from Rajesh Rajagopalan, "The Strategic Logic of the No First Use Nuclear Doctrine," Observer Research Foundation, 30 August 2019 https://www.orfonline.org/expert-speak/strategic-logic-no-first-use-nuclear-doctrine-54911/ (Accessed 7 July 2023)

15 The following is partly based on Rajesh Rajagopalan, "India's Nuclear Doctrine Debate", Carnegie Endowment for International Peace-Regional Insights, 30 June 2016 at https://carnegieendowment.org/2016/06/30/india-s-nuclear-doctrine-debate-pub-63950 (Accessed 7 July 2023).

16 Bharat Karnad, *Nuclear Weapons and Indian Security: The Realist Foundations of Strategy,* Macmillan, New Delhi, 2002, pp. 442-43.

17 Ibid., P. R. Chari, *India's Nuclear Doctrine: Stirrings of Change,* Carnegie Endowment for International Peace, Washington, D.C., 2014 at http://carnegieendowment.org/2014/06/04/indiasnucleardoctrinestirringsofchange/hcks; (Accessed 7 July 2023). Rajesh Basrur, *Minimum Deterrence and India's Nuclear Security,* Stanford University Press, Stanford, CA, 2006, p. 44.

18 Col. Rajesh Gupta, "India's NFU Stance: Need to Change Amidst the Changing Strategic Landscape," *CLAWS Issue Brief*, No. 351, July 2022 at https://www.claws.in/static/IB-351_India%E2%80%99s-NFU-Stance-Need-to-Change-Amidst-the-Changing-Strategic-Landscape-2.pdf. (Accessed 7 July 2023).

19 Sushant Singh, "Manohar Parrikar questions India's no-first-use nuclear policy, adds 'my thinking'," *Indian Express*, 11 November 2016 at https://indianexpress.com/article/india/india-news-india/manohar-parrikar-questions-no-first-use-nuclear-policy-adds-my-thinking-4369062/, (Accessed 7 July 2023)

20 "'No First Use' nuclear policy depends on circumstances: Rajnath Singh," *The Hindu*, 16 August 2019 at https://www.thehindu.com/news/national/no-first-use-nuclear-policy-depends-on-circumstances-rajnath-singh/article29109149.ece (Accessed 7 July 2023)

21 "Question No. 531 Basic Principle of Nuclear Doctrine" Rajya Sabha, 21 July 2022 at https://www.mea.gov.in/rajya-sabha.htm?dtl/35503/question+no531+basic+principle+of+nuclear+doctrine, (Accessed 7 July 2023)

22 Steven Lee Myers, "China Bolsters Its Nuclear Options With New Missile Silos in a Desert," *New York Times*, 3 November 2021 at https://www.nytimes.com/2021/07/02/world/asia/china-missile-silos.html, (Accessed 7 July 2023).

23 Rajat Pandit, "Army reworks war doctrine for Pakistan, China," *The Times of India*, 30 December 2009 at https://timesofindia.indiatimes.com/india/army-reworks-war-doctrine-for-pakistan-china/articleshow/5392683.cms, (Accessed 7 July 2023)

24 Huma Siddiqui, "Indian Army ready for a two-front war, Pakistan and China potent threat to India: Army Chief," *Financial Times*, 12 January 2021 at https://www.financialexpress.com/business/defence-indian-army-ready-for-a-two-front-war-pakistan-and-china-potent-threat-to-india-army-chief-2169506/, (Accessed 7 July 2023)

6

Nuclear Confidence Building Measures with India's Nuclear Neighbours

Kanica Rakhra

Introduction

India's nuclear history, like the history of any other State's nuclear programme, is primarily a reflection of its security concerns. While catering to its security concerns, India engages with its nuclear neighbours in NCBMs and CBMs, to ensure that it walks the fine line between deterrence and disarmament.

After conducting the nuclear tests in May 1998, the then Indian Prime Minister A.B. Vajpayee wrote an open letter to the then US President Bill Clinton[1] stating that the tests were not aimed at any state in the region or outside of it. This decision was representative of Indian strategic thought and presented India's reality and its concerns to the world. However, the May 1998 tests also resulted in India's Western neighbour – Pakistan becoming a nuclear weapons State and joining China, in surrounding India's northern borders by nuclear neighbours on both sides.

For India, as a responsible nuclear State, engagement with its nuclear neighbours has been a key aspect of its nuclear policy. India has chosen to engage repeatedly with NCBMs or CBMs as per the situational requirements. Unlike the American and Russian bilateral

CBMs or the multilateral CBMs between Europe and the Russia, the three Southern Asian States do not have all-encompassing CBMs. However, the three do have differing bilateral relationships, which impact the NCBMs undertaken in the region.

One criticism that India has faced in the last twenty-five years is of being reactionary in its approach, especially with regard to NCBMs. However, acknowledging the possible repercussions of being nuclear neighbours, India engaged in a number of NCBMs with Pakistan. These NCBMs stood the test of time, notwithstanding the tumultuous relationship shared by both the states. Despite having a stormy relationship with its other nuclear neighbour, China, the India-China CBMs are currently limited to being military in nature and have not officially ventured into the nuclear domain.

This chapter gives an overview of key developments in the nuclear programmes of the India and its two neighbours – China and Pakistan, the defined contours of their respective nuclear doctrines, and the difference in the dyadic relationships of the three states. It then goes on to discuss NCBMs undertaken in the region and outlines how India is managing its nuclear relationship under the shadow of regional security dynamics. The chapter also brings out the different Track-II initiatives and their impact on NCBMs between India and its two nuclear neighbours.

Nuclear Neighbours

India's relationship with its two nuclear neighbours is unique as it shares disputed land borders with both States, even though all three States have not deployed their nuclear weapons[2]. However, the dyadic relationship between the three States is very different from each other. India and Pakistan are proof of successfully engaging with an adversary and ensuring minimal repercussions. India and China, on the other hand, engage in limited confidence building measures but also exemplify how nuclear neighbours can maintain limited engagement without escalation to the level of nuclear weapons. The China-Pakistan dyad, however, is not an adversarial relationship and has grown from strength to strength. India's nuclear relationship with its two neighbours aims to reduce the chance of clashes, while growth of the China-Pakistan dyad from military to strategic, increases chance of a clash with India.

India's Nuclear Programme

May 1998 has become a milestone in Indian history for the way it catapulted India into the nuclear club. Twenty-five years since India's self-declaration as a NWS, the country has been able to overcome almost all criticisms that came its way with the execution of *Operation Shakti*. Any credibility that was lacking before was covered with the Indo-US Nuclear Deal (2005), which resulted in a 2008 waiver from the NSG.

In the last twenty-five years, India has been able to stay true to the two important aspects of its Nuclear Doctrine, released in 1999 – 'credible minimum deterrence' and 'NFU'. While being ambiguous on what it believes a "minimum credible deterrent" requires or when it expects to achieve the necessary deterrent, India has been able to build its nuclear arsenal from 40-50 weapons in 2005[3] to approximately 160 in 2022.[4] It has been able to expand on its air and land- based missiles and add the third leg of its triad with sea-based missiles. Ensuring that the missiles are non-deployed, the State also adhered to its NFU doctrine.

The Indian NFU, which has come under scrutiny repeatedly where some statements in the past have led to speculation regarding this segment of India's nuclear doctrine.[5] But with the most recent confirmation coming in 2020[6] from a Minister of the current Government, NFU has stood on firm ground and been accepted as an integral part of India's nuclear doctrine. Adding to this, India has also maintained 'strategic autonomy' as the primary driving factor for its nuclear arsenal. Whether it was with respect to the development of its nuclear programme or with respect to its nuclear deterrent.

Pakistan's Nuclear Programme

Pakistan's nuclear programme has seen development in terms of size and type of arsenal. From approximately 60 weapons in 2007[7] and 90 in 2009[8] to almost 165 in 2021,[9] Pakistan's nuclear arsenal comprises aircraft, land-based ballistic missiles, ground and air-launched cruise missiles along with a sea-based cruise missiles.[10] Pakistan has refused to declare a NFU policy or to articulate its nuclear doctrine. However, diversification of delivery means indicates a shift from massive retaliation to a graduated response.[11]

While the Pakistani nuclear programme has received assistance from India's other neighbour China,[12] it was the A.Q. Khan episode[13] that came to define how the other States viewed Pakistan's nuclear development. The A.Q Khan network shared nuclear designs with Iran, Libya and North Korea[14] and the revelation of the episode caused significant damage to Pakistan and its nuclear programme. Henceforth, Pakistani agencies began to focus significantly on establishing the necessary national authorities to maintain and secure its nuclear stockpiles. Especially after the September 11 attacks, there was significant effort from the Pakistani State to make its nuclear materials more secure.

As per reports, Pakistan worked to improve the military and scientific manpower within the nuclear establishments. To strengthen the SPD's security division, a reporting system was established for monitoring the movements of all officials. Added to this was another layer of employment security, in the form of the PRP and the Human Reliability Programme, for military and civilian personnel, respectively. Additionally, annual, semi-annual, and quarterly reviews of the security system were created and weekly, monthly, and quarterly reports initiated for the security of all organizations maintained by the SPD.[15]

China's Nuclear Programme

The PRC officially maintains a NFU,[16] which means, it will not be the first to use a nuclear weapon in a conflict; rather, it will only use nuclear weapons in retaliation to a nuclear attack against its territory or military personnel. The PRC has additionally committed itself not to use nuclear weapons against non-nuclear-weapon States or in nuclear-weapon free zones. Beijing's nuclear strategy centres on deterrence through "assured retaliation"[17] and its current nuclear stockpile stands at approximately 410 warheads.[18] Its deterrent capability covers all three legs of the triad and its near-continuous at-sea deterrence patrols with its six Jin-class nuclear-powered SSBN. Each SSBN can carry up to 12 SLBMs known as JL-2 and JL-3 missiles.[19]

For China, the main security threat has always been the US of America. PRC representatives often defend the Chinese State positions on nuclear issues as stemming from a defensive position. In his UNGA First Committee session speech on nonproliferation in October 2022, China's ambassador for disarmament affairs Li Song claimed that China "keeps its nuclear capabilities at the minimum level required for national security and does not engage in any nuclear arms race with any other country". He also claimed that, "China's nuclear strategy and policy have been long-standing and consistent with a high level of stability, continuity, and predictability, which are unique among nuclear weapon states as well as being the most responsible and transparent."[20] Thus, Chinese nuclear thought and doctrine does not engage with India and Pakistan in the manner that it focuses on the US, even though the language of the PRC is not country-specific.

China-Pakistan

China has a long history of providing nuclear and missile-related assistance to Pakistan, including weapons-grade uranium and warhead designs, with the majority of its assistance occurring in the 1980s and 1990s. Analysts generally interpret Beijing's motivation for assisting Pakistan as being rooted in its objective of containing India's regional power aspirations.[21]

China provided Pakistan with Highly-Enriched Uranium, ring magnets necessary for processing the uranium, and education for nuclear engineers. By helping Pakistan's nuclear programme, China has indirectly spread instability in regions outside of South Asia,[22] such as the Middle East. Strengthening the China-Pakistan dyad, the PRC aims to use its deepening ties with Pakistan to further add to the region's dynamics.

The China-Pakistan dyad, has strongly influenced Southern Asia's nuclear dynamics. Beyond the strategic partnership, Chinese investment initiatives, especially the CPEC, has raised doubts about its geopolitical intentions in the region.

India-Pakistan

Due to the timing of the Indian and Pakistani nuclear tests and their checkered history, South Asia was considered a highly volatile zone. Issues such as geographical proximity and protracted conflict zones made India-Pakistan a favoured area of study. A lot has been said and written about the India-Pakistan dyad. From Prof. Stephen Cohen (2004)[23] to Dr. Sameer Lalwani (2022),[24] the two States were in the line of fire for a significant period, with analysts repeatedly suggesting crisis escalation. Multiple factors played a role in each crisis not escalating to the nuclear level, but each crisis was a learning curve for the two States.

The Indo-US Nuclear Deal (2005) led to initiation of the geo-political de-hyphenation of India and Pakistan. But this did not translate into the nuclear dynamics of the region. When it came to nuclear crises, the India- Pakistan dyad was still considered volatile. A shift in world politics towards the Indo-Pacific, India's growing economic and political equity in the world, coupled with the deepening Pakistan-China dyad within the larger Indo-Pacific, brought China in a stronger manner into the Southern Asian dynamics.

India-China

Chinese assistance to Pakistan's nuclear programme deeply impacts the India-China nuclear relationship. Additionally, border skirmishes that are resulting in long standing conflicts are further stressing the India-China dyad. These in turn, affect India's evolving nuclear capabilities where India's concern lies in maintaining a modest nuclear arsenal which is capable of deterring China and Pakistan.

Chinese entry into the India-Pakistan dyad is the primary reason for Southern Asia facing a 'nuclear trilemma'. China's focus may be the US or its larger commitments to non-proliferation and disarmament; it may not consider India as a nuclear adversary, but its entry into the region has brought the PRC into the region's fold. Additionally, unresolved border issues between India and China play a significant role in the dyad's dynamics. While both have a policy of NFU and no crisis between India and China has escalated to the nuclear question, the dyad is evolving and both States are finding their space in the region.

India confronts challenges from two fronts that converge geopolitically into one at many levels.[25] Although the India-China nuclear dyad has not seen escalation, it is evolving and may require for the two States to engage in some NCBMs in the future.

Existing Nuclear CBMs

The two nuclear neighbours of India – Pakistan and China – have a unique relationship with each other and do not require CBMs. However, India engages in both its neighbours with CBMs. Within the India-Pakistan dyad, there are NCBMs that have managed to hold fort even during times of extreme crisis.

The success rate of NCBMs in the India-Pakistan dyad depends on the observer's vantage point. Many scholars are of the opinion that very little has been done in terms of NCBMs between the two States and there is space for a number of parameters to be brought into the discussions. This may primarily be, because for Pakistan, CBMs or NCBMs are not an act in themselves, but are a signboard to lead towards potential resolution of the Kashmir dispute. A case in point would be the confirmation of NCBMs in 2021, which was cited by Pakistan as a 'win' and by India as 'no change in positions'.[26]

Following are a list of India-Pakistan Nuclear Confidence Building Measures ranging from the official Lahore Declaration to Track II initiatives such as the Ottawa Dialogue.

Official NCBMs

1. Negotiations to merge the "No War Pact" (Pakistan's idea) and the "Mutual Treaty of Peace and Friendship" (India's)[27] (currently stalled)
2. The Zia-Gandhi pledge in December 1985 not to attack each other's nuclear installations.[28] This was subsequently formalized in the 1988 Non-Attack Agreement (1988) against nuclear installations and facilities.[29]
3. The Lahore Declaration signed in February 1999, states that India and Pakistan "shall take immediate steps for reducing the risk of accidental or unauthorised use of nuclear weapons and discuss concepts and doctrines with a view to elaborating measures for confidence building in the nuclear and conventional fields, aimed at prevention of conflict."[30]
4. The MOU, signed by Indian Foreign Secretary K. Raghunath and his Pakistani counterpart Shamshad Ahmed, emphasizing measures to improve nuclear security and prevent an accidental nuclear exchange. Agreeing to resolve remaining "technical details" in bilateral agreements by mid-1999, New Delhi and Islamabad commit to several steps to reduce the nuclear danger in the subcontinent.[31]
5. In the round of talks held between 2004 and 2007, five rounds focused on NCBMs talks and four on conventional CBMs. In the first round of nuclear talks in New Delhi, it was agreed that "the nuclear capabilities of each other, which are based on their national security imperatives, constitute a factor for stability", and that both countries were, "committed to work towards strategic stability". The achievements of the NCBMs talks were:
    - A hotline between the foreign secretaries;
    - Upgrading the existing hotline between the directors-general military operations;
    - Reaching an agreement on pre-notification of flight testing of ballistic missiles; and
    - An agreement on reducing the risk from accidents relating to nuclear weapons.

At the Foreign Secretaries' joint press conference in March 2007, it was stated:

> "...It is agreed that there should be regular expert -level discussions on doctrines for ensuring security in an environment of strategic deterrence that is maintained by the two countries and is a fact of life in South Asia."

The two States also went on to highlight what aspects would be discussed in the next NCBM talks. The following approaches are likely to be considered:

(a) Going beyond the 1999 Lahore MoU, on which talks have been based so far;
(b) Understanding perceptions on strategic stability and working towards the latter;
(c) Avoiding an arms race and promoting credible restraint in line with the declared responsible nuclear status of both countries;
(d) Evolving and implementing approaches guided by defensive rather than offensive doctrines;
(e) Inclusion of cruise missiles in the agreement on pre-notification of flight testing of ballistic missiles;
(f) Discussion on the impact of BMD on strategic stability; and
(g) Cooperation between the nuclear regulatory authorities of both countries on civil nuclear power plants after Fukushima.

The fundamental objective of these talks would be to remove or diminish mistrust and misunderstandings, and to ensure minimum deterrence, giving priority to socio-economic development in each country within the framework of improved bilateral relations.[32]

6. In 2011, India and Pakistan discussed Nuclear CBMs for the first time since 2007, reviewing existing agreements.[33] In their statement, the Foreign Secretaries said that India and Pakistan would work to build confidence over their nuclear and conventional weapons capability.[34]
7. Pakistan proposed a SRR, comprising conflict resolution, nuclear and missile restraint and conventional balance. Islamabad pushed

for the SRR soon after the nuclear tests conducted by the two countries.[35] Elements of the SRR are:[36]

- Conflict resolution through a sustained, result-oriented dialogue.
- Measures for nuclear restraint and conventional balance, to be discussed at the political and experts' level.
- Objective of minimum credible deterrence.
- Maintenance of nuclear weapons on low-alert status.
- No operational deployment of nuclear-capable ballistic or any other type of missiles / delivery systems.
- No acquisition or deployment of Anti-Ballistic Missile Systems.
- Avoidance of a nuclear, missile, or conventional arms race.
- Continuation of the national nuclear test moratoriums of both sides, as reaffirmed in the Joint Statement of 20 June 2004.
- Examination of the elements of the SSR proposal, and their potential elaboration in the form of implementable measures, in the meetings of the foreign secretaries and in subsequent expert-level talks.

Other proposed elements:

- Progress on substantive issues, Kashmir, Siachen, Sir Creek and Baglihar dam.
- India's conventional armed forces, armaments / military strength, arms acquisition, and doctrines, whose objective is to give an aggressive and coercive capability, should be realigned and reduced to make them defence-oriented and to remove the asymmetry, large disparity and imbalance that already exists between the conventional armed forces of India and Pakistan.
- Review of existing CBMs and other measures, periodically.
- Measures for the prevention of violations of airspace and territorial waters.
- Revival of pre-Shimla ground border rules.
- Prior notification of military exercises/manoeuvres and no joint military exercises with any foreign/third country in disputed areas.

- Enhancing the efficacy and upgrading the existing communication links between Directors-General, Military Operations.
- Non-acquisition or deployment of anti-ballistic missile systems.
- Linkage between nuclear and conventional CBMs.
- Clarification of security threat perception, which would reduce pretexts for unnecessary and destabilizing arms build-up.
- No permanent relocation of strike formations towards the Pakistan-India border.

8. Most recently, the Directors General of Military Operations of India and Pakistan held discussions over the established mechanism of contact through the hotline. The two sides reviewed the situation along the LOC and all other sectors in a free, frank and cordial atmosphere and released a joint statement on 25 February 2021.[37]

Track-II CBMs

Apart from these eight official programmes, there were also a number of Track-1.5 and Track-II dialogues that were held between Indian and Pakistani academicians and scholars that helped reduce the escalation during crisis. The Track-II paradigm has not been a steady interaction between the two countries, but has waxed and waned in accordance with India-Pakistan relations.

The Chaopraya Dialogue, which began in 2008, held meetings in Thailand. The Chao Track process conceptualized after the 26/11 Mumbai attacks, ran until December 2017. The process was resumed in August 2018, expanding its scope to regional stability in South Asia, under The Chaopraya banners. The Pakistan chapter of the project is managed by the Jinnah Institute and the India chapter by the Council for Strategic and Defence Research.[38]

Another such example was the Ottawa Dialogue[39] held in July 2011. The Ottawa Dialogue, a collaboration of the United States Institute of Peace, the University of Ottawa, and several other partners, recently produced a series of recommendations for reducing the threat of nuclear conflict between Pakistan and India. The final set of recommendations[40] from the Dialogue stated that their governments would,

1. Initiate an official, ongoing high-level dialogue on the impact of BMD on regional security;
2. Add cruise missiles to the Agreement on Pre-Notification of Flight Testing of Ballistic Missiles.
3. Sign a CBM to the effect that their land-based nuclear arsenals will remain "de-mated" and "de-alerted" in peacetime;
4. Initiate a high-level official dialogue over how new and emerging technologies, such as future sea-based systems and nuclear-armed cruise missiles, will impact upon strategic stability;
5. More generally, enter into a high-level official dialogue over "strategic sufficiency" – the question of how future nuclear force development can be kept to the lowest level consistent with national security needs;
6. Ensure that existing hotlines and communication channels are hardened, manned on a 24-hour, 7-day-a-week basis and supplemented with secure video links;
7. Ensure that a dedicated communication channel is established between the Indian National Security Advisor and the Pakistani counterpart; and
8. Ensure that each side establishes a "strategic risk management unit", which could serve some of the same communication functions as the Nuclear Risk Reduction Centres, in other contexts.

The last Ottawa Dialogue went so far as to list out possible CBMs categorized under the following sub-headings: Unilateral and/or Bilateral Declaratory Steps; Strategic Restraint Measures; Communication Measures; Physical Measures; and Cooperation between civilian nuclear establishments.

Both the Chaopraya Dialogue and the Ottawa Dialogue featured prominent strategic thinkers from India and Pakistan and brought forth valid considerations such as non-deployment of TNWs and agreement to share different experiences in creating and running

Nuclear Regulatory Authorities. However, neither governments have taken up the issue or have been willing to consider the suggestions offered by either of the groups. A primary reason for this may be that the trajectory of India's nuclear weapons development as well as its civilian programme, which has been very different from that of Pakistan.

The Future of NCBMs

Southern Asia as a region is traditionally bound by ecology. But given the deterrent capabilities of India and its nuclear neighbours, it is slowly being bound with nuclear weapons as well. China, India and Pakistan, as the three NWSs in the region, define how to approach and achieve nuclear stability and what an Asian understanding of nuclear weapons would entail. The rapid expansion of the nuclear deterrents of India and its nuclear neighbours has brought focus of a number of international organizations on the region.

With the security concerns of States evolving due to changes in geo-politics, there has been a recent spate of reports by SIPRI,[41] IISS[42] and APLN,[43] that suggest revisiting current NCBMs and updating them in keeping with newer threats and concerns. They highlight the long gap in discussions between India and its nuclear neighbours.

The Reports point to the yawning gap between nuclear developments and lack of conversation between the States. While IISS (2021)[44] focuses primarily on the India-Pakistan dyad, the other Reports from APLN[45] and SIPRI[46] point to the growing presence of China in the India-Pakistan dyad. SIPRI goes further to look at the US and Russian role as well, pointing towards the different actors involved in a South Asian nuclear dilemma. They also seem to draw on the pointers suggested by Indian and Pakistani experts during their agreements in the previously mentioned Ottawa and Chaopraya Dialogues.

In focusing on the India-Pakistan nuclear relationship, all three Reports suggest establishment of nuclear risk reduction centres and the need to modernise the 1988 Agreement on the Prohibition of Attack against Nuclear Installations and Facilities. However, they do not seem to take into account the recent accidental firing from India and its quick and effective management by the Indian and Pakistani officials. The IISS Report talks of CBM fatigue, but goes on to suggest more NCBMs. This seems contrary to the idea of CBM fatigue.

Many of the suggestions in the Reports are aspects that India has been pushing for in multiple international forums such as a NFU Agreement, pointed out in the APLN report. Of the three NWSs in the region, Pakistan is the only State that does not have an NFU and if it were to agree, the region may be able to work towards an NFU Agreement. The Report also suggests that the three countries should share best practices on nuclear safety and security of civilian nuclear facilities through their respective centres of excellence. As China refuses to acknowledge India's nuclear weapons programme, the suggestion again hits a roadblock. While situational escalation is a genuine cause of concern, the suggestions by States have not found favour with officials.

The SIPRI Report points out that China, India and Pakistan are all developing dual-capable missiles that could deliver conventional or nuclear warheads and that without China's participation in nuclear talks, the chance of long-term progress on a range of CBMs in South Asia remains low. The Report also suggests that Indian, Pakistani and Russian experts had a greater propensity to advocate for trilateral and multilateral talks than their Chinese counterparts. This may not be feasible. While Pakistan may be interested in such a proposition, Russian interests may not be served well if Russia gets caught in a Southern Asian quagmire.

Some suggestions that came forth from the Report are: China–India nuclear dialogues, a trans-regional forum on regional and global strategic stability, multilateral dialogues on non-weaponization of outer space, and consultations on the impact of AI and LAWS on nuclear risk. In line with the 2010 commitment towards global nuclear disarmament,[47] India and China held discussions on disarmament and non-proliferation in 2015,[48] prior to the Prime Minister's visit to Beijing, which was followed by a visit of the Chinese delegation to India for talk.[49] Bilateral dialogue on disarmament and non-proliferation continued till 2019.[50] They may have stalled due to the pandemic and other developments, but there were no indications that they may begin again.

The three Reports focus on the gap between the previous round of discussions and the nuclear developments of the three States. The Reports in themselves discuss the growing crevices in other aspects of the relationship between these States; however the recommendations do not reflect these changes. While there seems to be an understanding of shared risk between the two dyads of India-Pakistan and Pakistan-China, there is almost no understanding of shared risk between India and China.

The SIPRI and IISS Reports were written before the war in Ukraine. Nonetheless, military build-up within Europe along with and the US and Russian Federation withdrawal from treaties such as the INF and Open Skies respectively, has not been taken into consideration by the Reports. Such decisions are bound to have deep and lasting impact on how India and its nuclear neighbours interact with each other. Both the Reports seem to have left out this significant impact in their recommendations.

Thus, while suggestions provided in the above-mentioned reports are significant and warrant an internal discussion among officials, they do not take into account some international factors that deeply influence how States in the region react to situations.

Conclusion

The global nuclear order has had a deep impact on nuclearisation of the region, especially on India, Pakistan and China. From the developments of their nuclear deterrents to their want for NCBMs, the global influence has been consistent in its presence. At a time when there are almost no treaties on arms control, international institutions are unable to stay neutral in their approach to issues and new conflicts are sprouting every year, it may be difficult for India and its nuclear neighbours to develop processes that discuss risk reduction measures or nuclear confidence building measures.

Discussions on NCBMs in South Asia spans the period when both India and Pakistan became NWSs. The new reports highlight the growing relevance of China as a nuclear neighbour for India, but the recommendations do not seem to take other geo-political developments into consideration. In seeking a new approach,[51] it would be important to bring forth the interaction of Southern Asian States with other parts of the world and how evolving security dynamics impact regional dyads and vice versa.

In the last twenty-five years, however, there has been a significant shift in the debate. During the early 2000s, international literature highlighted the volatile nature of India- Pakistan relations and how their becoming nuclear would impact the region geo-politically as well as economically. Now, new elements have been added to the dyads – from AI to Multiple Independently targetable Reentry Vehicles or MIRVs. However, responsible behavior shown by States in the region or the sustained approach towards continued NCBMs has found little appreciation.

Another change that has taken place in recent years is the shift in focus to the Indo-Pacific and China. Evolution of the India-China relationship would play a significant role in determining how NCBMs are viewed in the region.

Every year, India and Pakistan celebrate their nuclearisation with a spate of articles. Although it is near impossible to negate the nuclear programme from the India-Pakistan dyad, the 25-year long journey has proved that there are multiple factors that influence how India interacts and engages with its nuclear neighbours. India, Pakistan and China, have traversed a long journey as NWSs and each is examining the situation on ground and taking measures to ensure State security while undertaking confidence building measures in the region.

India's nuclear journey has been a reflection of its evolving relationship with other States in and outside the region. Consistently engaging in the twin concepts of deterrence and disarmament, India has walked the thin line to prove its need for one and want for the other.

NOTES

1 "Excerpts from Letter written by Indian PM Atal Bihari Vajpayee to US President Clinton" at https://www.nytimes.com/1998/05/13/world/nuclear-anxiety-indian-s-letter-to-clinton-on-the-nuclear-testing.html (Accessed 12 April 2023)

2 "Status of World Nuclear Forces" *Federation of American Studies*, 28 March 2023.

3 Robert S. Norris and Hans M. Kristensen, "India's Nuclear Forces, 2005", Nuclear Notebook, *Bulletin of the Atomic Scientists,* September/October 2005.

4 Hans M. Kristensen and Matt Korda, "Indian nuclear weapons", *Bulletin of the Atomic Scientists,* 78(4), 2022, pp. 224-236.

5 Vishnu Som, "Defence Minister Manohar Parrikar's Nuclear Remark Stressed As 'Personal Opinion'" NDTV, 10 November 2016 and Rajnath Singh (@rajnathsingh), "Pokhran is the area which witnessed Atal Ji's firm resolve to make India a nuclear power and yet remain firmly committed to the doctrine of 'No First Use'. India has strictly adhered to this doctrine. What happens in future depends on the circumstances.", X, 6 August 2019.

6 Press Trust of India, "No change in India's nuclear doctrine: MEA" *The Hindu,* 4 March 2020.

7 R.S. Norris and H.M. Kristensen, "Pakistan's Nuclear Forces", *Bulletin of the Atomic Scientists,* 63(3), 2007, pp. 71–74 at https://doi.org/10.2968/063003016 (Accessed on 10 April 2023)

8 Robert S. Norris and Hans Kristensen, "Pakistani Nuclear Forces", *Bulletin of the Atomic Scientists,* 65 (5), 2009, pp. 82-89, DOI: 10.2968/065005008.

9 Hans M. Kristensen and Matt Korda, "Pakistani nuclear weapons", *Bulletin of the Atomic Scientists,* 7 (5), 2021, pp.265-278, DOI: 10.1080/00963402.2021.1964258.

10 Ibid.

11 Sadia Tasleem, *Pakistan's Nuclear Use Doctrine,* Carnegie Endowment for International Peace, 30 June 2016.

12 William Burr, "China, Pakistan, and the Bomb: The Declassified File on U.S. Policy, 1977-1997", *US National Security Archive,* 5 March 2004.

13 Shi-chin Lin, "The AQ Khan Revelations and Subsequent Changes to Pakistani Export Controls", *NTI Report,* 30 November 2004.

14 Rolf Mowatt-Larssen, "Nuclear Security in Pakistan: Reducing the Risks of Nuclear Terrorism", *Arms Control Association,* July 2009 (Accessed 12 April 2023).

15 Feroz Hassan Khan, "Nuclear Security in Pakistan: Separating Myth From Reality", *Arms Control Association* at https://www.armscontrol.org/act/2009-07/features/nuclear-security-pakistan-separating-myth-reality (Accessed 11 April 2023)

16 Annual Report to Congress, "Military and Security Developments involving the People's Republic of China 2022", *US Department of Defense,* 29 November 2022.

17 *Fact Sheet: China's Nuclear Inventory,* Centre for Arms Control and Non Proliferation, 2 April 2020.

18 Hans M. Kristensen, Matt Korda and Eliana Reynolds "Chinese Nuclear Weapons", *Bulletin of the Atomic Scientists,* 79 (2), 2023, pp. 108-133 at DOI: 10.1080/00963402.2023.2178713.

19 *Fact Sheet: China's Nuclear Inventory,* no. 17.

20 Minlu Zhang, "Diplomat: China's nuclear strategy 'transparent' ", *China Daily,* 19 October 2022.

21 Sharad Joshi, "The China-Pakistan Nuclear Deal: A Realpolitique Fait Accompli", *Nuclear Threat Initiative,* 10 December 2011.

22 John Dori and Richard Fisher, *The Strategic Implications of China's Nuclear Aid to Pakistan*, The Heritage Foundation, 16 June 1998.
23 Stephen P. Cohen, "India and Pakistan: Steps Towards Rapprochement", Brookings, 28 January 2004.
24 Sameer Lalwani, "How to Deal with the Risk of Nuclear Escalation in South Asia", United States Institute of Peace, 17 May 2022.
25 "Nuclear South Asia at 22" CSIS Commentary, 10 November 2020.
26 Suhasini Haidar and Dinkar Peri, "India, Pakistan agree to observe 2003 ceasefire", *The Hindu*, 25 February 2021.
27 "India-Pakistan: Prospects For Confidence-Building Measures", Central Intelligence Agency, 28 March 2012 at https://www.cia.gov/readingroom/document/cia-rdp90t00114r000700550001-1 (Accessed 13 April 2023).
28 Ibid.
29 "Agreement on the Prohibition of Attack Against Republic Of India and the Islamic Republic of Pakistan on 31 December 1988" at https://mea.gov.in/Portal/LegalTreatiesDoc/PAB1232.pdf (Accessed 13 April 2023).
30 "The Lahore Declaration", 21 February 1999 at https://peacemaker.un.org/sites/peacemaker.un.org/files/IN%20PK_990221_The%20Lahore%20Declaration.pdf (Accessed 13 April 2023).
31 Howard Diamond, *India, Pakistan Agree on Security, Confidence-Building Measures*, Arms Control Association, January 1999.
32 Tariq Usman Hyder, "Next Round of Talks" *The Dawn, 22* December 2011.
33 "Indo-Pak talks to discuss nuclear Confidence Building Measures" NDTV, 19 June 2011.
34 "Pakistan, India to explore new nuclear confidence building", Reuters, 24 June 2011.
35 "Pakistan proposes 20 CBMs: Secretary-level talks begin", *The Dawn*, 20 December 2004.
36 Ibid.
37 Ministry of Defence, "Joint Statement on 25 February 2022" at https://pib.gov.in/PressReleasePage.aspx?PRID=1700682 (Accessed on 12 April 2023).
38 https://csdronline.org/dialogue (Accessed 12 April 2023)
39 Ajit Jain, "Ottawa Dialogue leads to adoption of Indo-Pak nuclear confidence building measures", *Canada News*, 20 June 2011 at https://www.tvpaul.com/wp-content/uploads/2010/11/article1.pdf (Accessed 15 April 2023).
40 "Ottawa Dialogue makes further recommendations for India-Pakistan nuclear agreements on 22 December 2011" at http://ssms.socialsciences.uottawa.ca/vfs/.horde/newsfeed/000301_001324577320_Copenhagen_ENG%20(2).pdf (Accessed 13 April 2023).
41 Lora Salmaan and Petr Topychkanov, "Reinvigorating South Asian Nuclear Transparency And Confidence-Building Measures", *SIPRI Insights on Peace and Security* No. 2021/4, September, 2021.
42 Antoine Levesques, Desmond Bowen and Jack Gill, *Nuclear Deterrence and Stability in South Asia: Perceptions and Realities*, International Institute for Strategic Studies, 20 May 2021.
43 Salman Bashir, *The China–India–Pakistan Nuclear Triangle: Consequential Choices for Asian Security*, Policy Brief No 143, Toda Peace Institute and APLN, November 2022.
44 Antoine Levesques, Desmond Bowen and Jack Gill, no. 27.

45 Tanvi Kulkarni, *Managing the China, India and Pakistan Nuclear Trilemma,* Toda Institute and APLN, July 2022.

46 Lora Salmaan and Petr Topychkanov, no. 26.

47 "Joint Communiqué of the Republic of India and the People's Republic of China", 16 December 2010 at https://mea.gov.in/bilateral-documents.htm?dtl/5158/Joint (Accessed 10 April 2023).

48 "India-China Hold First Dialogue on Disarmament and Arms Control" on 17 April 2015 PTI at https://www.millenniumpost.in/india-china-hold-first-dialogue-on-disarmament-61371?infinitescroll=1 (Accessed 13 April 2023).

49 "Visit of Chinese Delegation for talks on Disarmament and Non-Proliferation on 13 September 2016" at https://mea.gov.in/press-releases.htm?dtl/27385/Visit+of+Chinese+delegation+for+talks+on+Disarmament+and+NonProliferation (Accessed 13 April 2023).

50 "India, China hold dialogue on disarmament and non-proliferation" on 03 June 2019 PTI at https://www.business-standard.com/article/pti-stories/india-china-hold-dialogue-on-disarmament-and-non-proliferation-119060301439_1.html (Accessed 14 April 2023)

51 Sobia Paracha, "India-Pakistan Nuclear CBMs: Internal Dialogue as Catalyst for Peace?" *The Diplomat,* 07 June 2016.

7

The Difficult Road to Nuclear Disarmament: What can India Offer?

Manpreet Sethi

Introduction

India conducted five nuclear tests in 1998 and declared itself a state with nuclear weapons. Non-proliferation activists around the globe immediately cried foul and chastised the country for having done grievous harm to the regime. Meanwhile, the disarmament proponents felt betrayed since a champion of their cause had chosen to move towards nuclear weapons. Both assumptions were, however, baseless as India's action did not compromise its position on either non-proliferation or disarmament.

To introduce its new nuclear self, India presented to the public a draft of its nuclear doctrine on August 17, 1999. Besides outlining several issues related to operationalisation of nuclear deterrence, the document also expressed support for elements of the non-proliferation regime. India has upheld the principles espoused by the NPT, despite being outside it), and has over time undertaken harmonisation of its export controls, accepted IAEA safeguards on its civilian nuclear infrastructure, and ensured compliance with nuclear security measures. On disarmament too, India supports all such measures at the UN and CD that show the promise of achieving a universal, verifiable, multilaterally negotiated world without nuclear weapons.

Of course, post-1998, India has focussed on building a credible nuclear deterrent to meet the security challenges of an adversarial nuclearised neighbourhood. It has not led any high-profile[1] initiatives towards nuclear disarmament for the last 25 years. This has at times been interpreted as waning of India's interest in disarmament and pre-dominance of realpolitik in its nuclear inclinations. There is also a sense of cynicism at the lack of seriousness on the part of the NWS for disarmament at the global level.

Indeed, as things stand in 2023, nuclear disarmament looks distant. The number of nuclear weapons may have reduced since the peak of the Cold War, but there is no hope that national nuclear arsenals will move to zero anytime soon. Rather, all states possessing such weapons continue to ensure well-funded, elaborate modernization plans that have them trapped in an offence-defence spiral. The NPT RevCon could not achieve a consensus final document in 2022, and frustration of the NNWS at the lack of effort by the NWS to move towards nuclear disarmament is not a secret.

This is ironical since the first meeting of States Parties to the TPNW, which today has close to 90 signatories and 65 ratifications, successfully concluded in Vienna in 2022. An Action Plan was adopted to advance progressive steps towards disarmament. It emphasizes on inclusion of the ideas and energies of all stakeholders —civil society, affected communities and indigenous people, gender and youth. But, the one group that the treaty has not been able to convince to join are the nuclear weapon possessors. And, unfortunately, they are the ones that really matter if efforts towards elimination of nuclear weapons are to succeed. For now, though, the nuclear weapon possessing states appear to have steadfastly turned their back to such a future.

Consequently, the shadow of nuclear weapons, including the possibility of their use, hangs ominously over the global landscape. The use of force against Ukraine by a nuclear Russia has shown the value of nuclear weapons for both nuclear deterrence and nuclear coercion. In this rather fractious atmosphere, can India bring the need for nuclear disarmament back to the consciousness of the NWS? Should it make this effort? Would it be in its national interest to do so? What exactly can India offer?

To answer these questions, this chapter starts by mapping the contemporary nuclear reality to show where the dangers are lurking, especially for Asia and India. The second part of the paper explains why it is in India's interest to elucidate its own interpretation of a NWFW and its suggestions on possible pathways to elimination of nuclear weapons. The paper concludes by arguing that despite the apparently low appeal for nuclear disarmament in today's world, it is in India's interest to support and encourage efforts in this direction. As said by António Guterres, UN Secretary General, on 26 September 2022 on the occasion of the International Day for Total Elimination of Nuclear Weapons, 'We must eliminate these weapons before they eliminate us.'[2]

Contemporary Nuclear Reality: Understanding the Dangers

During the long years of the Cold War, there was only one adversarial nuclear dyad of significance. The US–the USSR confrontation was premised on mutually assured destruction owing to a rough parity in their nuclear arsenals. While this may still be true for US and Russia, it is not so for the many other dyads that populate the global nuclear landscape. Given that nuclear weapons are available today with nine countries, there is a multiplicity of deterrence equations. There are also significant variations in how deterrence is practiced. Each one of the dyads has its own frame of reference in terms of threat perceptions, the method of establishing deterrence and the trajectory of capability build-up. There are also asymmetries in capabilities, differences in the role accorded to nuclear weapons in national security strategies. Meanwhile, there is also a lack of transparency. Rather, strategic ambiguity is the hallmark of doctrines of many nuclear possessors and this tends to generate hedging strategies as each adversary assumes the worst of the other. Relations between major nuclear players are indeed experiencing severe stresses, trust deficits and lack of strategic dialogue.

In 2022, the biggest nuclear reality show since the Cuban missile crisis unfolded in Europe. The theatre of conflict, duration, as well as the practice of nuclear brinkmanship were both unexpected developments, especially for the US and its NATO allies. Russia's frequent references to its nuclear weapons during the last 14 months has contributed to the fear that Moscow might use them. But, Moscow's behaviour is not an isolated instance. Western media and analysts seemed to have been overly alarmed by this and expressed their fear that there was a near certainty of use of nuclear weapons by Russia. Projection of a low nuclear threshold, however, is a way of practising deterrence. In Asia, which really is the 'most nuclearised of all continents,'[3] this has been repeatedly demonstrated by Pakistan and North Korea to enhance deterrence.

Nuclear Complexities of Asia

Nuclear equations in Asia make for a rather complicated web of inter-state relations. It is a region that includes many kinds of nuclear countries – those recognized as nuclear weapon states by the NPT, those that are protected by American extended deterrence commitments, those that are nuclear armed but outside the NPT, those with the potential to go nuclear, those that could be tempted to acquire weapons, and those that have been engaged in wilful nuclear proliferation. Many of these nations are also geographically proximate and suffer from unresolved territorial conflicts. In contrast, the US and the USSR were physically separated by an ocean. Their conflicts too were never in the form of a direct engagement between the two, but as proxy conflicts in third countries that were themselves non-nuclear.

Another troublesome reality of Asia's nuclear weapons possessing countries is that they espouse diverse nuclear doctrines, including those that project a readiness to use nuclear escalation to de-escalate a crisis. Consequently, battlefield nuclear weapons are touted as a way of enhancing deterrence. Some countries have also deployed dual-use capable delivery systems at the same location or under the same command. Such measures, ostensibly taken to deter conflict, can significantly heighten the possibility of accidental or inadvertent escalation every time a crisis erupts between nuclear armed nations. As put aptly by a strategic analyst, 'The weapons we task with securing our nation are the same weapons that hold the potential to destroy other nations and to trigger an attack that will destroy our own.'[4]

Yet another danger felt palpably in the region is that of nuclear terrorism. This danger is more pronounced in Asia for two reasons – one there is greater availability of nuclear material and technology owing to the spread of nuclear power programmes; the second is the presence of terrorist organizations of all hues, which in countries like Pakistan enjoy state support and sponsorship. Modern day terrorist organizations are also far better networked and well endowed. Hence, their reach into nuclear establishments and their potential influence over insiders with lure of lucre or ideology is not a small cause of concern.

A further complication arises from the spread of new technologies such as those related to cyber, AI, unmanned systems and hypersonics. Each one of these impacts nuclear deterrence, especially by bringing in new challenges to nuclear command and control. Even as the imminent dangers are yet to be wholly understood, the technological advances continue with no arms control in place. Rather, trust deficits are encouraging hedging strategies that create new security dilemmas that propel another round of mitigation attempts.

Undoubtedly, the hold of nuclear weapons on national security in nations that possess such weapons has proven to be tight. In the wake of the Russia-Ukraine conflict, whispers are getting louder on whether vertical, and even horizontal proliferation will increase, as NWS scramble for greater 'security,' and NNWS feel threatened by NWS and lose faith in negative security assurances. Absence of strategic dialogues and tense inter-state relations are leading to an appraisal of national security in which nuclear weapons are beginning to look attractive once again. With every act of proliferation, however, nuclear risks will increase. All in all, we are in a highly risk prone nuclear reality.

India's Stake in NWFW

In this apparent free fall of nuclear relations, should India give up on its long-standing pursuit of universal nuclear disarmament? Should it opt to be a passive observer, or should it actively participate in shaping the debate on disarmament by promoting its desirability and feasibility? The following paragraphs argue that for the sake of its national security, India must remain engaged in efforts that promote nuclear disarmament. While there are also moral, ethical, legal, humanitarian or environmental considerations for pursuing a world without nuclear weapons, which are worthy causes in and of themselves, for India, a NWFW is a desirable objective from the national security perspective too.

India accords a narrow role to nuclear weapons. These are meant only for nuclear deterrence; not for warfighting, nor for influencing the scope and conduct of a conventional conflict, or for any revisionist purpose. With the objective of the weapon restricted to safeguarding India against the possibility of nuclear coercion or blackmail, the need for nuclear weapons would disappear if there was universal nuclear disarmament. If steps and mechanisms could be devised to verifiably and universally move towards nuclear abolition, India could shed its nuclear baggage without any loss of security. Rather, it is the presence of these weapons with its nuclear armed adversaries in the neighbourhood that brings several risks for India.

Nuclear weapons have been used by Pakistan to perpetrate cross border terrorism while protecting itself from behind the shield of nuclear weapons.[5] Pakistan's nuclear weapons, therefore, complicate India's national security and their disappearance from the arsenals of the two as part of a global zero plan would not adversely impact, but rather benefit, India's security calculations. They would liberate India from the risk of inadvertent escalation in case of every crisis that may erupt between the two.

Meanwhile, China's nuclear weapons expose India to the possibility of nuclear coercion and blackmail. While India is engaged in building credible nuclear deterrence to counter this possibility, China's rapid pace of nuclear expansion and upgradation threatens to pull India into a nuclear arms race if it feels the need to mirror Chinese capabilities. Such a nuclear arms race would sap India's resources since sustained modernization of conventional capabilities also remains a security necessity. Therefore, a non-nuclear China would let India concentrate on building conventional strength. Of course, much will depend on how and what kind of a nuclear world the nations arrive at. This is a space where India can exercise some of its influence to nudge nations along its own vision of nuclear disarmament.

India's Definition of Nuclear Disarmament

The journey to nuclear disarmament must begin with clarity on the end goal. Should it be a world with no nuclear weapons, few weapons, weapons with a few nations or with an international authority of some kind? India interprets nuclear abolition as the complete removal of these weapons from the world. Some, however, contend that an international authority consensually negotiated might be made the repository of a few nuclear weapons in case of an unthinkable eventuality. Meanwhile, most NWS are unable to accept or even envision a situation with no or zero nuclear weapons.

Interestingly, most roadmaps to an NWFW too have stopped short of zero. For instance, the report *Eliminating Nuclear Threats* brought out by the ICNND in 2009, outlined short term, medium term and long-term measures for nuclear disarmament. But it could not identify the year by which the world might get to a state of zero. It stated, 'we have found it impossible credibly to do so [identify a particular target date for achieving the complete elimination of nuclear weapons], given the nature and complexity of the conditions that will have to be satisfied in the final elimination phase move from low numbers to zero.'[6]

Envisioning a world without nuclear weapons has proven to be especially difficult as the theory and practice of realism that today holds sway over international relations can only visualize competitive inter-state relations. This is a *real* challenge since unless nations begin to visualize disarmament as a state of zero, we would be always looking at half measures that will not be able to address trust deficits in inter-state relations. It is only when *all NWS express their willingness to give up all their nuclear weapons* and the attendant fissile material, delivery systems, infra-structure, etc., that there would be a complete change in how inter-state relations get perceived and conceived for the future.

As it did several centuries ago, India needs to help the world rediscover the meaning of zero, this time in the nuclear realm. universal nuclear disarmament has to be a state of zero nuclear weapons – not of fewer weapons or in fewer hands because as long as even one country retains even one nuclear weapon, an NWFW cannot be realized and proliferation cannot be stopped.

For the path to now change, there obviously is need for significant transformation of the geopolitical environment. As opined by the ICNND 15 years ago, 'political-security relations among the nuclear-armed states and their neighbours will have to be cooperative and balanced enough....'[7] But it is clear that this is not easy to achieve. In the prevalent state of international relations, there is a particularly high focus on hard power and military capability as the means to secure a nation. So, is the sense of nationalism and need to secure narrow national interests, even at the cost of other's security. The ongoing conflict in Europe is a good illustration of this approach. President Putin has justified his actions as a way to 'right' several wrongs that he perceived the 'West' has perpetrated on Russia. On the other hand, US/NATO are fixated on their version of the rules-based order. In the bargain, millions of lives in Ukraine have been disrupted and countries across the world impacted as they grapple with energy and food insecurity.

India drew attention to this at the 77th session of UNGA in September 2022. EAM, S. Jaishankar, chose the global platform to draw attention to the fragility of international security when narrow national interests are pursued. Not many remember that India's first

Prime Minister Jawaharlal Nehru used to emphasize the goal of peace over security. The reason behind such an approach was well explained by India's foremost strategic analyst Jasjit Singh in these words, 'An environment of peace would naturally provide security, whereas mere security may or may not bring peace. For example, security in Europe during the Cold War was ensured for 45 years by something like 60,000 nuclear weapons, 94,000 combat airplanes, about 110,000 tanks and massive quantities of other weapons and military systems....' And yet despite all these security measures, peace proved to be elusive owing to the continued attempts to build competitive spheres of influence. The acquisition of nuclear weapons, whether as a national possession or through extended deterrence, brought an ephemeral sense of security but not peace. It is time, as Singh said in 2008, 'Peace has to be given a chance in shaping future paradigms.'[8]

India is best endowed to bring renewed focus to this thought process as the driver of conduct of inter-state relations. Cooperative security, in place of the current competitive security, is needed to meet the many challenges of the twenty-first century. Can nations bring themselves to rise above existing paradigms of security to envision a different world order premised on cooperation and the objective of peace rather than security? Can we at least begin to talk, write and debate the contours of a post-nuclear world so that its appeal and advantages can begin to pervade wider spaces – geographical, and of the mind. And as mindsets change, so will the reality of the day. This is a fact proven in history and the abolition of well entrenched systems such as slavery and apartheid bear testimony to this.

Raising its voice over the cacophony of realism, India must remind the world that the right route to collective survival lies in a world order based on the principles of coexistence, non-use of force, non-intervention in the internal affairs of others and the right of every state to pursue its path of development. These principles, in fact, are enshrined in the UN Charter, but appear to have faded from immediate consciousness. India must help revive their importance in the present moment if the world is to be stopped from sliding into a realist's vision of 'nasty, brutish and short', for any use of nuclear weapons would certainly make it so.

India's Proposed Pathways to NWFW

In October 2006, India presented a Working Paper at the UNGA that encapsulated a set of proposals that could lead to the elimination of nuclear weapons. These included:

- Reaffirm the unequivocal commitment by all NWS to the complete elimination of nuclear weapons;
- Reduce the salience of nuclear weapons in security doctrines;
- Reduce nuclear danger, including the risk of accidental nuclear war, by de-alerting nuclear weapons to prevent unintentional or accidental use of nuclear weapons;
- Negotiate a global agreement among NWS on NFU of nuclear weapons;
- Negotiate a universal and legally binding agreement on non-use of nuclear weapons against NNWS;
- Negotiate a convention on the complete prohibition of the use or threat of use of nuclear weapons; and
- Negotiate a Nuclear Weapons Convention prohibiting the development, production, stockpiling and use of nuclear weapons and on their time-bound destruction, leading to the global, non-discriminatory and verifiable elimination of nuclear weapons.

As is evident, India's articulation of nuclear disarmament is anchored in the eventual conclusion of a Nuclear Weapons Convention akin to the CWC and BWC that would be uniformly applicable to all nations and have the necessary provisions for verification of compliance. Clearly, this objective cannot be achieved in one leap. The entrenched mindsets and logistic complexity of the task of achieving an NWFW make it impossible to expect that all countries would at some fortuitous dawn see sense in arriving at a comprehensive treaty on nuclear abolition. En route to such a world, several smaller steps as part of a process will have to be taken, in a spirit of sincerity and mutual confidence. Any half-hearted measures that reveal a lack of commitment would do more harm than good to the cause of disarmament by eroding faith in the feasibility of the exercise for the future.

The paper suggests urgent and immediate action on two fronts whose successful conclusion has the highest chance of getting to disarmament by loosening the hold of nuclear weapons over national security: first, target nuclear doctrines to reduce the role of nuclear weapons; and second, work towards the conclusion of a universal NFU treaty. This is not to suggest that these are the only steps that need to be taken. But, movement on these would certainly help to create an environment in which more will be possible.

Relook at Nuclear Doctrines to Narrow Down the Role of Nuclear Weapons

Countries have accorded many varied roles for their nuclear weapons. For instance, countries use them to offset conventional inferiority (Russia and Pakistan), to deter chemical and biological weapons (the US, Russia, France and India), to guard against regime change (North Korea and China), to retain prestige and status (the UK and France), and to deter interference in the conduct of their foreign policy (Russia and China). A belief in multi-purpose utility of nuclear weapons, beyond its primary purpose of nuclear deterrence, adds to their appeal and desire for holding on to them.

However, the ongoing Russia-Ukraine conflict is a good study to understand the role of nuclear weapons and their limitations. Though it would be premature to make any definitive pronouncements since the war is still on, but as of now two aspects certainly stand out: the first is the political value of nuclear deterrence. Russia used nuclear threats as soon as it started its military operations to deter the US/NATO from interfering. Moscow's repeated recall of its nuclear capability has deterred the West from providing all the weapons that Ukraine has demanded. Clearly, nuclear weapons play a role in constraining the nature and scope of conflict; second, the efficacy of nuclear weapons as militarily usable instruments is questionable. Despite possessing a large nuclear arsenal, Moscow has not brought nuclear weapons into play even in the face of significant losses. In fact, even 'TNW', which have often been touted as *the* weapons to 'escalate to de-escalate' have not been used. This casts doubts on how to use nuclear weapons to achieve a meaningful politico-military outcome.

Therefore, the only credible role of nuclear weapons is to deter nuclear use. If the nuclear doctrines of the NWS could at least start curtailing the role of nuclear weapons to the basic purpose of nuclear deterrence alone, then over time, the attraction of nuclear weapons would reduce, enabling their proscription and eventual renunciation.

Acceptance of NFU to Restrict Circumstances of Use of Nuclear Weapons

While limiting the role of nuclear weapons to dealing with only nuclear contingencies would provide credible Nuclear Security Assurance to NNWS, accepting NFU would further reduce the possibility of their use against NWS too. Therefore, the adoption of NFU can be a crucial step towards reducing salience of nuclear weapons since it would involve an assurance from every country that it would not be the first to introduce nuclear weapons into a conflict. Since there will not be a first, it would effectively mean no use of the nuclear weapon.

This would lessen the drive of each NWS for new and modernized nuclear arsenals and thus lower inter-state tensions. Even if NFU would allow the NWS to retain the notional sense of security that they derive from their national nuclear arsenals, an agreement to renounce first use would reduce danger. Gradually, the desire to even retain, or improve an unusable weapon would lessen, making it easier to give it up. Therefore, this step would work towards enhancing the gradual irrelevance of the nuclear weapon.

Of course, there are critics of the NFU who dismiss it as nothing more than a declaratory policy that would mean little once hostilities break out between nuclear nations. Such criticism, however tends to overlook some facts. First, that the adoption of NFU automatically translates into a nuclear force posture and deployment pattern that, as different from first use doctrines, does not adopt launch on warning or launch under attack postures. NFU also allows for greater response time for the self and a more relaxed posture for the adversary. Therefore, acceptance of NFU can allow nations to adopt de-alerting, de-mating and de-targeting – steps that can reduce risks of inadvertent escalation. This would not only reduce the dangers of an accidental launch of nuclear weapons, but also heighten the chances of no use of nuclear weapons by granting legitimacy to a norm of non-use. Even if declaratory, such positions have an impact on strategy and psychology of the conduct of war.

It may be recalled that India has annually tabled at the UNGA since 1982, a draft Resolution entitled 'Convention on the Prohibition of the Use of Nuclear Weapons'. This resolution aims at prohibiting the use or threat of use of nuclear weapons *under any circumstances*, a step that can substantially reduce the prospect of nuclear use and contribute towards the creation of a climate for a subsequent agreement on the prohibition of nuclear weapons in *toto*. In case every nation has the assurance that it will not be subject to the use of nuclear weapons, or threat of their use to exert pressure, intimidate or indulge in blackmail, the temptation to acquire the same would be curbed since most nations decide to go down the nuclear path only for the purpose of self-defence. The Resolution introduced by India has, nevertheless, been consistently opposed by NATO and European states.

Moving Forward

Nuclear disarmament has eluded mankind from the time when the scope and intensity of the problem was far lesser than what it has acquired today. Complete elimination has often been dismissed as unattainable unless war as a means of settling disputes between states is first abolished and a state of general and complete disarmament is enforced through a system of world governance. Since the attainment of these pre-requisites appears utopian, nuclear disarmament too tends to be dismissed as unattainable. But, simple and easily implementable steps to devalue nuclear weapons in national doctrines and mindsets can possibly lead to universal nuclear disarmament.

India must not opt to sit on the sidelines or dismiss the process because of cynicism based on its experience of non-interest in its initiatives of the past. Prudence demands that the country proactively participate in the ongoing debates to shape the discourse as it desires and serve as a bridge on divisive issues. In case something worthwhile does fructify from this churning, it would be a gain for India's national security. In case the attempts fizzle out, as many have done in the past, India would have still gained by maintaining its credibility as a sincere aspirant of universal nuclear disarmament and a responsible member of the international community. India's Defence Minister, V.K. Krishna Menon had said before the UNGA in 1953, 'Disarmament is a matter for all nations, great or small, in whatever continent they may be and in whatever climate....'[9]

Seven decades later, in his address at the UNGA, India's present EAM mentioned that today's India is willing to take on greater responsibilities because it 'believes that national good and global good can be entirely in harmony'.[10] As powerful nations of the world appear to move away from their nuclear responsibilities, India today has the capacity and sagacity to step up and make the case for ridding the world of the risk of nuclear war. India has the locus standi to play a role in stirring issues on nuclear disarmament and claim the status of a Vishwa guru that Prime Minister Modi believes India has the capability to be.

It would be in India's interest from the military and political point of view, if it could trigger and support nuclear disarmament discussions once again. Nuclear restraint and responsibility that India has shown in force structure and posture, role of the weapon, and circumscribing circumstances of its use can be a model for emulation by other NWS. If nuclear possessors could agree to subscribe to even this much as a first step, it would temper down the nuclear heat and prepare the world for taking next steps towards nuclear disarmament. Indeed, nuclear India @ 25 has much to offer the world.

NOTES

1 The last such initiative that India championed was at the 1988 third Special Session on Disarmament when then Prime Minister Rajiv Gandhi had presented an elaborate, three-phase Action Plan for a Nuclear Weapons Free World (NWFW) to be obtained by 2010, each phase covering one decade. For the action plan see Manpreet Sethi, ed., *Towards a Nuclear Weapons Free World*, Knowledge World, New Delhi, 2009, Appendix 1, pp. 151-156.

2 António Guterres, at https://www.un.org/sg/en/content/sg/speeches/2022-09-26/secretary-generals-remarks-for-the-international-day-for-the-total-elimination-of-nuclear-weapons, 2022. (Accessed 10 April 2023).

3 Brad Roberts, 'Asia's Major Powers and the Emerging Challenges to Nuclear

Stability among them', Institute for Defence Analyses, Paper no. P-4423, February 2009, pp. S-1.

4 Richard Falk and David Krieger, *The Path to Zero: Dialogues on Nuclear Dangers,* Routledge, New York, 2012, p. 38

5 For more on Pakistan's nuclear doctrine see Manpreet Sethi, 'Pakistan's Nuclear Doctrine and Strategy', *Air Power Journal,* 2(3), July-September, 2007.

6 International Commission on Nuclear Non-proliferation and Disarmament, 2009, *Eliminating Nuclear Threats: A Practical Agenda for Global Policy Makers,* p. 204. at http://www.icnnd.org/reference/reports/ent/index.html. (Accessed 29 September 2022).

7 Ibid, p. 205.

8 Jasjit Singh, 'Introductory Remarks to the New Delhi Conference', in Manpreet Sethi (ed.), *Towards a Nuclear Weapon Free World,* Knowledge World, New Delhi, 2009, p. xvi.

9 As cited in A.K. Chopra, *India's Policy on Disarmament,* ABC Publishing House, New Delhi, 1984, p. 3.

10 Shubhajit Roy, "World needs to hear reason, experience goodwill, India willing & able on both: EAM Jaishankar at UNGA", *Indian Express,* New Delhi, 25 September 2022.

8

The Role of Nuclear Energy in Achieving Net Zero Target

R.B. Grover

Introduction

Energy is a necessary input for the economic growth and improvement in the quality of life of the citizens of a country. Energy use in India has been steadily growing and the CAGR of year-wise energy consumption between 2012-13 and 2021-22 was 2.94 per cent.[1] In terms of end-user convenience, electricity is the best carrier of energy. Electricity generated by utilities and non-utilities in 2021-22 was 1720 TWh and its CAGR for the decade 2012-13 to 2021-22, was 5 per cent.[2] Energy use in India is lower than the world average and for improvement in the quality of life of the citizens, it needs to increase. The GoI, in the Nationally Determined Contributions updated in August 2022, committed to decarbonizing the energy sector by 2070.[3] Thus, on the energy front, India faces twin challenges: to decarbonize the energy sector, and to increase per capita energy consumption

Technically well-developed, commercially deployable at scale, and low-carbon energy sources are hydro, nuclear, solar, and wind. Lifecycle GHG emissions in grams of CO_2 equivalent per kWh for these technologies, are 8.1 to 147 for hydro, 5.1 to 6.4 for nuclear, 8 to

The Chapter was submitted on April 21, 2023.

83 for solar Photo-Voltaic (PV), 14 to 122 for CSP, and 7.8 to 23 for wind.[4] Most GHG emissions for renewable technologies are embodied in the infrastructure. Fossil fuels emit carbon, and technologies to capture and use or sequester the emitted carbon have been developed, but are yet to be deployed at scale. For coal, emissions vary from 751 to 1095, and when equipped with carbon capture and storage, emissions come down to 147- 469 g CO_2 equivalent per kWh, but are still higher than that from low-carbon technologies. The cost of CCUS technologies is high and needs significant improvement before they become commercially viable. The main cost driver in the CCUS value chain is the capture cost, which varies from sector to sector. They are amongst the highest for coal-based power plants due to low concentrations of CO_2 and when deployed, will have a significant influence on the electricity tariff.[5] Biomass is a renewable energy technology, but its carbon neutrality and the contribution biomass use can make towards the net-zero goal, is contentious.[6] It can take decades for trees to grow enough, to offset the carbon released from wood pellets made by cutting down trees.

The carbon flux of the bio-power generation technology will depend on the feedstock type, time frame for biomass replenishment, management and harvesting of feedstock, and the distance through which biomass is transported before use. Overall, there are "serious questions about the net life-cycle greenhouse gas benefits of biomass from both managed forests and dedicated energy crops."[7] These observations are not applicable to the use of bagasse and crop residue-based bioenergy. While they should be exploited as their use is associated with positive externalities, their potential is limited as compared to India's energy needs. Also, the burning of biomass has an adverse effect on the air quality of areas surrounding bio-power plants.

All low-carbon technologies that are commercially well-developed (hydro, nuclear, solar, and wind) generate electricity. Future developments can change this, but as of today, for reaching a net-zero energy mix, one has to plan for the deployment of hydro, nuclear, solar, and wind, and to the extent possible, the end-use sectors have to be electrified. However, in many sectors, fossil fuels also provide reducing agents (as in steel making in the blast furnace) or molecules (as in syngas), and such uses cannot be electrified. For those sectors, an alternative to the use of fossil fuels is to use hydrogen produced by low-carbon sources. Hydrogen has to be produced in electrolysers, and certain types of electrolysers (for example, alkaline) are already well-developed.

The first step in preparing for decarbonisation by 2070 is to estimate electricity needs including that for the production of hydrogen.

One such estimate was made by Rupsha Bhattacharyya et al. using the correlation between HDI and total final energy requirement.[8] The study builds several scenarios and concludes that India will need to generate 24,000 billion kWh per annum. A part of it (about 60–70 per cent) will be used as electricity and the rest for the generation of hydrogen by electrolysers. This estimate accounts for likely improvements in the efficiency of energy use, but one must note that the turnover of the existing stock to realize the benefits of efficiency improvement is a challenge for a price-sensitive market like India.

Technology development in the coming decades can make it possible to produce hydrogen using high-temperature heat from nuclear reactors or CSP plants. Nevertheless, these have to be built to provide high-temperature heat. Another study that forecasts energy requirements similar to Rupsha Bhattacharyya et al., is by the CEEW, New Delhi.[9] There are more studies, but they are based on assumptions that can be challenged.[10] To achieve the target of generating 24,000 TWh per annum by 2070, India has to maintain the present CAGR of about 5 per cent for the next five decades, and also nurture all low-carbon electricity-generating technologies.

Potential and Characteristics of Various Technology Options[11]

First, we examine the potential of solar, wind, and hydro. One optimistic estimate is by S.P. Sukhatme[12] that accounts for all solar, wind, hydro, biomass, wave, marine currents, ocean thermal, and tidal energy. According to this estimate, the total electricity generated could range from 1803.9 to 5854.6 TWh per annum, with the actual generation achieved somewhere between the two extremes. To arrive at the solar potential, Sukhatme assumed a range of areas devoted to the installation of solar PV plants, resulting in a range of generation capacities (500–2000 GW). He also assumed a very large generation capacity based on wind, an estimate at variance with the estimate by the GoI as included in the latest edition of *Energy Statistics*.[13] The GoI estimates the total solar potential as 750 GW, wind as 695 GW at a hub height of 120 metres, small hydro potential as 21 GW, and bio-energy potential as 25 GW. One can expect the solar potential to improve with technological advances resulting in increased efficiency of solar panels and that of wind due to a further increase in hub height. The large hydro-installed capacity is about 50 GW with a generation of about 160 TWh per annum. Further addition of hydro is a challenge, though there is potential for it. To decarbonize the energy sector, the total potential of hydro, solar and wind has to be exploited, but the potential is short of the projected requirements. The balance has to be met by nuclear and fossil energy with CCUS, as and when it becomes competitive.

Nuclear power generation is characterized by low carbon emissions (measured in grams of CO_2 equivalent per kWh, data given in the second paragraph), very low land use (measured in TWh/km^2, data in Table 1), and a very good safety record (measured as the

Table 1: The median land-use intensity of electricity (LUIE) showing total direct and indirect land use (ha/TWh per annum)

Energy Source	*Biomass*		*Coal*	*Gas*		*Hydro-power*	*Nuclear*	*Solar*		*Wind*	
	R	*D*		*F*	*S*			*G*	*C*	*F*	*S*
LUIE	130	58,000	1000	410	1900	650	7.1	2000	1300	130	12,000

Legend: R: Residue; D: Dedicated;F: Footprint; S: Spacing;G: Ground-mounted PV.

Notes: For gas and wind, two areas are given. The footprint area represents land directly covered by infrastructure (turbine pads and access roads for wind, and well pads, access roads, and pipelines for gas) while the spacing area is the entire area within the perimeter of a production site.

Land use for fuel sourcing for coal, natural gas, and biomass is a larger share of LUIE than direct land use. Indirect land use comprises over 90 per cent of total land use for natural gas, 55 per cent for coal, and over 99 per cent for dedicated biomass. For nuclear, land use for uranium mining is only 10 per cent of the total.

For further details, refer to Jessica Lovering, Marian Swain, Linus Blomqvist, and Rebecca R. Hernandez, "Land-use intensity of electricity production and tomorrow's energy landscape", *PLoS One*, 17(7): e0270155 at https://doi.org/10.1371/journal.pone.0270155 (Accessed on 18 April 2023)

Table 2: The mortality rate from accidents and air pollution per thousand TWh of energy production

Energy source	*Biomass*	*Brown coal*	*Coal*	*Gas*	*Hydro-power*	*Nuclear*	*Solar*	*Wind*
Mortality rate	4.63	32.72	24.62	2.82	1.30	0.03	0.02	0.04

Source: https://www.statista.com/statistics/494425/death-rate-worldwide-by-energy-source/ (Accessed on 18 April 2023).

mortality rate per TWh, data in Table 2).[14,15] Nuclear power plants operate at high capacity factors which makes nuclear power dispatchable (thereby providing firmness to the grid) and also results in lower transmission costs. Nuclear power can also be used to generate low-carbon hydrogen, using electrolysers. High-temperature reactors, when developed, can be used to provide high-temperature heat for the thermo-chemical splitting of water to generate hydrogen. Nuclear power plants normally operate at fixed power to provide baseload, while some designs of nuclear power plants can be operated flexibly, to respond to demand variation. However, as the demand for low-carbon hydrogen increases, electrolysers powered from the grid can be used to shape demand so that there is no need to flex nuclear power plants or curtail renewable power.[16]

Prior to the advent of renewable sources of energy, the metric LCOE generation was devised to compare various technology options having different life spans. Since intermittency was not a characteristic of any of the sources at that time, the metric LCOE has no parameter to account for intermittency. Even after the advent of renewable sources, energy professionals have continued to use this metric, resulting in the narrative that solar and wind are competitive.[17] Between the generators and consumers of electricity lies the transmission and distribution system, also called the grid. The grid controller has to ensure that electricity demand and supply always match and this leads to system costs. With the increasing penetration of variable solar and wind, consumers demanding reliable round-the-clock electricity supply, and the demand profile varying according to the time of the day and the season, the system cost is increasing.

The cost becomes exorbitant when the level of penetration of renewables in the grid becomes high. This has been highlighted in several studies and also from experiences in the recent past. Here, relevant studies are reviewed that consider the necessity of having firm low-carbon electricity sources as a part of the electricity grid. To start with, one needs clarity on the terminology used to refer to various generation sources. Building on the classification by N.A. Sepulveda et al,[18] by integrating what has been left out, the following classification is presented for low-carbon technologies.

(1) *VRE resources:* These include run-of-river hydropower,[19] solar PV, concentrating solar power without storage, and wind power.

(2) *Storage, balancing, and demand-shaping technologies:* These technologies are key to integrating intermittent VRE and include short-duration energy storage as in Li-ion batteries, synchronous condensers, long-duration storage as in PHS, demand-shaping technologies such as vehicle-to-grid technologies and electrolysers for producing hydrogen, or price-responsive demand-shaping by deploying smart meters, geographical aggregation by grid extension over a large area, etc. Technologies such as battery storage are energy-constrained, and their future role depends on steep price reductions and the continued availability of critical materials. The dispatchable load provided by hydrogen electrolysers has good potential and also provides green hydrogen, but price reduction is key to their large-scale deployment. All technologies in this category add to costs, but are necessary for large-scale deployment of VRE resources.

(3) *Firm low-carbon resources:* These technologies can meet demand during all seasons, over long durations, and some can even flex in response to demand. These include nuclear power plants (which may or may not be capable of flexible operation), hydroelectric plants with high-capacity reservoirs, coal and natural gas plants with CCUS and capable of flexible operations, biomass, and biogas fuelled plants, and geothermal power. These plants provide power at all times,

> except when they are under maintenance and repair. The scheduled maintenance period of firm low-carbon plants is known well in advance.

Sepulveda et al.[20] analysed two US regions, a northern system with modest renewable resource potential (New England) and a southern system having a significant renewable resource (Texas). The study concluded that firm low-carbon resources contributed to containing the overall cost of decarbonisation even in regions with abundant renewable resources. It reported that "in the absence of firm low-carbon resources, affordable decarbonisation of the power sector would simultaneously require further steep reductions in the cost of VRE and battery storage technologies, significantly over-sizing installed capacity relative to peak demand, significantly greater demand flexibility, and expansion of long-distance transmission capacity connecting wide geographical regions." The study did not model technologies capable of long-term storage, such as PHS that can moderate the cost of integrating VRE. It advocated greater public support for firm low-carbon sources.

The study by Jane C.S. Long et al.[21] focused on California, and arrived at similar conclusions. Three groups were convened to model California's energy system and despite distinct approaches to the calculations, all the models concluded that "solar and wind can't do the job". The study referred to a large-scale weather pattern extending over large geographical areas and driving out solar and wind. It concluded, "If wind and solar are pushed to do all the heavy lifting themselves, the system requires enormous excess generating capacity and storage (most of which is seldom used) to provide reliable electricity and completely drive out greenhouse emissions. The strategy is much more expensive and demanding of land and infrastructure than other possible pathways." Finally, the study recommended developing clean firm power by saying that "Nuclear power can steadily provide very large amounts of energy in a small footprint."

The relationship between electricity supply and demand in low-carbon systems was analysed by the IEA.[22] The analysis revealed that due to the presence of VRE, multiple services are needed to provide electricity reliably, and these include "meeting peak capacity requirements, keeping the power system stable during short-term disturbances, and having enough flexibility to ramp [it] up and down in response to changes in supply or demand". The IEA study quantified the energy and service contribution of different technologies to maintain electricity security in China in the *Announced Pledges Scenarios, 2060*. While VRE majorly contributes to energy, contribution to system stability comes from firm power sources, namely nuclear and abated thermal. The contribution of VRE to even the peak capacity is much less than its contribution to energy. Using Monte Carlo assessments to simulate the power system under many possible conditions, analysis by IEA captured aspects like the amount of load not served or frequency of the unserved load. The analysis concluded that "Maintaining operational security requires both system stability – supported by power system inertia and operating reserves – and the flexibility to ramp up and down to maintain a balance between supply and demand". VRE doesn't provide system inertia, flexing, or operating reserves (at all times).

Global Scenario Regarding New Nuclear Build

Overall studies such as by Lei Duan et al. have come to the conclusion that deep decarbonisation cannot be provided by solar and wind alone, and firm power sources like nuclear are necessary.[23] It is particularly so for countries that are not endowed with high-capacity wind energy sources. This conclusion is embedded in the plans being unveiled by different countries. System-level modelling studies done in the US suggest that the US would need significantly more firm capacity to reach net zero. According to a USDOE Report, limitations on renewable buildout estimates "come from current understanding of land-use intensity, regional siting requirements, supply chain, transmission, and interconnection difficulties that increasingly impact utility-scale deployment."[24] The Report opines that achieving net zero in the US would require approximately 550-770 GW of additional clean, firm capacity, and out of that, nuclear has to be about 200 GW. This is in addition to 100 GW of nuclear already in operation.

The UK envisages increasing deployment of civil nuclear to up to 24GW by 2050 – three times more than at present and representing up to 25 per cent of the projected electricity demand in the country. This could involve constructing up to eight more large reactors and also financial support to develop SMRs in partnership with Rolls Royce.[25] France has announced a programme for the construction of six large reactors by 2035 and to consider building a further eight, and is developing NUWARD, an SMR[26] at the same time.

Russia and China are moving forward to ensure that nuclear power has an expanded role in their energy mix and are developing advanced reactor technologies. However, consolidated reports outlining their low-carbon strategy like those from the US, France, and the UK are not available from them. Many countries in Europe and elsewhere have firmed up plans to add nuclear. For example, the Netherlands has announced plans to build two new nuclear units, and Finland has five operating units and has announced plans to add one more to take the nuclear contribution to about 60 per cent. The website of the World Nuclear Association provides country-wise details of the status of nuclear power.

Status of Nuclear Power Development in India

PHWR Programme

Decisions taken during the early days of the nuclear power programme in India included the pursuit of a closed fuel cycle, the selection of PHWRs as the reactor system for implementation, exemplary stress on nuclear safety, and the indigenization of the complete fuel cycle. In the beginning, several 220 MW PHWRs were set up, and then the capacity was raised to 540 MW. NPCIL has acquired experience in designing, constructing, operating, and aging management of PHWRs, and equipment manufacturing capability has been established in the country. Based on this capability, a state-of-the-art 700 MW PHWR was designed and the first such unit has been connected to the grid. Being the FOAK unit, it did have some teething troubles, but they have been addressed and the power is being raised in a step-by-step manner. As on 21 April 2023, it is working at 60 per cent power and the power will be raised gradually in consultation with the AERB. B.C. Pathak et al.[27] provide all details of this reactor system and a passage quoted here *in extenso* informs its important features.

The following distinguishing features make the 700 MW PHWR worthy of being replicated to enhance nuclear-installed capacity in India:

- Improved layout features such as interleaving of feeders to improve safety.
- Advanced control systems.
- Introduction of a MTM[28] to handle higher fuelling requirements.
- Improved containment features, including a steel lining that eliminates the need for evacuation even in an extreme emergency.
- Incorporation of systems to handle severe events postulated as part of the design.

To increase capacity addition through these units, the measures incorporated include standardized layout and design leaving re-engineering and qualification limited to site-specific inputs; standardization of safety analysis and procurement specifications and adoption of bulk procurement for multiple units. Experience indicates that it will be possible for NPCIL to construct 700 MW PHWRs at Rs 15 crores per MW – a globally competitive cost. Considering the competitive cost and advanced safety features, and the fact that more than 95 per cent of equipment and components are manufactured in India, several 700 MW PHWRs should be constructed to achieve the target of a net-zero energy mix by 2070.

While the first 700 MW unit has been connected to the grid, three more units are in an advanced stage of construction. Pre-project activities are ongoing for two more units. In 2017, NPCIL obtained sanction for constructing ten more units in fleet mode. The supply chain within the country for 700 MW units has been established and bulk procurement activities are in progress.

Simultaneously with the development of reactors, fuel cycle facilities have also been developed. Exploration for uranium is done by the Atomic Minerals Directorate for Exploration and Research, mining by the UCIL, fuel fabrication by the Nuclear Fuel Complex, heavy water production by the Heavy Water Board, and fuel reprocessing and waste management by the Nuclear Recycle Board (it is a part of BARC). While mining by UCIL is limited by the extent of domestic uranium reserves, the capacities for fuel fabrication, heavy water production, and spent fuel reprocessing can be expanded to match the demand, as the necessary technologies have been developed indigenously.

Light Water Reactor Programme

To speed up nuclear power addition, it was decided to set up large light water reactors in technical collaboration with foreign vendors; two 1000 MW reactors are already operating at Kudankulam in Tamil Nadu. Four more are under construction at the same site.

Dialogue is also ongoing with vendors from France and the US to set up light water reactors, but the progress is slow.

Light water reactors have higher burn-up as compared to PHWRs. This reduces the tonnage of fuel to be reprocessed, but the technology for reprocessing high burn-up fuel is yet to be demonstrated at scale in India.

SMRs

In the case of SMRs, capital investment per reactor is low, but to start with, capital investment per MW will be high. It might improve after several units have been constructed. Their economic competitiveness, at this stage, is an expectation. For example, a Report by DOE, USA states,[29]

To unlock deployment at scale, NOAK advanced nuclear overnight capital costs may need to approach ~$3,600 per kW. While the estimated FOAK cost of a well-executed nuclear construction project is ~\$6,200 per kW, recent nuclear construction projects in the US have had overnight capital costs over \$10,000 per kW. Delivering FOAK projects without cost overrun would require investment in extensive upfront planning to ensure the lessons learned from recent nuclear project overruns are incorporated. Subsequent nuclear projects would be expected to come down the cost curve to ~\$3,600 per kW after 10-20 deployments depending on learning rate; this cost reduction would largely be driven by workforce learnings and industrial base scale-up.

Therefore, at this stage, SMRs are being considered as an addition to deploying large reactors. A programme to develop SMRs has been initiated in India as well and they will be useful for deployment at places like Andaman and Nicobar Islands. As their economic viability gets proved in the future, they can be deployed at scale. Though the IAEA limits the definition of SMRs to those having an electric power output of less than 300 MW, Rolle Royce has proposed a design having a power output of 470 MW. GE Hitachi has developed BWRX, a 300 MW Boiling Water Reactor. Natrium, a 345 MWe sodium-cooled fast neutron reactor, is being developed by TerraPower and GE Hitachi. These larger units have a higher probability of achieving commercial success.

SMR designers have to demonstrate the effectiveness of fundamental safety functions so that the likelihood of occurrence of an accident with serious radiological consequences is very low and the radiological consequences in the event of such an unlikely accident should be practically eliminated. Nuclear waste generation from SMRs vis-a-vis large reactors also needs examination. Relative to a large reactor, neutron leakage is higher in the SMR core reducing fuel burnup. An analysis of three distinct SMR designs shows that relative to GW-scale PWR, these reactors will have higher spent nuclear fuel arising per MWh and larger amounts of nuclear waste.[30] This needs further studies to ensure that planning for SMRs addresses this aspect.

Depending upon the design of the SMR selected, the corresponding reprocessing technology also needs to be developed.

Manpower Development

Regarding manpower development in the nuclear field, India has a very good track record. A Training School was started in the Atomic Energy Establishment (now BARC) in 1957 as a non-formal programme to train manpower for the nuclear sector. In 2005, with the setting up of the Homi Bhabha National Institute (a deemed-to-be-university), the Training School programme has been converted to coursework for an M.Tech programme.[31]

During the initial years, NPCIL was drawing trained manpower from the BARC Training School. In view of its large manpower requirements, it has started its own Training Schools. Branches of the training school have also been established at units other than BARC. The intake capacity of training schools can be scaled up to match the demand.

A unique feature of the training school is its hidden curriculum. Every Institute has an explicit curriculum that is written down and taught to students on a formal basis. However, a student imbibes certain values and culture as he/she passes through the corridors of the Institute, interacts with faculty and senior students, and debates with fellow students on issues confronting them. The hidden curriculum of the training school inculcates respect for nuclear safety and a striving for indigenisation among all students. Anyone who wants to take up nuclear power plant construction and operation in India has to imbibe the nuclear safety culture. Also, India is able to build nuclear power reactors at a competitive cost as the supply chain has been indigenised.

Governance Framework

A framework for the governance of nuclear power has been established in India. This includes the Atomic Energy Act, 1962 and rules thereunder. The AERB has been constituted under the Atomic Energy Act and has evolved into an internationally recognised professional organisation.

India has served on the Board of Governors of the IAEA since its inception. It is a part of several international Conventions like the Convention on Early Notification of a Nuclear Accident, the

Convention on Assistance in the Case of a Nuclear Accident or Radiological Emergency, the CNS, the Convention on Physical Protection of Nuclear Material and its 2005 amendment, and implements the IAEA code of conduct on the safety and security of radioactive materials.

Expanding nuclear power, particularly siting of nuclear reactors near international boundaries, prompted India to enact the Civil Liability for Nuclear Damage Act in 2010. Its feature regarding the liability of suppliers is unique as compared to liability acts of other nations which had to be explained to suppliers.[32] India has also signed the Convention on Supplementary Compensation for Nuclear Damage.

In the implementation of nuclear power and non-power applications, India strives to achieve the highest standards of radiation and nuclear safety, based on a scientific approach, operating experience, and best practices followed by the nuclear industry. It also ensures that the use of radiation and atomic energy in all its applications is safe for the health of radiation workers, members of the public, property and the environment. India is pursuing a closed fuel cycle to minimise nuclear waste requiring deep geological disposal, extract maximum power per tonne of nuclear fuel, and enable the use of thorium for power generation. All this is embedded in publications and speeches by Homi Bhabha, the first Chairman of the AEC, and it is desirable that these be issued as policy statements by the DAE.

Role of Hydrogen

In a deep decarbonisation scenario, hydrogen will have a crucial role. Bhattacharyya et al.[33] estimate that about 30 to 40 per cent of final energy consumption in net-zero India in 2070 may be in the form of low-carbon hydrogen. Several countries including India have come up with policies or plans to promote the use of hydrogen in the industry as a substitute for fossil fuels. The US is promoting nuclear hydrogen, and a demonstration facility to produce hydrogen from the electricity from the Nine Mile Point Nuclear Station in New York is already in operation since February this year. This is one of the four projects supported by the US DOE to demonstrate clean hydrogen production at nuclear power plants.[34]

After a debate, the EU has reached a compromise that includes counting hydrogen generated by nuclear power as low-carbon, as part of separate targets for renewable hydrogen used by industry.[35] The UK is moving in the direction of including nuclear in its green taxonomy.

India has also announced a National Hydrogen Mission for the production of hydrogen from renewable energy, but the plan is silent about nuclear hydrogen. Considering the scarcity of low-carbon energy options, it is desirable for India to follow a technology-agnostic policy when it comes to low-carbon initiatives. This has already been laid out by India in many policy documents by including "non-fossil energy" sources, and should be done for low-carbon hydrogen as well.

Future Directions

Several factors make it necessary to look at nuclear energy as an essential part of India's energy mix. India has land use constraints because of its high population density. Large land areas cannot be diverted for use for locating solar PV or for cultivation of energy crops. Wind resources in India are limited. India has exploited 29 per cent of the total hydro potential and further 10.3 per cent is under construction. Exploitation of the remaining potential is a challenge.[36] As stated earlier, studies have shown that deep decarbonisation cannot be provided by solar and wind alone, and it is necessary to have firm low-carbon sources like nuclear and coal with CCUS as a part of the energy mix. Assuming that 20 to 30 per cent of the electricity generation target (24,000 TWh per annum) has to be provided by nuclear energy and nuclear power plants operate at a capacity factor of 85 per cent, India would need nuclear-installed capacity in the range of 650 to 1000 GW by 2070. This number might come down if energy efficiency improvements are more than what has been assumed by Rupsha Bhattacharyya et al.[37] in arriving at the figure for target generation, and India's success in making 'LIFE' – 'Lifestyle for Environment' – a mass movement. Even after providing 20 to 30 per cent by nuclear, one question remains: wherefrom will India get what cannot be provided by renewables and nuclear? To get the balance, research and development for deployment of CCUS at scale needs to be accelerated.

To implement a large nuclear power programme, India has to deploy PHWRs, light water reactors as well as SMRs. The sanction obtained by NPCIL in 2017 for the construction of ten 700 MW PHWRs in fleet mode was a step in the right direction and was a signal to equipment suppliers in India to be ready to execute orders. It demonstrated India's commitment to nuclear power. Now that the first unit of 700 MW is close to reaching full power, sites for setting up sanctioned 700 MW PHWRs have been selected and in most cases acquired, the GoI should consider mandating NPCIL to start work on one or two additional fleets. Simultaneously, the development of fast reactor technology needs to be expedited and new reactor concepts such as molten salt breeder reactors, need to be developed.

Looking at the larger role to be played by nuclear power, public sector undertakings other than NPCIL are looking forward to setting up nuclear power plants. Therefore, the policy statements referred to in the previous section should be issued by the Department of Atomic Energy and the regulatory framework strengthened as necessary.

Considering that India is a country with a high-density of population and cannot divert large tracts of land for solar and wind, and has limited sources for generating hydropower, it is desirable that all low-carbon technology options be pursued based on policies that are technology-agnostic and provide a level playing field. Without nuclear, achieving a net zero energy mix by 2070 will not be affordable.

Epilogue

By the beginning of this century, India had mastered PHWR technology and the associated fuel cycle, established the supply chain in the country, and acquired operating experience. The 540 MW reactors at Tarapur were constructed within budget and as per schedule. However, all operating reactors were working at low-capacity factors due to the non-availability of domestic uranium, and it was not possible for India to buy uranium from the international market due to the then-prevailing guidelines of the NSG. However, in 2008, the NSG relaxed its guidelines to facilitate civil nuclear trade with India. Since then, India has been importing uranium for its reactors under safeguards by IAEA. The agreement to construct four additional reactors at Kudankulam was signed only after the relaxation of guidelines. The relaxation of NSG Guidelines to facilitate civil nuclear trade was a diplomatic triumph for India based on its strength in science.[38] I have always wondered: would this have been possible if the *Shakti* series of tests had not taken place?

NOTES

1 *Energy Statistics India – 2023*, Ministry of Statistics and Programme Implementation.
2 Ibid.
3 "India's updated first nationally determined contribution under Paris Agreement, (2021-2030)", August 2022 submission to UNFCCC, GoI.
4 "Carbon Neutrality in the UNECE Region: Integrated Life-cycle Assessment of Electricity Sources", United Nations Economic Commission for Europe, 2022.
5 Atanu Mukherjee and Saurav Chatterjee, "Carbon capture, utilization and storage (CCUS): Policy framework and its deployment mechanism in India", *NITI Aayog*, 2022.
6 K. Bracmort, "Is biopower carbon neutral?", Congressional Research Service, R41603, 2016.
7 J.D. Jenkins, Max Luke, and Samuel Thernstrom, "Getting to Zero Carbon Emissions in the Electric Sector", 2 July 2018, pp.2487-2510.
8 R. Bhattacharyya, K.K. Singh, R.B. Grover and K. Bhanja, "Estimating Minimum Energy Requirement for Transitioning to a Net-zero, Developed India in 2070", *Current Science*, 122(5), 2022, pp. 517–527.
9 V. Chaturvedi and A. Malyan, "Implications of a Net-zero Target for India's Sectoral Energy Transitions and Climate Policy", Working Paper by Council on Energy, Environment and Water, New Delhi, October 2021.
10 R.B. Grover, "Need for Evaluation of Near-term Energy Transition Policies of India Based on Contributions to Long-term Decarbonization Goals", *Current Science*, 123(11), 2022, pp.1309–1316.
11 This section is based on a paper by the author cited at no. 10.
12 S.P. Sukhatme, "Can India's Future Needs of Electricity be Met by Renewable Energy Sources? A Revised Assessment", *Current Science*, 103(10), 2012, pp. 1153–1161.
13 *Energy Statistics India – 2023*, no. 1.
14 B.W. Brook and C.J.A. Bradshaw, "Key Role for Nuclear Energy in Global Biodiversity Conservation", *Conservation Biology*, 29(3), 2014, pp. 702-712.
15 US DOE, "Pathways to Commercial Liftoff: Advanced Nuclear", March 2023.
16 R.B. Grover, no. 10.
17 R.B. Grover, "An Examination of the Narratives about the Electricity Sector", *Current Science*, 119(12), 2020, pp. 1910-1918.
18 N.A. Sepulveda, J.D. Jenkins, F.J. de Sistemes and R.K. Lester, "The Role of Firm

Low-carbon Electricity Resources in Deep Decarbonization of Power Generation", 2 July 2018, pp. 2403–2420.

19 In case of some run of river projects, limited storage, for up to 24 hours, is available.

20 N.A. Sepulveda, J.D. Jenkins, F.J. de Sistemes and R.K. Lester, no. 18.

21 C.S. Jane Ejeong Baik Long, Jesse D. Jenkins, Clea Kolster, Kiran Chawla, Arne Olson, Armond Cohen, Michael Colvin, Sally M. Benson, Robert B. Jackson, David G. Victor, Steven P. Hamburg, "Clean Firm Power is the Key to California's Carbon-free Energy Future", *Issues in Science and Technology*, 2021, at https://issues.org/california-decarbonizing-power-wind-solar-nuclear-gas/ (Accessed 15 April 2023).

22 International Energy Agency. "Energy Transitions Require Innovation in Power System Planning" at https://www.iea.org/articles/energy-transitions-require-innovation-in-power-system-planning (Accessed 15 August 2022).

23 Lei Duan, Robert Petroski, Lowell Wood, Ken Caldeira, "Stylized Least-cost Analysis of Flexible Nuclear Power in Deeply Decarbonized Electricity Systems Considering Wind and Solar Resources Worldwide", *Nature Energy*, 7, March 2022, pp 260-269.

24 US DOE, "Pathways to Commercial Liftoff: Advanced Nuclear", no. 15.

25 "Policy paper on British Energy Security Strategy", at https://www.gov.uk/government/publications/british-energy-security-strategy/british-energy-security-strategy#nuclear (Accessed 27 February 2023).

26 "Nuclear power in France", at https://world-nuclear.org/information-library/country-profiles/countries-a-f/france.aspx (Accessed 28 March 2023).

27 B.C. Pathak, C.P. Kaushik, K.N. Vyas and R.B. Grover, "The Status of Nuclear Power Development in India", *Current Science*, 123(3), 2022, pp.281-292.

28 Mobile Transfer Machine.

29 US DOE, "Pathways to Commercial Liftoff: Advanced Nuclear", no. 15.

30 L.M. Krall, A.M. McFarlane, and R.C. Ewing, "Nuclear waste from small modular reactors", Proceedings of National Academy of Sciences, 119 (23), 2022, e2111833119.

31 R.B. Grover, A.P. Tiwari, and P.R. Vasudeva Rao, "From the Atomic Energy Training School to the Homi Bhabha National Institute", *Current Science*, 123(3), 2022, pp. 441-450.

32 R.B. Grover, "The Civil Liability for Nuclear Damage Act of India: An Engineering Perspective Regarding Supplier's Liability", *Progress in Nuclear Energy*, (101), pp. 168-175.

33 R. Bhattacharyya, K.K. Singh, R.B. Grover and K. Bhanja, no. 8.

34 "Nine-Point Mile Begins Hydrogen Production, 7 March 2023 at https://www.energy.gov/ne/articles/nine-mile-point-begins-clean-hydrogen-production (Accessed 11 March 2023).

35 NucNet, 31 March 2023.

36 "Utilisation of Hydro Power Potential", *Ministry of Power* at https://pib.gov.in/PressReleasePage.aspx?PRID=1909276 (Accessed 22 April 2023).

37 R. Bhattacharyya, K.K. Singh, R.B. Grover and K. Bhanja, no. 8.

38 R.B. Grover, "Resumption of International Civil Nuclear Cooperation: a Diplomatic Triumph Based on Strength in Science", Science Diplomacy Case Studies No. 2, Forum for Science Diplomacy, RIS, New Delhi, 2019.

9

The Commitment to *Vasudhaiva Kutumbakam*: Peaceful and Constructive use of nuclear energy in India

K.N. Vyas and M. Ramanamurthi

Introduction

The era of science, from the late nineteenth century to mid-twentieth century, beginning with the discovery of radioactivity and culminating with the horrendous nuclear explosions over Japan, is considered by many as the Golden Age of Nuclear Physics. Despite the two world wars during this period, it saw a tremendous surge of discoveries and innovations in the field of nuclear physics, including the discovery of natural and artificial radioactivity, the structure of the atom, and the properties of subatomic particles. The works of scientists such as Becquerel, Curies, Thomson, Rutherford, Fermi, Bohr, Chadwick, Szilard, Hahn and Strassman, etc. were fundamental to our understanding of the nature of matter, energy, and the universe. Their work laid the foundation for later discoveries in nuclear transmutation, nuclear fission, and the development of nuclear power, nuclear weapons, and other practical applications of nuclear technology, which continue to have a significant impact on our lives today.

Atoms for Peace

After the devastation caused by World War II, there was growing concern about the potential dangers of nuclear weapons and the need to prevent their proliferation. The Atoms for Peace initiative was launched under the auspices of the UNGA in December 1953 to promote international cooperation on peaceful uses of nuclear energy and to control the spread of nuclear weapons. The first international conference on Peaceful Uses of Atomic Energy was held in Geneva in 1955. Homi Jehangir Bhabha (Figure 1) represented India and he was unanimously selected as Chairman of the conference. In a memorable Presidential address, Bhabha said, 'In a broad view of human history, it is possible to discern three great epochs. The first is marked by the emergence of the early civilizations in the valleys of the Euphrates, the Indus and the Nile; the second by the industrial revolution, leading to the civilization in which we live; and the third by the discovery of atomic energy and the dawn of the atomic age, which we are just entering. Each epoch marks a change in the energy pattern of society.'

Figure 1: Dr. Homi Jehangir Bhabha

The IAEA was created in 1957 as part of the Atoms for Peace initiative, with the goal of promoting the safe and peaceful use of nuclear technology and preventing the spread of nuclear weapons.

Nuclear India

Recognizing the importance of nuclear energy as a potential source of power for India's growing economy, the Indian nuclear energy programme was launched in 1948, shortly after India gained independence from British rule. The AEC was constituted in 1948 and the DAE was established in 1954. Thus began India's journey for harnessing nuclear energy and radiation technology for peaceful purposes in the areas of power production, and applications of radioisotopes in the fields of medicine, agriculture, industry and research. The programme was pioneered by Homi Jehangir Bhabha. The initial thrust to the nuclear programme was provided with the commissioning of a research reactor 'APSARA' in 1956 at Trombay, Mumbai, which was in fact the first reactor in Asia. This was followed by the second research reactor CIRUS in 1960 and a third one 'DHRUVA' in 1985 (Figure 2).

Figure 2: CIRUS and Dhruva Reactors

The CIRUS reactor has now been decommissioned after almost 50 years of operation. Parallelly, the nuclear power programme also began its journey with the establishment of the first power reactor at Tarapur in 1969. The power programme has now expanded significantly with 22 reactors being currently operational in the country and many more are under construction. Today India has the sixth largest fleet of nuclear reactors in the world and second largest fleet of reactors under construction.

Thrust Areas of the Indian Nuclear Energy Programme

In addition to the nuclear power programme, radioisotopes produced in research and power reactors have played a key role in the programmes of DAE. They are used widely in the development of applications in healthcare, agriculture, food preservation, and several other societal programmes of DAE. Numerous spin-off technologies have also emerged from the DAE centres towards urban waste management, water purification, water desalination, sewage sludge hygienization and many other applications, directly benefiting human society. These technologies are widely shared with entrepreneurs, industrial houses and government agencies, for implementation in rural and urban centres around the country, and are also shared with other countries around the world. In the next few pages, we shall be describing some of the noteworthy contributions of DAE, which serve the cause of humanity and live up to the *Vasudhaiva Kutumbakam* philosophy.

Nuclear Medicine

Nuclear medicine is a branch of medicine that uses trace amounts of radioactive substances for the diagnosis and treatment of various ailments and organs such as cancer, neurological and cardiac disorders. Nuclear medicine procedures are generally non-invasive and can diagnose abnormalities in the early stages of diseases, facilitating timely commencement of treatment.

Early History: The earliest example of the use of radiation medicine dates back to 1941 when a patient with basal cell carcinoma, a type of skin cancer, was successfully treated using Phospherous-32. The use of Phospherous-32 for skin cancer treatment was a significant breakthrough in the field of radiation therapy and helped pave the way for further research and development of other radioisotopes for medical applications.

In India, the use of nuclear medicine techniques, or radiation medicine, as it was then known, was pioneered by Lt. Col. S.K. Mazumdar, who was posted as a Specialist Medical Officer to the DSL, Delhi in August 1956. The activities started on a modest scale, with radioiodine thyroid uptake studies and blood volume estimations on the diagnostic side, and treatment of thyrotoxicosis with Iodine-131 and polycythaemia vera with Phospherous-32 on the therapeutic side.

Present Status: With increasing indigenous availability of radiopharmaceuticals, particularly after the commissioning of CIRUS and DHRUVA reactors, the scope of work has expanded considerably and millions of procedures for diagnostic and therapeutic purposes are now being carried out annually around the country using radiopharmaceuticals prepared with radio isotopes emerging from research and power reactors of DAE.

DAE is involved in the production of radiopharmaceuticals as well as the development of novel organ and disease-specific radiopharmaceuticals for improved outcomes. Table 1 lists some of the more recently developed radiopharmaceuticals that have been deployed for various treatment procedures.

India's recently commissioned medical cyclotron facility in Kolkata, Cyclone-30 has facilitated the production of cyclotron-based radioisotopes for healthcare applications. Flourine-18, a radioisotope of fluorine produced here, is used to synthesize labelled Sodium Fluoride (^{18}F-NaF), which is a radiopharmaceutical used for bone scanning applications. Bone scanning is carried out to initially diagnose benign and malignant diseases of the skeleton. A PET scan is subsequently carried out to obtain more detailed images for deciding treatment protocols.

Production and regular supply of ^{18}F-FDG, an extremely critical

Table 1: Recently Developed Radiochemicals/ Radiopharmaceuticals/ Freeze-dried Kits

Sl. No.	*Product Name*	*Application*
1	^{99m}Tc-Hynic-TOC/HYNIC-TATE	Neuroendocrine tumour imaging
2	^{99m}Tc-HSA-Nanocolloid	Detection of sentinel nodes in breast and other cancers
3	^{99m}Tc-UBI (29-41)	Infection imaging
4	^{99m}Tc-HYNIC-[cyclo(RGDfk)]$_2$	Malignant tumour imaging
5	^{18}F-FDG	Cancer diagnosis
6	Na^{18}F	Bone imaging
7	^{18}F-FLT	Tumour proliferation marker
8	^{68}Ga-DOTA-TOC/DOTA-TATE/DOTA-NOC	Neuroendocrine tumour imaging
9	^{68}Ga-PSMA-11	Prostate cancer imaging
10	^{64}CuCl$_2$	Cancer imaging and ^{64}Cu-radiopharmaceutical preparation
11	^{131}I-Lipiodol/^{188}Re-DEDC-Lipiodol	Liver cancer therapy
12	^{188}Re-HEDP/^{177}Lu-EDTMP/^{177}Lu-DOTMP	Bone pain palliation
13	^{177}Lu-DOTA-TATE	Neuroendocrine cancer therapy
14	^{177}Lu-Hydroxyapatite/^{90}Y-Hydroxyapatite	Radiation synovectomy
15	^{177}Lu-PSMA-617	Prostate cancer therapy
16	^{177}Lu-Rituximab	Therapy of Non-Hodgkin's Lymphoma
17	^{177}Lu-Trastuzumab	Breast cancer therapy
18	^{90}Y-glass microsphere (BhabhaSphere)	Treatment of liver cancer

short-lived radiopharmaceutical used in the PET detection of cancer, Gallium-68 used in Gallium-based radiochemicals such as $^{68}GaCl_3$ used for imaging of neuroendocrine cancers and prostate cancer as well as $^{201}TlCl$ for myocardial perfusion imaging studies are other examples of radioisotopes being produced in the country for the first time using this medical cyclotron.

Cancer Therapy

Radiation has the property of killing cancerous cells. Radiation therapy can be administered externally for treatment of tumours that are approachable from outside without collateral damage to healthy tissues. For the treatment of deep seated tumours as well as tumours of sensitive organs, radiation sources in sealed condition are placed closed to the location of the tumour. Some examples are described below.

A technology for cobalt teletherapy has been developed for the selective destruction of cancerous growths in tissues using external radiation from Cobalt-60, a radioactive element produced in nuclear reactors. A teletherapy machine, called Bhabhatron has been developed for this purpose, which has been deployed extensively in India and some centres abroad as well. (Figure 3)

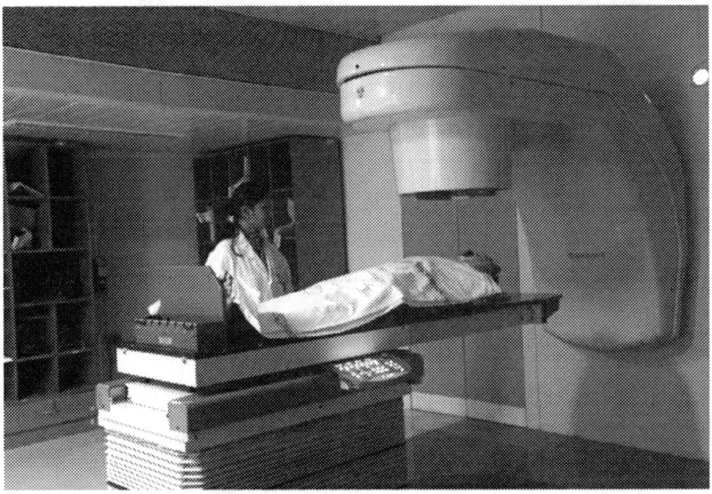

Figure 3: Bhabhatron

Ru-106 Eye Plaque for Treatment of Ocular Cancer

A recent contribution of DAE has been the development of an eye plaque for treatment of ocular cancer. Ruthenium-106, a radioisotope recovered after nuclear fission from spent fuel is integrated into circular eye plaques for use in the treatment of eye cancer. The plaques were extensively tested as per the specifications approved by the AERB and have also received endorsements through independent evaluations carried out by leading ophthalmic centres such as Dr. Rajendra Prasad Centre for Ophthalmic Sciences, All India Institute of Medical Sciences, New Delhi, Centre for Sight Hospital, Hyderabad and Sankara Eye Hospital, Bangalore. The handling of the BARC plaque during the treatment procedure was found to be surgeon-friendly and at par with international standards in all respects. Figure 4 shows the plaque, along with its specifications and the insertion procedure for treatment.

Material	**: Silver, 99.99%**
Diameter	**: 15.8 mm**
Spherical radius	**: 12 mm**
Total thickness	**: 1 mm**
Source strength	**: 300-600 μCi**
Useful life	**: 1 year**
Total No. patients can be treated	**: 50**

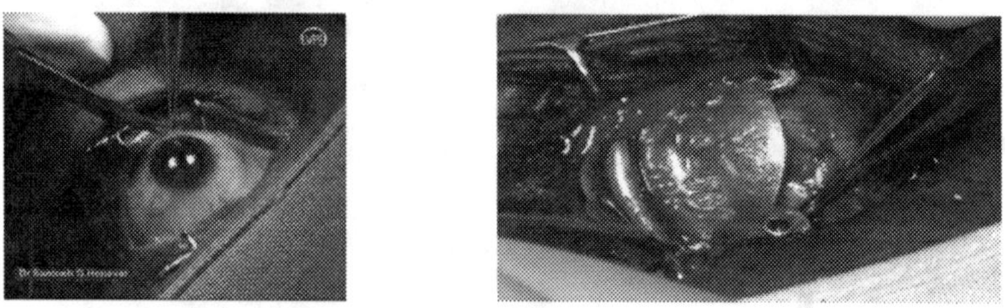

Figure 4: Ru-106 Plaques and procedure for treatment

Other Applications

Very small sized Yttrium-90 glass spheres (with a size of about 30 micro-metre, called Bhabhasphere) have been developed, which can be used for treating a specific type of liver cancer. I-131 based radiopharmaceuticals for thyroid cancer, Lu-177 based radiopharmaceuticals for treatment of neuroendocrine cancer and Sm-153 based radiopharmaceuticals for bone pain palliation are some other prominent examples.

All of these are low-cost import substitutes, costing considerably less than equivalent imported products, thereby substantially lowering the cost of treatment procedures. More than 5 lakh patients receive affordable treatment every year at Tata Memorial Centre, a constituent unit of DAE.

NCG: The NCG is a network of cancer centres and research institutions in India that collaborate to provide standardized, high-quality cancer care and treatment across the country. The NCG was established in 2012 with the aim of creating a coordinated system for cancer care that would ensure that patients receive the best possible treatment, regardless of their location or socio-economic status.

The NCG includes more than 294 cancer centres and research institutions across India, and it is supported by the DAE and the Tata Memorial Centre. The network provides a range of services to cancer patients, including diagnosis, treatment planning, and access to advanced treatments and clinical trials.

One of the key objectives of the NCG is to improve the quality of cancer care in India by promoting the use of evidence-based treatments and best practices. The network also facilitates collaboration between different cancer centres and institutions, enabling the sharing of knowledge and resources and promoting innovation and research.

The NCG is a significant initiative that is helping improve cancer care in India and promote greater collaboration and co-ordination in the fight against cancer.

Nuclear Agriculture

Biological systems continuously undergo mutations on a very slow time scale, governed by environmental conditions or on exposure to other drastic external influences. The mutations can be favourable as well as unfavourable to the system. Natural selection tends to retain the species, which have developed traits favourable to its propagation. Direct exposure to ionising radiations such as gamma rays from a radioisotope can induce accelerated mutations. BARC has an extensive programme on creating induced mutations in various crops, a technique known as mutation breeding. The method involves exposing seeds to controlled beams of gamma radiation, leading to favourable as well as unfavourable mutations in them. Seeds with desirable traits are selected and multiplied. 60 Trombay crop varieties including groundnut, rice, mustard, mung bean, cow peas, chick peas, etc., with improved characteristics like higher yield, early maturity, improved disease, draught resistance, etc., have been developed using the technique of mutation breeding and are cultivated extensively in the country (Figure 5 and Chart 1).

Figure 5: Trombay Crop Varieties

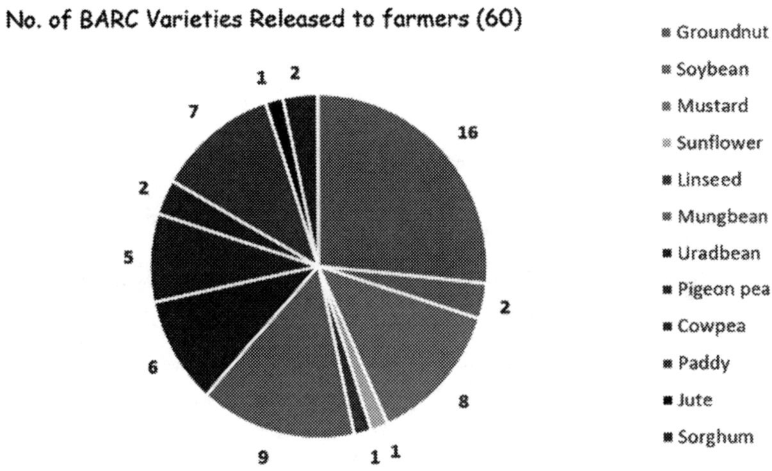

Chart 1: List of crops developed by Mutation Breeding

Food Preservation

Pest infestation, contamination and mould infestation are some of the major problems being faced by the agricultural sector, leading to substantial losses to the extent of 20-30 per cent of the produce. Prevention of post-harvest spoilage is therefore of great significance. Radiation processing provides an eco-friendly solution to this problem. The method involves exposure of food and agricultural commodities to measured doses of gamma radiation. This process results in favourable outcomes such as disinfestation of pests, delayed ripening, inhibition of sprouting and elimination of pathogens and micro-organisms causing spoilage. Radiation processing is the only method of killing pathogens in raw and frozen food. The radiation beam produces its effect by merely depositing its energy and does not lead to any radioactivity being generated in the target material. Radiation processing of food is a method approved by various organizations such as IAEA, World Health Organization, Food and Agriculture Organization and FSSAI. DAE has developed irradiation technology for preservation of fruits, vegetables, pulses, spices, sea food, etc. by radiation processing and has transferred the technology to private entrepreneurs. Several such commercially operated facilities are available around the country (Figure 6).

Figure 6: Krushak: An Onion Potato Irradiation Facility

Sludge Hygienization

This is a dual-purpose technology for the hygienization of sewage sludge as well as for its conversion to organic fertiliser. Dried sewage sludge is irradiated with gamma rays to eliminate pathogens and dormant seeds. The irradiated sludge is then enriched with micronutrients by inoculation with Bio-NPK and used as fertiliser. A plant for sewage sludge hygienization has been commissioned by Ahmedabad Municipal Corporation in collaboration with DAE and serves as a technology demonstration facility (Figure 7).

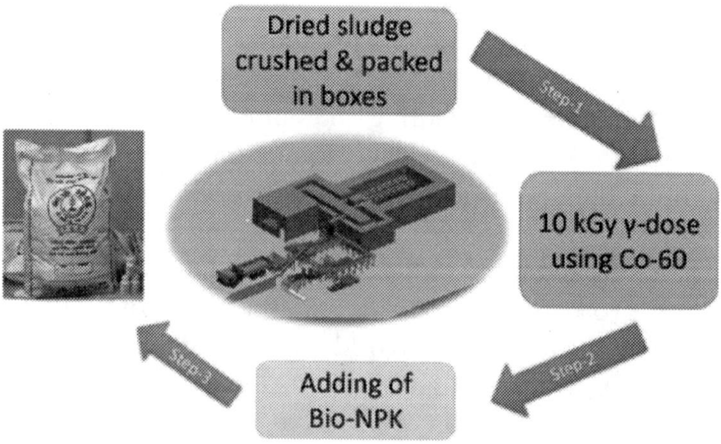

Figure 7: Sewage Sludge Hygienization

Non-Nuclear Technologies

The intense technological challenges of the nuclear sector create several technologies, which have appreciable spin-off benefits in other vital domains of the society. Most of these technologies, though employed at DAE institutions, are also readily transferred to the societal domain for commercial exploitation as well as community welfare schemes. Some of them are listed below.

Nisargruna

Nisargruna (repaying our debt to nature) is an organic waste management technology for the treatment of biodegradable waste such as food waste, municipal waste, abattoir waste, faecal matter, etc. Organic manure and biogas are useful by-products. The technology has a modular design and is therefore scalable from 10-100 kg/ day, making it amenable for installations in small as well as large establishments generating such waste (Figure 8).

Figure 8: Nisargruna Plant

Water Purification

The DAE has developed low-cost water purification systems using membrane filters for ultrafiltration of impurities. These systems require no electricity and call for minimum maintenance, thereby making them rugged and versatile. Technology has been transferred to several entrepreneurs and the systems are commercially available and in wide use.

Water Desalination

A technology for desalination of sea water has been developed using nuclear waste heat. Two such plants have been set up at Kalpakkam and are supplying potable water to the nearby township. The fresh water resources of the country are rapidly depleting due to overuse and sea water desalination technologies will be required in the future. This technology provides a cost effective and viable solution and can be considered as a technology for the future. RO based desalination plants for generating potable water have also been set up by DAE in nearly 200 villages under its CSR programme. RO based plants have been supplied to BSF and the plants have been found to be very good help to the persons living in very difficult locations. (Figure 9).

Figure 9: BARC Desalination Plant for BSF

Hybrid Granular Sequencing Batch Reactor (hgSBR) for Sewage Water Treatment

Wastewater contains fibrous impurities that are difficult to separate. DAE has developed a technology to cause the fibrous impurities to aggregate into large particles and settle at the bottom of the treatment vessel. The treatment effectively lowers organic carbon, nitrogen and phosphorous and other contaminants to acceptable levels and eliminates foul odour. Pure water can be decanted and recirculated for industrial purposes and if subjected to tertiary treatment, could also be made potable. The footprints as well as the operation and maintenance costs of the hgSBR treatment plants are lower compared to the conventional sewage treatment plants.

Reefer

A liquid nitrogen-based system for storage and transport of vegetables, fruits, seafood, etc. has been developed. Considerable quantities of produce wasted due to spoilage caused by lack of cold chain facilities can be avoided using these refrigerated and mobile systems, which can be deployed for use over land routes, railways as well as water ways, making them highly versatile. An agreement has been signed with Tata Motors Limited to jointly develop these vans, known as SHIVAYs (Sheetal Vahak Yantra) for vehicular applications (Figure 10). In a recent development, these systems are being adapted for use in fishing trawlers in order to increase the shelf life of the catch and avoid the need to carry large quantity of ice in fishing trawlers.

Figure 10: SHIVAY

Potential of Nuclear Energy and Radiation Technology

The above description provides a few glimpses of the vast potential of the applications of nuclear energy and radiation technology in all aspects of our lives. Maintaining and sustaining our ecosystem and biodiversity without compromising on the developmental agenda calls for innovative solutions. Many of the technologies delivered by DAE as seen above, are efforts in that direction, providing far reaching benefits in energy, healthcare, nutrition and general well-being in a sustainable manner.

Vasudhaiva Kutumbakam symbolizes the idea of universal

brotherhood, where all living beings are considered members of a global family. It encompasses love, kindness, unity, harmony, mutual respect, understanding and compassion amongst all beings of the world, irrespective of their species, race, religion, nationality, or social status, with a view to creating a peaceful and prosperous world for all. This message of unity and inclusiveness is a call for people to work together to build a better world for all.

The phrase has its roots in the ancient Hindu scriptures, but its significance has resonated with people of many different cultures and faiths around the world, and has become a popular expression of the idea of global unity and brotherhood. The philosophy has become even more relevant today, where the world is becoming increasingly interconnected, and any event or happening in any corner of the globe impacts the entire humanity.

The culture, philosophy and thought process of the Indian Government not only resonates with these ideals in numerous ways, but is also visibly demonstrated in its conduct of international diplomacy. We have always believed in extending the hand of friendship and cooperation to neighbours as well as distant nations, which are in need of help and support from us in numerous domains. In this spirit, DAE is actively involved in numerous regional cooperation agreements for sharing and transfer of knowledge, experience and expertise. Equipment and technical knowhow is shared in international forums such as the IAEA, multilateral mega-science projects such as CERN and ITER as well as through a platform specifically created for this purpose, namely the GCNEP situated near Delhi. *Vasudhaiva Kutumbakam* for us is not merely a slogan but a way of life.

Acknowledgements: We gratefully acknowledge the support of Scientific Information Resources Division, BARC for providing the figures, charts and quotations from the BARC archives, and Director, RRCAT for providing the photograph of Shivay.

10

Nuclear India and the Global Nuclear Governance

Roshan Khanijo

We have been and will continue to be in the forefront of the calls for opening negotiations for a Nuclear Weapons Convention, so that this challenge can be dealt with in the same manner that we have dealt with the scourge of two other weapons of mass destruction through the Biological Weapons Convention and the Chemical Weapons Convention.

– PM Atal Bihari Vajpayee[1]

Introduction

India was one of the few countries to understand the implications of nuclear explosion early on, as Pt. Jawaharlal Nehru on 26th June 1946 at Bombay, had said: "As long as the world is constituted as it is, every country will have to devise and use the latest scientific devices for its protection. I have no doubt India will develop her scientific research and I hope Indian scientists will use the atomic force for constructive purposes. But if India is threatened, she will inevitably try to defend herself by all means at her disposal."[2] This clearly posited India's nuclear trajectory, an amalgamation of morality and geopolitical realism. With the PNE in 1974, India demonstrated its nuclear technological capability, however, it was only after "Operation Shakti", on the 11th and 13th May 1998, that India declared herself as a NWS. In 1974, when India conducted the PNE, the philosophical narrative as suggested by the then PM Indira Gandhi was still rooted in nuclear disarmament, as she stated that "it is only through nuclear disarmament that discrimination would be eliminated and equality between nations re-established", and this is in the "best interests of the country". This posture was vociferously propagated by Rajiv Gandhi in his Action Plan for ushering in a "Nuclear Weapon-Free and non-violent World Order".

Notwithstanding, this policy of disarmament post 1998 has broadly remained the same. Post Pokhran II, as commented, "India got room to rework its nuclear diplomacy. From being a protestor against discrimination in the nuclear order, India was now transforming itself into a nation that was ready to support the existing order and calling for its incremental reform. The essence of the change in the Indian nuclear policy after Pokhran-II rested in the shift from the past emphasis on disarmament to a new one on pragmatic arms control. The former called for a total abolition of nuclear weapons. The latter focussed on the challenge of reducing the nuclear threat in the short term."[3] Further, with India opting for a unilateral voluntary moratorium on nuclear testing, and her consistent take on proliferation issues, gave India the leeway, to diplomatically negotiate and share with major powers, as also with the nuclear non-proliferation regimes, her goals and aspirations, to become an active and responsible member, in creating a non-biased nuclear architecture. This was evident in the then US President George W. Bush's proclamation of India as a responsible state with advanced nuclear technology.[4] India has come a long way since then and this 13th May 2023, India will complete 25 years of being a responsible NWS. Although the global architecture has been a complex one, but India's nuclear journey has been impressive and this paper tries to highlight some of the milestones.

Global Nuclear Governance Architecture

Global Nuclear governance is a complex architecture which attempts to address the challenges to nuclear proliferation, nuclear safety and security and initiates dialogues for nuclear disarmament and arms control. It encompasses wide range of domestic and international rules and regulations, guiding principles as enunciated in international treaties, which help nations in strengthening the domestic architecture. The global apex body, for nuclear governance and guidance is the IAEA. In addition, there are several nuclear industry and non-governmental professional institutions, including the WANO, the INPO, and the World Institute for Nuclear Security that develop and share "best practices" that extend beyond regulatory standards.[5] To prevent issues of proliferation, prevent nuclear testing, and eliminate nuclear weapons, some significant treaties namely, the NPT, The CTBT, and the TPNW have been formed. Further, in the past, if the PTBT discussed the banning of nuclear test in the atmosphere, outer space and under water, then 'The Outer Space Treaty' prevented deployment of nuclear weapons in outer space. Further, various NWFZ were created which banned the testing as well as deployment of nuclear weapons in those regions. The central treaty for the nuclear safety and security is the CNS which mandates the nations' to domestically assess the nuclear regulatory standards and safety issues. This is supplemented by the CPPNM and its 2005 Amendments, the ICSANT. Further, through Zangger Committee the export of nuclear equipment and material is being kept under IAEA safeguards as also NSG seeks to give guidelines for nuclear export. Additionally, MTCR aims "to limit the spread of ballistic missiles and other unmanned delivery systems that could be used for chemical, biological, and nuclear attacks"[6] and through 'The Australian Group' nations' "coordinate their national export controls to limit the supply of chemicals and biological agents-as well as related equipment, technologies, and knowledge-to countries and non-state entities suspected of pursuing chemical or biological weapons capabilities."[7] Nuclear governance is thus, a multifaceted, intricate system, where both international and national technical and legal systems need to not only complement each other, but also require constant improvements, to adapt to the emerging international environment and address effectively the challenges.

Nuclear India: A Historical Perspective

In 1998 the then PM Atal Bihari Vajpayee after the nuclear tests had stated, "We do not intend to use these weapons for aggression or for mounting threats against any country, these are weapons of self-defence, to ensure that India is not subjected to nuclear threats or coercion. We do not intend to engage in an arms race."[8] True to his words India through her NFU policy has steadfastly chosen a responsible non escalatory path. Whether it is nuclear non-proliferation or nuclear disarmament, India has been a pioneer in championing this cause, although, the same cannot be said about India's two nuclear neighbours who have been involved in nuclear proliferation and nuclear arms race.

Historically, in "1965, along with a small group of non-aligned countries, India had put forward the idea of an international non-proliferation agreement under which the nuclear weapon states would agree to give up their arsenals provided other countries refrained from developing or acquiring such weapons."[9] Further, in 1978, India was involved in the negotiations to prohibit the use or threat of nuclear weapons, as also in 1982 India had called for prohibiting the production of nuclear fissile material through its initiative of 'nuclear freeze'. In the same decade the then PM Rajiv Gandhi had put the action plan for phased elimination of nuclear weapons. Had this proposal been followed, today world would have been a nuclear free world. However, post 1998, India's emphasis has been on having a consensus on crafting practical steps to address nuclear proliferation. Also, the policy in totality addresses not only the dangers of proliferation, but also of nuclear terrorism, which India has been highlighting regularly in international forums. Further, India has been actively participating in multilateral treaties whether it is NSS or other UN based negotiations like ICSANT, GICNT, etc,.

Moreover, India has continued to shape the global nuclear course through her positive role in the establishment and support of the IAEA, as she is conducting number of regional training seminars on nuclear security in cooperation with the IAEA. From 2010 to 2016

India had actively participated in the NSS and hosted meetings of NSS Sherpas. In 2016 during Prime Minister Narendra Modi's visit to Washington to attend the fourth edition of the NSS, India announced a $1-million grant for the IAEA.[10] Consequently, India has voiced her opinion on global terrorism, and it's a known fact that the doomsday clock is inching closer to midnight as world is becoming more and more vulnerable to nuclear terrorism. Thus, India has played a significant role in developing meaningful nuclear architecture.

India and Nuclear Non-proliferation Governance

The then EAM Jaswant Singh made a suo motu statement in Parliament: 'India's policies have been consistent with key provisions of NPT that apply to weapon states. India has been a responsible member of the non-proliferation regime and will continue to take initiatives to bring about stable and lasting non-proliferation."[11] Despite being an outlier state, India has upheld the ethos of non-proliferation objectives, and India has set an example for other states by virtue of its nuclear behaviour, thus India's dual and conflicting position has been gradually recognised by the international community.[12] This is so because India's civilizational ethos talk about global peace and that is why even India's Draft Nuclear Doctrine reiterates that "the use of nuclear weapons in particular as well as other weapons of mass destruction constitutes the gravest threat to humanity and to peace and stability in the international system."[13] Historically, it is a known fact that India was involved in the negotiations of NPT. As Scott Sagan points out, "In the actual negotiations creating the NPT text, Sweden and India proposed to include a commitment to a number of 'tangible steps,' including security assurances for NNWS, an end to nuclear testing, and a freeze on the production of nuclear weapons in the treaty, however, the US and the Soviet Union refused to allow such specific measures to be included in the final text of the NPT."[14] However, for India "attempts to promote non-proliferation would be merely a first step toward the ultimate goal of universal nuclear disarmament."[15] Notwithstanding, India supports the view that if a country has signed the NPT, then it should honour the commitments, as in the past it had criticised North Korea and Iran for the same reasons.

Further, there has been zero proliferation links as far as India is concerned and in spite of having nuclear weapons India refused to transfer technology to other countries, the case being Libya in 1978 when India refused to give the technology. On the contrary the same cannot be said about India's nuclear neighbours, where cases of proliferation were quite evident like Pakistan's AQ Khan's network as also China-Pakistan-North Korea nexus. China has been a signatory to NPT as well as a participant of the NSG but still questions are being raised about her clandestine proliferation of nuclear technology to Pakistan. Additionally, India did not go into the arms race mode, as it continued with her NFU and avoided the development of the escalatory TNWs. India's nuclear policy stands on the pillars of Disarmament and non-proliferation often a barometer for nuclear behaviour and if global ranking is based on that, then India will be ranked much higher than other countries like China and Pakistan. As far as India's response to nuclear proliferation is concerned India has taken an active part in nuclear disarmament, diplomacy and seeing the elimination of nuclear weapons as both a way of dealing with the threat of proliferation as also a way of avoiding the unpleasant decision about building its own nuclear weapons.[16] To prevent proliferation, India supported and implemented the UN Security Council Resolution 1540 (2004). Also to prevent and control the export of material India has adopted the global best practices. India has aligned her domestic export control with that of control list required by international export control organizations and as Rajiv Nayan writes: "The SCOMET list is the principal regulatory mechanism for Indian export controls. It is regularly updated and expanded frequently, depending on the pace of technology.... The Indian export control system was revamped in keeping with the guidelines and technology control lists of the NSG and the MTCR as per the July 18, 2005 joint statement."[17] Thus, this SCOMET is a classic example, and through 'Category Zero' India has tried to bring nuclear related material and technology in the legal gambit. Further the

Chapter IVA of Foreign Trade (Development & Regulation) Act, 1992, "was incorporated by way of amendment in 2010 to regulate brokering, transhipment and export of specified goods, services and technology which have applications as weapons of mass destruction, in aligning it with the provisions of The WMD Act, 2005."[18] Internationally, India had also supported the FMCT which was thwarted by the Pakistanis. The Indian efforts have been acknowledged, and the US recognized India as a responsible nuclear weapon power in 2005[19] through the operationalization of the 123 Agreement in 2008.[20]

India and Nuclear Terrorism

India's foreign secretary S. Jaishankar in his Welcome Address at the Implementation and Assessment Group Meeting GICNT, stated that "terrorism remains the most pervasive and serious challenge to international security...the dangers of discriminating among terrorists – good or bad or even yours and mine – are increasingly recognized. Terrorism is an international threat that should not serve national strategy."[21] Since the time the first nuclear power plant came in the 1950s the number of countries involved in the nuclear energy has increased tremendously. Nuclear energy now provides about 10% of the world's electricity from about 440 power reactors and over 50 countries utilize nuclear energy in about 220 research reactors.[22] In addition to research, these reactors are used for the production of medical and industrial isotopes, as well as for training.[23] The nuclear inventory including research reactors, fuel cycle facilities, and radioactive sources are increasing, hence, the issue of nuclear safety and security is of utmost significance. Nuclear terrorism especially the 'Dirty Bombs', which is the DD, or in other words a conventional bomb spiked with radioactive material is becoming a reality. Additionally, countries like Pakistan have got TNWs which makes it vulnerable to theft, thus, making the regional environment susceptible to nuclear terrorism. Moreover, nuclear sabotage and cyber-attacks on power grids are concerns for any country. India feels that this issue of nuclear terrorism has often not got the requisite attention it should, therefore India's endeavour has been to bring it, to the forefront by highlighting it in the UNGA, as also co-sponsor resolutions on "Measures to prevent terrorists from acquiring weapons of mass destruction". India is more concerned about it due to her geographical location, as it is flanked by nations which harbour terrorist activities. The AF-Pak region has some of the deadliest terrorist organisation like Al-Qaida, ISIS, Jaish-e-Mohammed, Hizbul Mujahideen, etc. Thus, India has been proactive in not only highlighting the issue of nuclear terrorism globally, but has also adopted the twin strategy of firstly, signing international treaties like ICSANT, GICNT, etc. Secondly, considering India has 22 operating reactors, so, domestically India has been following a stringent policy, as far as nuclear safety and security of India's nuclear power plants are concerned. India on her part has separated the weapons programme from the civilian nuclear energy programme. India's civilian nuclear power plants are under the safeguards of IAEA. India and the IAEA signed an Agreement for Application of Safeguards to Civilian Nuclear facilities in India and an Additional Protocol to the Safeguards Agreement between the Government of India and the IAEA for the Application of Safeguards to Civilian Nuclear Facilities entered into force on 25 July 2014.[24] Also, India believes that tracking and controlling radiological and fissile materials, and preventing nuclear terrorism requires international cooperation, hence it has not only signed but also ratified CPPNM and its 2005 amendment, thus bringing the domestic transportation of nuclear material under the ambit of the convention.[25] However, it is prudent here to discuss in brief about India's nuclear safety and security architecture.

Nuclear Safety and Security in India

India has a unique civilian nuclear programme which ranges from using Uranium to Thorium in various nuclear fuel cycles. From developing PHWR to developing LWR in collaboration with foreign firms and now the indigenous Fast Breeder Reactors to use the abundant thorium, depicts the fascinating journey of India's civilian nuclear programme. India has 22 nuclear power plants and has an installed capacity of 6780 Mwe, amongst these eighteen reactors are PHWRs and four are LWRs.[26] All this requires seamless coordination with national and international organisations, as also following stringent nuclear safety and security standards. India has a strong legal framework which includes the Atomic Energy Act which created the AEC in 1948 and later on the DAE was created in 1954. Further, number of other acts to address specific areas were created like Atomic Energy (Safe Disposal of Radioactive Wastes) Rules, 1987; Atomic Energy (Radiation Protection) Rules, 2004; the WMD Act 2005, etc. Significantly, the AERB was created in 1983 which is responsible for both nuclear safety and security of civilian nuclear power plants. Internationally, India is party to all the 13 anti-terrorism conventions. Additionally, India has placed voluntarily her civilian plants under IAEA safeguards and WANO has conducted Peer Review of India's power plants[27] Post Fukushima, India's DAE and the AERB have 24×7 emergency control rooms that have a human crew who monitor and respond to emergencies, additionally, India has on-site emergency response centres to plan and initiate actions based on the phase and level of emergencies, and India also has off-site emergency support centres for intermediate phase-level emergency.[28] Further, India's National Disaster Management Authority has its own system as well, and coordinates with other agencies on safety measures.[29] Technologically, also the newer reactors have better built in safety facilities and GCNEP is also through research and development trying to develop reactors which are safe, and secure. Though India has tried to plug in the gaps but still there are certain loopholes which needs to be addressed. The start point can be in having an independent AERB. Considering, nuclear safety and security is an ongoing dynamic process hence, it is imperative that nations' not only constantly review their systems but also participate in international conventions to understand and learn the best practices adopted by other nations.

Legal and Regulatory Support: India's Tryst with Multilateral Nuclear Arrangements

India had been quick to navigate from an outlier nation to becoming an intrinsic part of the global nuclear governance through its journey of joining major nuclear multilateral treaties. Continuing with its foundational ethos of "commitment to promoting and working with the international community in advancing the common objectives of global non-proliferation and international security."[30] India has been voicing concerns over the Proliferation of WMD as well as their delivery systems. On her part, India has promulgated the WMD Act, under which it "authorizes the Government of India to regulate the export, retransfer, re-export, transit, and trans-shipment of any items related to the development, production, handling, operation, maintenance, storage, or dissemination of a WMD or missile delivery device. It also established a catch-all control that restricts exports of non-listed items destined for a WMD end-use, and it provided a rudimentary legal basis to regulate technology transfers."[31] India was also negotiating to become a member of the MTCR and which it joined in 2018. Similarly, it joined the Wassenaar Arrangement, and the Australia Group. It had implemented UN Security Council Resolution 1540. As far as NSG is concerned it is a known fact that this treaty has more to do with power politics, than any technical deficiencies. Moreover, India does not lose much if it does not become a member, considering the US 123 Agreement has given India the necessary leeway for supply of fissile material.

With regard to IAEA activities, "Being a 'designated Member', India has served on the Board of Governors of the IAEA since its inception and India actively participates in IAEA's Advisory Groups and Technical Committees, as also India also contributes to the Agency's activities by way of providing experts and conducting training programs, workshops and occasionally providing equipment."[32] India has contributes $50,000 annually to IAEA's INPRO and it was also one of its founding members.[33] Further, India has supported the 5th revision of IAEA's INFCIRC/225 and participated in the IAEA's Illicit Trafficking Database, as also India has cooperated with the Interpol's Radiological and Nuclear Terrorism Prevention Unit, the World Customs Organization-on nuclear trafficking issue, and is a party to the GICNT.[34] Additionally, India's civilian nuclear power plants were reviewed by the OSRT of the IAEA and the WANO.

As also, IRRS and the Peer Review Mission of IAEA conducted a review of the nuclear power plants in India, and in its report, the Executive Vice President Ramzi Jammal had concluded that there is a strong commitment to safety in India.[35] Thus, India has slowly tried to integrate with the global nuclear community.

Institutional Framework: GCNEP

Under the aegis of DAE the government of India has established a Centre of Excellence called the GCNEP. The main aim is to enhance nuclear safeguards to effectively and efficiently monitor nuclear materials and facilities as also promote and to develop advanced, and more proliferation resistant nuclear power reactors.[36] The five schools under it namely; Advanced Nuclear Energy Systems, Nuclear Security Studies, Radiation Safety Studies, Nuclear Material Characterisation Studies, and lastly the Application of Radioisotopes and Radiation Technology in healthcare, agriculture and food, encompasses the entire gambit of nuclear energy. On one hand through its training, lecture-series, seminars and workshop schedules, organised either independently or in collaboration with the international organisations, this centre tries to create a trained pool of human resource faculty. On the other hand through nuclear research it tries to aid in the design and development of nuclear systems that are intrinsically safe, secure, proliferation resistant and sustainable. Thus, the GCNEP has been successful in its objective "to provide a world class research and development, test and evaluation, information security, training and exercise facility for different areas of nuclear security to national and international audience."[37]

Challenges and Way Forward

India in the past had to travel a bumpy road as it refused to sign the NPT and the CTBT due to complex security architecture in its neighbourhood, as also the geopolitics and power play had curtailed India's membership to the NSG. However, through her voluntary moratorium of not undergoing nuclear tests, as also her participation and signing of major treaties mentioned in earlier paragraphs and her impeccable record in nuclear non-proliferation, her efforts has ultimately been recognised.

However, the global trends in the last few years, has been alarming, especially, the pace with which nations are modernisation their weapons and the development of niche and disruptive technologies. Especially, the trajectory of China in developing disruptive technologies and adopting coercive strategies, has been a cause of concern for many nations. Also, the US-China competition in space and development of AI and automation led technological innovations are changing the military landscape, as new dual use LAWS is transforming the nature of warfare. This will have a cascading effect globally. Further, with the Russian-Ukraine conflict and the intervention of US and NATO, has complicated, the already tense environment. It is more visible in the nuclear field as US-Russia nuclear cooperation has taken a major beating. The Russians have suspended its participation in the New Start Treaty and may go in for nuclear testing if provoked. All this proves that, some of the challenges cannot be addressed by the old dyadic architecture, for example nuclear disarmament talks cannot be just limited to US-Russia when China is emerging as a major technological disruptor, hence it is high time that China is pushed to take more responsibility and participates in arms talk.

The war has also brought to the forefront the issue of nuclear safety and security of power plants as also the role of IAEA. Further, the war may lead to the resurgence of nuclear power plants as the supply chains have been disrupted. We are already talking about modular nuclear reactors, hence, in future nuclear safety and security as also proliferation of fissile material will become issues of utmost importance, hence it is essential that a more inclusive nuclear environment is created. India through her GCNEP has already started the process and coming years will see India emerge as a more proactive player globally.

Conclusion

India has come a long way from being an outlier to becoming a responsible nuclear weapon state. Her non-proliferation credentials, her role in highlighting nuclear terrorism, and her becoming a major treaty partner, whether it is the MTCR or the Wassenaar agreement or her role in the IAEA, the circle has been completed. Her participation in NSS and the promise of creating GCNEP with the vision "of promoting safe, secure, and sustainable nuclear energy for the service of mankind through global partnership", is a positive contribution to the global community. However, the security is a dynamic concept and new paradigms keep emerging and one such domain is the emergence of disruptive technology. These technological innovations are bound to create new challenges and the global architecture will require to adapt and change. India too will need to adjust her policies and become more proactive in highlighting the challenges, as also become a part of the solution.

NOTES

1 Twelfth Lok Sabha, Session: 2, Date: 27-05-1998, Participants: Vajpayee Prime Minister Atal Bihari. Source: Lok Sabha, Debates, at http://164.100.47.194/Loksabha/Debates/Result12.aspx?dbsl=248

2 "Speech by Shri K.R. Narayanan, President of India, at the Inauguration of The Birth Centenary Celebrations of Dr. K. S. Krishnan", Bangalore, Tuesday, 28 July 1998 at http://www.krnarayanan.in/html/speeches/others/jul28_98.htm

3 C Raja Mohan, *Crossing the Rubicon: The Shaping of India's New Foreign Policy*, Viking, New Delhi, 2003, pp.15

4 "Joint Statement by President George W. Bush and Prime Minister Manmohan Singh", at https://2001-2009.state.gov/p/sca/rls/pr/2005/49763.htm, 18 July 2005.

5 Evolving Nuclear Governance for a new Era, Policy and Memo Recommendations, Global Nexus Initiative, April 2017 at https://globalnexusinitiative.org/wp-content/uploads/2017/04/GNI-Policy-Memo-3.pdf

6 Arms Control Association, The Missile Technology Control Regime at a Glance, Factsheet, at https://www.armscontrol.org/factsheets/mtcr

7 Arms Control Association, The Australia Group at a Glance,Fact Sheet at https://

www.armscontrol.org/factsheets/australiagroup

8 XII Lok Sabha Debates, Session *II, (Budget)* Wednesday, 27 May 1998 / Jyaistha 6, 1920 (Saka), Type of Debate: Statement By Prime Minister, Title: Made a statement on nuclear tests in Pokhran. At https://parliamentofindia.nic.in/ls/lsdeb/ls12/ses2/04270598.htm

9 Ibid.

10 Iftikhar Gilani, "Nuclear Security Summit: PM Modi announces paradigm shift in nuclear policy", DNA, 4 April 2016 at https://www.dnaindia.com/india/report-nuclear-security-summit-pm-modi-announces-paradigm-shift-in-nuclear-policy-2197847

11 Suo motu statement made in Parliament by the Minister of External Affairs on the NPT Review Conference, 9 May 2000, at http://meaindia.nic.in/disarmament/dm10may00.html (Accessed 23 June 2008).

12 Reshmi Kazi & Ashlid Kolas, *India in global nuclear governance,* Routledge Publication, New Delhi, 2020

13 "Draft Report of National Security Advisory Board on Indian Nuclear Doctrine", 17 August 1999, http://mea.gov.in/in-focus-article.htm?18916/Draft+Report+ of+National+Security+Advisory+Board+on+Indian+Nuclear+Doctrine

14 Scott D. Sagan, "Convenient Consensus and Serious Debate about Disarmament," Discussion Paper Presented to the Working Group on an Expanded Non-Proliferation System, Washington, DC, 8-9 June, 2010. Available at http://www.nti.org/media/pdfs/ConvenientConcensusDebateDisarmament-ScottSagan-060610_2.pdf?_=1326132026

15 S. Ganguly, "India's Pathway to Pokhran II: The Prospects and Sources of New Delhi's Nuclear Weapons Program," *International Security,* 23 (4), 1999, pp. 148-177.

16 Rajesh Rajagopalan, 'Nuclear Non-Proliferation: Indian Perspective', FES Briefing Paper 10 | October 2008, at https://library.fes.de/pdf-files/iez/global/05793.pdf

17 Rajiv Nayan, "Integrating India with the Global Export Control Systems: Challenges Ahead", *Strategic Analysis,* 3, 2011, p. 443.

18 India's Export Control System, Ministry of Commerce & Industry Department of Commerce Directorate General of Foreign Trade, at https://ibkp.dbtindia.gov.in/DBT_Content_Test/CMS/Guidelines/20181115135754468_Export%20of%20 SCOMET %20guidelines.pdf

19 US Department of State Archives, "Joint Statement by President George W. Bush and Prime Minister Manmohan Singh," 18 July 2005, https://2001-2009.state.gov/p/sca/rls/pr/2005/49763.htm (Accessed 10 October 2021).

20 US. Department of State Archives, "US-India Civil Nuclear Cooperation Initiative – Bilateral Agreement on Peaceful Nuclear Cooperation," 10 October 2008, https://2001-2009.state.gov/r/pa/prs/ps/2008/oct/110920.htm

21 Welcome address by Foreign Secretary at Implementation and Assessment Group Meeting Global Initiative to Combat Nuclear Terrorism (GICNT), New Delhi, 08 February 2017, MediaCenter, Ministry of External Affairs, Government of India at https://mea.gov.in/Speeches-Statements.htm?dtl/28012/Welcome_address_by_Foreign_Secretary_at_Implementation_and_Assessment_Group_Meeting_Global_Initiative_to_Combat_Nuclear_Terrorism_GICNT_New_Delhi

22 "Nuclear Power in the World Today", World Nuclear Association, at https://world-nuclear.org/information-library/current-and-future-generation/nuclear-power-in-the-world-today.aspx

23 Ibid.

24 IAEA, Ministry of External Affairs, 7 April 2023 at https://eoi.gov.in/eoisearch/MyPrint.php?8838?001/0029#:~:text=India%20actively%20participates%20in%20IAEA's,workshops%20a

25 Nuclear Security in India, Document, Ministry of External Affairs, 18 March 2014 at http://www.mea.gov.in/in-focus-article.htm?23091/Nuclear+Security+in+India

26 Atomic Energy Regulatory Board, 'Nuclear Power Plants', at https://www.aerb.gov.in/english/regulatory-facilities/nuclear-power-plants last updated 24-03-2023

27 Nuclear security India at https://www.mea.gov.in/Images/pdf/Brochure.pdf

28 Rajeshwari Rajagopan & Pulkit Mohan, "Nuclear Safety and Security in India: Emerging Threats and Response Preparedness",ORF, 31 Sepember 2021, at https://www.orfonline.org/research/nuclear-safety-and-security-in-india

29 Ibid.

30 Draft Report of National Security Advisory Board on Indian Nuclear Doctrine", 17 August 1999, at http://mea.gov.in/in-focus-article.htm?18916/Draft+Report+of+National+Security+Advisory+Board+on+Indian+Nuclear+Doctrine

31 "India's Export Controls: Current Status and Possible Changes on the Horizon", securus Strategic Trade Solutions, 2011 at: http://securustrade.com/Indias_Export_Controls_Article_July_2011_FINAL.pdf

32 IAEA, Ministry of External Affairs, 7 April 2003 at https://eoi.gov.in/eoisearch/MyPrint.php?8838?001/0029#:~:text=India%20actively%20participates%20in%20IAEA's,workshops%20a

33 "India and the IAEA," Indian Embassy (Vienna), Government of India. at http://www.indianembassy.at/pages.php?id=64.

34 Roshan Khanijo "Global Nuclear Governance and India", in Reshmi Kazi &Ashild Kolas (eds.), *India in Global Nuclear Governance*, Routledge Publication, New Delhi, 2020

35 IAEA Mission Concludes Peer Review of India's Nuclear Regulatory Framework, IAEA, 27 March 2015 at https://www.iaea.org/newscenter/pressreleases/iaea-mission-concludes-peer-review-india-nuclear-regulatory-framework

36 Government of India, Department of Atomic Energy, Global Center for nuclear energy Partnership at https://www.gcnep.gov.in/about/about.html

37 "India's Export Controls: Current Status and Possible Changes on the Horizon," SECURUS Strategic Trade Solutions, 2011 at http://securustrade.com/Indias_Export_Controls_Article_July_2011_FINAL.pdf

11

India and the Non-Proliferation Regime

Abhishek Verma and Niranjan C Oak

> *"The present decision and future actions will continue to reflect a commitment to sensibilities and obligations of an ancient civilisation, a sense of responsibility and restraint, but a restraint born of the assurance of action, not of doubts or apprehension."*[1]
>
> – Shri Atal Bihari Vajpayee

Introduction

India's approach towards nuclear weapons and nuclear-related regimes reflects a remarkable consistency with its overall foreign policy orientation. Indian political leaders consistently tied India's prospects of acquiring nuclear weapons with the country's national interests. This chapter discusses the evolution of India's approach towards nuclear non-proliferation regimes. The chapter argues that 25 years of Indian journey as a NWS can broadly be categorised into four phases – Estrangement, Engagement, Integration and Accommodation. Since 1998, these broad phases have not been strictly compartmentalised but have entailed certain overlaps. A consistent running theme throughout these three phases, as also before them, is India's consensus-driven nuclear policy that innately supported non-proliferation and disarmament.

Indian Approach towards Nuclear Non-proliferation Regimes

India's approach towards nuclear non-proliferation has been consistent since the late 1950s. Inspired by the guiding principles advocated by Mahatma Gandhi and Gautam Buddha, as well as the ancient dictum of '*Vasudhaiva Kutumbakam*', New Delhi has staunchly advocated disarmament, not only in a normative sense but also through concrete, tangible initiatives. As early as 1954, Prime Minister Jawaharlal Nehru called for a Standstill Agreement on nuclear testing.[2] The proposed agreement was the foundation of the PTBT adopted in 1963 by the US, USSR and the UK. Continuing the thread, after 34 years, in 1988, PM Rajiv Gandhi proposed an "Action Plan for ushering in a nuclear-weapon-free and non-violent world order."[3] After the nuclear tests of 1998, India's advocacy for non-proliferation and disarmament continued. In 2007, India presented a Working Paper on Nuclear Disarmament at the CD.[4] Additionally, India's Resolutions in the First Committee of the UNGA in 2013 bear testimony to India's unflinching commitment to nuclear disarmament. Further, India has always supported a global, non-discriminatory multilateral framework for nuclear non-proliferation.

In the UN-sponsored ENDC negotiations between 1962 and 1969, New Delhi for the first time, brought the world's attention from 'non-dissemination' of nuclear technology to 'non-proliferation' (both vertical and horizontal). However, India did not accept the NPT – a cornerstone of the global non-proliferation regime and a product of the ENDC negotiations – on the principled stand that the country could not accept externally prescribed norms or standards on matters within the jurisdiction of its Parliament, which were not consistent with India's constitutional provisions and procedures. Besides, they were contrary to India's national interests, leading to the infringement of its sovereignty.

The then Joint Secretary in the Ministry of External Affairs, Shri M.A. Hussain's note brought forth four apprehensions[5] that India had:

(a) "It (the NPT) does not stop vertical proliferation

(b) It does not explicate pathways for general and complete disarmament

(c) It will obstruct the developmental use of nuclear energy

(d) It will impose control, inspection and verification over non-weapon powers".

Jaswant Singh reiterated similar concerns in an article published in *Foreign Affairs*, where he emphasised the arbitrariness of the NPT for dividing the world into nuclear haves and have-nots. He stated:

> "In the absence of universal disarmament, India could scarcely accept a regime that arbitrarily divided nuclear haves from have-nots. India has always insisted that all nations' security interests are equal and legitimate."[6]

New Delhi rightly brought forth the dichotomy questioning why possession of nuclear weapons among the five States would enhance international security and establish deterrence, while India's acquisition of nuclear weapons would be detrimental to global peace. K. Subrahmanyam, India's foremost national security analyst, criticised the NPT and asserted that "indefinite and unconditional extension of NPT provided legitimacy to the nuclear weapons with NWS under NPT."[7] Thus, India criticised the discriminatory provisions of the non-proliferation regime while consistently supporting the regime in principle. India co-sponsored the CTBT in 1993.[8] Simultaneously, it vehemently opposed the discriminatory approach followed by the Treaty and the provision allowing a State to withdraw if national security interests so demanded.[9] The Indian approach saw a remarkable continuity even after the *Shakti* series of nuclear tests conducted in 1998. The then PM Atal Bihari Vajpayee declared emphatically in the Parliament that. "....in the absence of universal and non-discriminatory disarmament, we cannot accept a regime that creates an arbitrary division between nuclear haves and have-nots".[10]

India's support for the cause of nuclear non-proliferation was evident when it interdicted the North Korean cargo ship *MV San* in August 2009 as per the sanctions adopted by the UN Security Council. This interdiction was due to the apprehension that the ship was ferrying nuclear material. Despite not being a member of an informal US-led Proliferation Security Initiative, India remained alert and aware of its prominent role in thwarting malign proliferation intent. The interdiction in 2009 was not the first time India had interdicted a suspicious ship. In 1999, too, the Indian Navy interdicted a North Korean ship allegedly carrying missile parts to Pakistan.

In the last decade, India's international stature and willingness to take a position on prominent nuclear-related global issues of concern have enhanced her legitimacy and acceptance of viewpoints. In 2020, India's decades-old proposals – 'Reducing Nuclear Danger' tabled in 1998 and CPNW tabled in 1982, were adopted by the UNGA First Committee with a substantive majority. The former emphasised reducing the risk of unintentional or accidental use of nuclear weapons through improvisation in nuclear doctrines like de-alerting and de-targeting nuclear installments. The latter sought to promulgate a legally binding, universal and multilateral international agreement to prohibit the use or threat to use of nuclear weapons under any circumstances. Both the Resolutions conspicuously brought out India's solemn commitment towards nuclear disarmament.[11] In a recently concluded plenary meeting of the CD, an Indian representative reiterated New Delhi's stand on disarmament, stating that "India is committed to the goal of universal, non-discriminatory and verifiable nuclear disarmament and has called for complete elimination of nuclear weapons through a step-by-step process."[12]

India's Non-Proliferation Commitments post-Shakti Series of Nuclear Tests

The then PM, P.V. Narasimha Rao decided to conduct the nuclear test towards the end of 1995 amidst structural changes in the international nuclear order in terms of a permanent extension of NPT (institutionalising nuclear status quo) and negotiations over CTBT.[13] However, New Delhi could not proceed with the tests due to prevailing political conditions and an unfavourable international atmosphere. In the ensuing years, things changed for the worse from India's perspective. Pakistan-China collaboration in missile development reached its zenith in 1998 when Islamabad conducted the *Ghauri* missile test. The missile's trajectory and the absence of Pakistan's Notice to Airmen led the then Indian Defence Minister, George Fernandes to declare *Ghauri* as a Chinese missile.[14] Moreover, the US appeared amenable to Pakistan's explanation of the test. Further, Washington seemed to turn a blind eye to China's role in Pakistan's missile development programme.[15] As a result, the Indian government decided to undertake the nuclear test. In May 1998, Prime Minister Atal Bihari Vajpayee and his National Security Advisor, Brajesh Mishra, presented a *fait accompli* by announcing the five nuclear tests conducted on 11 and 13 May 1998.

> *"Today at 1545 hours, India conducted three underground nuclear tests in the Pokhran range. These tests conducted today were one with a fission device, a low yield device, and a thermonuclear device. The measured yields are in line with expected values. Measurements have also confirmed that there was no release of radioactivity into the atmosphere."*[16]
>
> – Atal Bihari Vajpayee, 11 May 1998.

The announcement astonished the international community in general and the nuclear weapon States in particular. In the immediate aftermath, PM Vajpayee sent a letter explaining the rationale for conducting nuclear tests to each of the major powers. The letter's content to President Bill Clinton brought forth India's steadfast support for non-proliferation and disarmament. The letter stated:

> "...I assure you that India will continue to work with your country in a multilateral or bilateral framework to promote the cause of nuclear disarmament. Our commitment to participate in non-discriminatory and verifiable global disarmament measures is amply demonstrated by our adherence to the two conventions on Biological and Chemical Weapons. In particular, we are ready to participate in the negotiations to be held in Geneva in the Conference on Disarmament for the conclusion of a fissile material cut-off treaty."[17]

Thus, India's record of accomplishment in nuclear non-proliferation remains clean. As we celebrate the silver jubilee of the Indian nuclear tests, India's journey since the *Shakti* series of nuclear tests can be divided into four broad phases – Estrangement, Engagement, Integration, and Accommodation.

Phase I: Estrangement from the West

The decade of the 1990s was an important phase for global non-proliferation efforts. The NPT was reviewed in 1995, culminating in an indefinite extension of the Treaty. The CTBT opened for signature in September 1996. In the early 1990s, two remaining nuclear weapon States – France and China – joined the NPT, consolidating the five nuclear-weapon States under the Treaty. The Indian decision-makers had discerned that India's nuclear test would attract international criticism, even sanctions. Still, India went ahead with the nuclear tests, which were followed by sanctions from the West. Commenting on the extent of sanctions, Shakti Sinha, Private Secretary to PM Vajpayee (1998-99), in his book *Vajpayee: The Years that Changed India* stated[18] that "while some sanctions could be predicted, it was impossible to know how different countries would actually react."

One of the first reactions from the international community was the passage of the UN Security Council Resolution 1172 on 6 June 1998. It condemned the nuclear test conducted by India and Pakistan and urged them to find mutually acceptable solutions to the outstanding issues. It also urged India and Pakistan to sign the NPT and CTBT "without conditions."[19] The Organisation of Islamic Cooperation countries supported Pakistan, with some expressing complete solidarity with Pakistan and condemning India.[20] US President Clinton remarked that "India's actions threaten the stability of Asia and challenge the firm international consensus to stop all nuclear testing. So, again, I ask India to halt its nuclear weapons program and join the 149 nations that have already signed the Comprehensive Test Ban Treaty."[21] The US invoked provisions of the Glenn Amendment to the Arms Export Control Act 1976. Under the Amendment, the country imposed prohibitions on foreign assistance, foreign military sales, foreign military finance and other dual-use exports.[22]

Meanwhile, Japan froze 'Yen-loan for new projects to India' and started cautiously examining the loans extended to India by international financial institutions.[23] Germany withheld developmental aid worth a few million dollars in response to the nuclear test.[24] China and Russia expressed their displeasure over the nuclear test, while Canada moved a step ahead, criticising the nationalistic orientation of the then-Indian regime. Australia and Denmark also moved to restrict the flow from aid programmes to India.

On its part, India tried to assuage the misgivings about Indian nuclear intentions by putting out a White Paper on India's nuclear doctrine. Alongside, PM Vajpayee gave interviews to a number of foreign and domestic journalists. In an interview with *India Today*, PM Vajpayee alluded to the 'consistency with the nuclear disarmament policy' of successive governments in India and denied his government's radical departure from the past policy by conducting nuclear tests. The phase of estrangement did not last long due to an understanding of legitimate Indian security concerns in some quarters of the US administration and also by a few of the major powers.

Phase II: Engagement with the International Community

When the initial opprobrium vis-à-vis the Indian nuclear test subsided, various contrary voices emerged, contextualising the Indian nuclear test with the ensuing regional security complex. While France, the UK and Russia decided not to impose sanctions, some in the US Congress criticised Washington for imposing sanctions against New Delhi. Congressman Frank Pallone and House Speaker Newt Gingrich criticised[25] Clinton for ignoring India's legitimate concern about the China-Pakistan axis. A few years later, former Secretary of State Henry Kissinger supported the test, acknowledging India's case for deterrence.[26] Analysing the nuclear test by India and Pakistan, Kissinger, in an article published in *The Washington Post*, wrote that "while Clinton has every reason to pursue the (non-proliferation) objectives he is seeking, the Prime Ministers of India and Pakistan are equally reasonable in pursuing their own nuclear objectives."[27]

Again, in 2006, Kissinger wrote, "In 1998, I opposed the sanctions against India's nuclear tests, suggesting that India should be treated as a nuclear country whose progress in the nuclear field had become irreversible."[28]

As early as November 1998, the US government lifted[29] sanctions imposed on India. Continental-sized India, with a rising economy and demography, proved too big a country for the US to keep alienated. Exercising Presidential authority, Clinton decided to take several initiatives to normalise the strained bilateral relations with India. The Kargil Review Committee, in its Report, concluded that "the progress of economic reforms in India and the attraction of a burgeoning middle-class market with rising purchasing power was a factor in the toning down of Western rhetoric on the nuclear tests."[30]

India, on its part, took several initiatives to undo the clamour around its nuclear test. Alongside media interactions, interviews, parliamentary debates and letters to the major countries, the newly formed NSAB released a draft nuclear doctrine on 17 August 1999, explaining India's stand vis-à-vis the use of nuclear weapons. The motive behind the draft appeared to ward off nuclear ambiguity regarding New Delhi's nuclear intentions. This preliminary document[31] contained broad principles for the 'development, deployment and employment of India's nuclear forces'. The document reflected the rationale for acquiring the weapon and drew consonance with the global norms and the UN Charter. For instance, the 'effective, credible minimum deterrence' and 'adequate retaliatory capability' in the absence of global consensus on disarmament was proved consistent with the right of self-defence sanctioned under the UN Charter.

As a nuclear weapons State, India declared through this document that she would not use or threaten to use nuclear weapons against NNWS. India provided an unqualified negative security assurance to NNWS and committed itself to work towards internationally binding unconditional negative assurances by NWS under NPT. The policy of 'NFU' and advocacy of a global NFU further provided India with international support as a responsible NWS. Reflecting India's benign intentions behind nuclear tests, New Delhi declared a moratorium on further nuclear tests.

Beginning 12 June 1998, the then EAM Jaswant Singh and the US Deputy Secretary of State, Strobe Talbott, held fourteen rounds of talks to manage the effects of the Indian nuclear weapons test through July 2000. Negotiations proceeded over five major issues of concern– signing of CTBT; a permanent ban on the production of fissile materials; a strategic restrain regime; adoption of stringent "world-class" export controls over dangerous material, technology and know-how; and resumption of dialogues to address the root cause of tension.[32] These talks proved educative and opened a new chapter in India-US strategic relations, culminating in a Civil Nuclear Agreement and more entrenched defence cooperation. The ground for the civil nuclear agreement was laid in January 2004. Both the Indian and US governments agreed to expand cooperation, in a series of dialogues hereafter, in three specific areas, under the NSSP – civilian nuclear activities, civilian space programmes and high-technology trade. Additionally, it was agreed to extend dialogues on missile defence.[33]

Phase III: Integration with International Nuclear Order

The story of India's integration into the international nuclear non-proliferation regime is fascinating. After the 'PNE' of 1974, the international community tried to alienate India and its nuclear programme by establishing what later became known as the NSG, a group of suppliers regulating the flow of nuclear materials. Nearly 35 years later, the same NSG provided a unique exception, a waiver, for India to conduct nuclear commerce, even without signing the NPT. The waiver granted by NSG was testimony to India's statesmen-like responsibility and attitude towards nuclear weapons. The India-US Civil Nuclear Deal appeared as validation and acceptance by the international community led by the US of India's enhancing politico-economic and technological prowess. The prevalent belief at the time was that India was too important a country to remain out of nuclear-related international deliberations.

On 18 July 2005, Indian Prime Minister Dr. Manmohan Singh and President George W. Bush issued a joint statement[34] in Washington D.C. where both were satisfied with the "convergence of interests reflected in common understanding on the implementation of" the civil nuclear deal. The agreement proved consequential for India for more than one reason. First, the India-US nuclear deal assured India of a consistent nuclear fuel supply to run the country's nuclear reactors. In doing so, the US incorporated assurances regarding the fuel supply under Section 123 of the US Atomic Energy Act. Washington also agreed to support New Delhi in developing a strategic reserve of nuclear fuel and to negotiate with the IAEA, an India-specific fuel supply agreement. Second, the deal committed both parties to mutually transfer information regarding the use of nuclear energy for peaceful purposes. This information pertains to the production and use of nuclear reactors, fuel cycle activities, and research on various applications. Third, nuclear materials, equipment, sensitive nuclear technology, natural-low enriched Uranium, special fissionable material, and heavy water production technology were agreed to be transferred under the agreement.

Fourth, an India-Specific safeguard agreement was signed between India and the IAEA under which India put its civilian nuclear reactors under the IAEA. Further safeguards were maintained on all the nuclear materials and equipment being transferred. Fifth, under India's Separation plan, it was decided that out of 22 thermal power reactors in operation or under construction, 14 reactors would be identified and offered IAEA safeguards. India decided to place all future civilian thermal power reactors under IAEA safeguards, and the sole authority to determine such reactors would remain with the GOI. The overarching criterion for subjecting a nuclear facility to IAEA safeguard would be its strategic significance in terms of securing India's national security interest.[35] Sixth, India denied accepting any safeguards on its Prototype FBTRs and FBTRs located at Kalpakkam due to their strategic significance.

Prime Minister Dr. Manmohan Singh stated in Parliament on 7

March 2006, "In terms of the Separation plan, there is an assurance of uninterrupted supply of fuel to reactors that would be placed under safeguards together with India's right to take corrective measures in the event fuel supplies are interrupted. The House can rest assured that India retains its sovereign right to take all appropriate measures to fully safeguard its interests."[36] The consensus on a civil nuclear agreement gave further credence to India's solid non-proliferation record with responsible handling of nuclear and related activities. Unlike Pakistan, which helped countries like North Korea build its nuclear capability, India had a well-established, open and transparent nuclear doctrine. Moreover, India intended to implement IAEA safeguards, working alongside other nations on the FMCT and joining export control regimes.[37] On 20 October 2008, the then EAM Pranab Mukherjee stated[38] in the Lok Sabha that "taken together the India-specific Safeguards Agreement, the NSG decision and the bilateral cooperation agreements provide the basis for us to engage in international cooperation in civil nuclear energy on a long term and sustainable basis with interested international partners. We regard these decisions as a vindication and recognition of India's impeccable non-proliferation credentials." In fulfilment of the commitments undertaken, India harmonised its export controls with those of the NSG and the MTCR guidelines by notifying and implementing these guidelines and control lists. Even though India is not a member of either group, undertaking such an obligation reflects New Delhi's intention and approach towards non-proliferation. Besides, India expressed willingness to work with the US to conclude the multilateral FMCT.[39]

It was India's solemn commitment towards non-proliferation and an impeccable track record as a responsible nuclear weapon State that she managed to diplomatically negotiate all the hurdles in materialising a civil nuclear agreement with the US. New Delhi was granted an NSG waiver on 6 September 2008. Former Foreign Secretary and National Security Advisor Shiv Shankar Menon wrote in his book *Choices: Inside the Making of India's Foreign Policy*,

> "India's red lines were respected, namely, no reference to testing, no discriminatory provisions and no periodic review of India's behavior or the exemption, thus permitting permanent full civil nuclear cooperation-the 'clean' exemption that India sought."[40]

The India-US Civil Nuclear Agreement manifested international legitimacy accorded to Indian nuclear enterprises. The deal further opened the hard shells of nuclear institutional architecture, recognising India's legitimate need for nuclear energy. Speaking in Parliament on 20 October 2008, the then Minister of External Affairs, Shri Pranab Mukherjee, stated, "This initiative marks the end of the technology-denial regimes which have restricted India for over three decades. These developments are the beginning of a new chapter for India – of engagement as equal partners in civil nuclear energy cooperation with other countries. As we move forward, it will help us to expand high technology trade with technologically advanced countries."[41] Thus, the India-US Civil Nuclear deal gave India international legitimacy as a de-facto nuclear power.

Phase IV: Accommodation into the Global Nuclear Regime

Having acknowledged India as a responsible nuclear power, the credibility of Indian voices on nuclear high tables strengthened manifold. This reflected New Delhi's burgeoning and stable economy, commercial benefits and strategic value. On its part, India made diplomatic efforts to let the international community align their approach towards Indian nuclear tests with that of India. In a similar effort, India explicitly committed to aligning its export control regime with the NSG's guidelines and the MTCR specifications under the NSSP initiative signed in 2004 with the US. In conformity with the UN Security Council Resolution 1540, the Indian government enacted the WMD Act in 2005.

The efforts, coupled with the growing economic prowess and strategic significance – particularly regarding China's rise – made India too big and significant to have been kept off the nuclear tables. India took long strides in its journey of engagement with multilateral nuclear regimes. Despite being a non-signatory to the NPT, India could enter into a civil nuclear agreement with NSG members and others to supply nuclear materials. Through the NSG waiver, India was further accommodated within the international nuclear architecture through civil nuclear agreements for peaceful uses of nuclear energy with the US, the UK, Japan, France, Mongolia, Russia, Kazakhstan and Australia, among others.

India's comprehensive nuclear security commitments are manifested in New Delhi's membership in international nuclear security regimes. Besides being a party to the CPPNM and the GICNT, India is also a party to the ICSANT.[42]. In June 2016, India extended its commitment to the joint statements on strengthening Nuclear Security Implementation, as contained in INFCIRC/86,[43] aimed at a sustainable and effective nuclear security regime.

The NSS is another platform where the international community recognises India's contribution. As a demonstration of nuclear responsibility, following the NSS communique on the reduction of reliance on HEU, India shifted the HEUs from the Apsara research reactor to a safeguarded facility in 2010.[44] At its first summit, India took the initiative to establish the GCNEP. The GCNEP would conduct extensive research, development and training on Advanced Nuclear Energy System Studies, Nuclear Security, Radiation Safety, and the application of Radioisotopes and Radiation Technology in the areas of healthcare, agriculture and food. The Centre's mandate would also entail Research & Development over the development of system designs that are intrinsically safe, secure, proliferation-resistant, and sustainable. This would further strengthen nuclear security in the long run.

India's reputation as a responsible nuclear State is further enhanced by her joining various export control regimes even without being a signatory to the NPT. Besides the NSG waiver, India joined the Australia Group in 2018 as its 43rd member. Similarly, the MTCR, formed in 1987, aims to restrict the flow of missiles and relevant technology capable of delivering 500 kg WMD at least 300 km. Due to India's adherence to the guidelines of the Regime, she was inducted into the MTCR in 2016.[45] The fourth export control regime, the

Wassenaar Arrangement, was formed in 1995 to control conventional arms and dual-use goods and technologies. New Delhi became its 42nd member in 2017, further enhancing India's non-proliferation credentials.

India's entry into international export control regimes manifests New Delhi's enhanced diplomatic and political stature among the comity of nations. Besides, India's moratorium on further nuclear testing, her NFU, negative security assurances, her unflinching adherence to non-proliferation norms, and engagement with the major nuclear non-proliferation institutions have made her a quintessential nuclear power. The accommodation has purely been on India's own merits, manifested in her exceptional non-proliferation record, unprecedented economic growth, and better adherence to the principles of NPT than some of the other signatories.

Conclusion

India had to opt for the nuclear option, given her national interests due to the complexities in its neighbourhood. To quote former PM, Vajpayee, "...these tests are not directed against any country; rather these were intended to reassure the people of India about their security and convey determination that this Government, like previous Governments, has the capability and resolve to safeguard their national security interests."[46] The path, however, was not smooth, and India's nuclear journey had to be undertaken in phases. The phase of estrangement largely saw sanctions and a moratorium on international aid. The withdrawal of sanctions and diplomatic overtures characterised the engagement phase. This led India to the phase of integration, where the India-US Civil Nuclear Cooperation Agreement saw intense political and diplomatic heavy lifting, ultimately culminating in an India-specific NSG waiver. The accommodation phase gave New Delhi membership in several non-proliferation and nuclear security groups. Over the years, India has developed a doctrinal approach towards nuclear weapons, which dictates that they are, at best, for deterrence against other nuclear forces.

NOTES

1 "Nuclear Weapons for Self-Defence" *Prime Minister Atal Bihari Vajpayee Select Speeches Vol-1* (March-1998-March 1999)", Publication Division, Ministry of Information and Broadcasting, 2000.
2 Standstill Agreement, 2 April, 1954 at https://pmindiaun.gov.in/public_files/assets/pdf/Agreement_6sep.pdf (Accessed on 22 July 2023)
3 Permanent Mission of India to the Conference on Disarmament, Geneva, "India's Disarmament Initiatives", 9 June 1998 at https://meaindia.nic.in/cdgeneva/?0424?000
4 Ibid.
5 "N.P.T. and Security Guarantees", Note from M.A. Husain, 11 April 1968, *P.N. Haksar Papers,* IIIrd Instalment, Subject File No. 200, Nehru Memorial Museum and Library (NMML), New Delhi.
6 Jaswant Singh, "Against Nuclear Apartheid." *Foreign Affairs,* 77(5), 1998, pp. 41–52; *JSTOR,* https://doi.org/10.2307/20049049 (Accessed 18 April 2023).
7 K Subrahmanyam, 'Nuclear Indian in Global Politics', *World Affairs: The Journal of International Issues,* 2(3), 1998, pp. 12-40
8 India co-sponsored the CTBT Resolution in the United Nations. India withdrew in 1995 due to domestic and strategic compulsions.
9 "N.P.T. and Security Guarantees", no.5.
10 Government of India, "Evolution of India's Nuclear Policy" *Prime Minister Atal Bihari Vajpayee Select Speeches Vol-1* (March-1998-March 1999), Publication Division, Ministry of Information and Broadcasting.
11 United Nations First Committee, "Reducing Nuclear Danger" 4 April 1998 at https://digitallibrary.un.org/search?f1=author&as=1&sf=title&so=a&rm=&m1=p&p1=UN.+ General+ Assembly+ %2853rd+sess.+%3A+1998-1999%29&ln=en
12 Permanent Mission of India to the Conference on Disarmament, "Statement by Ambassador Pankaj Sharma, Permanent Representative of India to the Conference on Disarmament, Geneva during the Plenary meeting of the Conference on Disarmament held on 24 January 2022" at https://pmindiaun.gov.in/Cdgeneva/statement_content/OQ (Accessed 16 April 2023).
13 K. Subrahmanyam "Indian Nuclear Policy- 1964-98" in Jasjit Singh (Ed.) *Nuclear India,* Knowledge World, 1998.
14 "India, Pakistan Nuclear Test and US Response", Congressional Research Service, 4 November 1998 at https://www.everycrsreport.com/reports/98-570.html
15 K. Subrahmanyam, no. 13; Shakti Sinha, *Vajpayee: The Year that changed India,* Penguin Random House, 2020, p. 106.
16 "India Achieves Nuclear Capability" *Prime Minister Atal Bihari Vajpayee Select Speeches Vol-1* (March-1998-March 1999), Publication Division, Ministry of Information and Broadcasting, Government of India.
17 "Nuclear Anxieties: Indian's letter to Clinton on the Nuclear Testing", 13 May 1998 at https://www.nytimes.com/1998/05/13/world/nuclear-anxiety-indian-s-letter-to-clinton-on-the-nuclear-testing.html
18 Shakti Sinha, no. 15.
19 United Nations Security Council, "RESOLUTION 1172 (1998) Adopted by the Security Council at its 3890th meeting", 6 June 1998 at S_RES_1172(1998)-EN.pdf (Accessed 23 July 2023)
20 *Kargil Review Committee Report,* National Security Council Secretariat, New Delhi, 1999, p. 175.

21 "USA - Clinton speaks on India's nuclear tests" at https://www.youtube.com/watch?v=KXFGkVvMYzk (Accessed 28 May 2023).

22 The White House, "Glenn Amendment" 18 March 2000 at https://clintonwhitehouse4.archives.gov/WH/New/SouthAsia/fact_sheets/india3.html

23 "Comments by the Chief Cabinet Secretary on Measures in Response to the Second Nuclear Testing conducted by India", 14 May 1998 at https://www.mofa.go.jp/announce/announce/1998/5/0312-09.html

24 Sheryl Wudunn "Nuclear Anxiety: The Allies – Japan Freezes Some Grants; Other Nations Seem Doubtful", *The New York Times,* 14 May 1998 at https://www.nytimes.com/1998/05/14/world/nuclear-anxiety-the-allies-japan-freezes-some-grants-other-nations-seem-doubtful.html

25 P.M. Kamath, "India's Nuclear Test, Then and Now: An Analysis of US and Canadian Responses", *Strategic Analysis,* 23(5), August 1999.

26 Shakti Sinha, no. 15.

27 Henry Kissinger, "India and Pakistan: After the Explosions", 8 June 1998 at https://www.washingtonpost.com/archive/opinions/1998/06/09/india-and-pakistan-after-the-explosions/c8cd600a-a090-48e3-9979-c5ba5bf5274a/

28 Henry Kissinger, "Working With India", 20 March 2006 at https://www.henryakissinger.com/articles/working-with-india/

29 The White House, "The President's Trip to South Asia", 18 March 2000 at https://clintonwhitehouse4.archives.gov/WH/New/SouthAsia/fact_sheets/india3.html#:~:text= Glenn%20Amendment%20%2D%20India,as%20well%20as %20other%20 activities.

30 *Kargil Review Committee Report*, no. 20.

31 "Draft report of National Security Advisory Board on Indian Nuclear Doctrine" at https://nuke.fas.org/guide/india/doctrine/990817-indnucld.htm (Accessed 20 April 2023).

32 Strobe Talbott, *Engaging India: Diplomacy, Democracy and the Bomb,* Penguin Viking, New York, March, 2006.

33 "Joint Press Statement: Next Steps in Strategic Partnership between India and the US", Press Releases, Embassy of India, Washington DC.

34 *Joint Statements India-US,* Ministry of External Affairs", Government of India.

35 "Suo-Motu statement by Prime Minister Dr. Manmohan Singh on Discussions on Civil Nuclear Energy Cooperation with the US: Implementation of India's Separation Plan" Ministry of External Affairs, Government of India, 7 March 2006 at https://mea.gov.in/Speeches-Statements.htm?dtl/2167/suomotu+statement+by+prime+minister+dr+manmohan+singh+on+discussions+on+civil+nuclear+energy+ cooperation+with+the +us+implementation+of+indias+separation+plan (20 May 2023).

36 Ibid.

37 Shivshankar Menon, *Choices: Inside the Making of India's Foreign Policy,* Penguin Random House, New Delhi, 2016.

38 "The Minister of External Affairs laid a statement regarding India's civil nuclear energy initiative-laid." Lok Sabha Secretariat, Government of India at https://eparlib.nic.in/bitstream/123456789/732821/1/10246.pdf#search= Civil%20 Nuclear %20Agreement (Accessed 24 April 2023).

39 "Implementation of the India-United States Joint Statement of 18 July 2005: India's Separation Plan" at https://mea.gov.in/Uploads/PublicationDocs/6145_bilateral-documents-May-11-2006.pdf (Accessed 22 May, 2023).

40 Shivshankar Menon, no. 38, p. 77.

41 "The Minister of External Affairs makes a statement regarding India's civil nuclear energy initiative-laid." Lok Sabha Secretariat, Government of India at https://eparlib.nic.in/bitstream/123456789/732821/1/10246.pdf#search=Civil%20 Nuclear % 20Agreement (Accessed 24 April 2023).

42 "Nuclear Security Summit National Progress Report India", Prime Minister's Office, Government of India, at https://pib.gov.in/newsite/PrintRelease.aspx?relid =81755 (Accessed 24 April, 2023).

43 "Communication of 20 June 2016 from the Permanent Mission of India concerning its commitment to the Joint Statement on Strengthening Nuclear Security Implementation", International Atomic Energy Agency at https://www.iaea.org/sites/default/files/infcirc897.pdf (Accessed 20 April, 2023).

44 "Nuclear Security in India", Ministry of External Affairs, Government of India, at https://www.mea.gov.in/Images/pdf/Brochure.pdf (Accessed 22 April 2023).

45 Missile Technology Control Regime at https://mtcr.info/partners/?lang=en (Accessed 1 September 2023).

46 "India Achieves Nuclear Capability" *Prime Minister Atal Bihari Vajpayee Select Speeches Vol-1* (March-1998-March 1999)", Publication Division, Ministry of Information and Broadcasting, Government of India.

Conclusion

The chapters of this book reveal a distinct trend that has emerged over more than 25 years of India's nuclearisation. India had compelling security reasons for conducting its nuclear weapons tests in 1998, a point all the authors agree upon. Professor Rajesh Rajagopalan argues that India should have pursued the nuclear option decades earlier. Various political and technical factors delayed this decision; however, the eventual choice to go nuclear was both timely and necessary to reassure citizens that national security would not be subject to the whims of either declared or undeclared nuclear States.

During India's nuclear discussions and subsequent tests, China's nuclear capabilities loomed large. Despite this, the Indian government has generally refrained from explicitly naming China or any other nation as its motivation for acquiring nuclear weapons. Officially, India asserts that its nuclear arsenal is not targeted at any specific country and has rejected the outdated Western narrative that confines India's nuclear posture to the South Asian context, particularly the Pakistan-India conflict. India maintains that its nuclear capabilities have no regional role, whether in a narrow South Asian context or a broader Southern Asian framework that includes China.

The authors emphasize India's determination to counter misrepresentations of international law. While India's approach to these unjust legal instruments has evolved, it has occasionally found itself confronting aggressive powers. Indian diplomacy has played a crucial role in resisting the manipulation of international law that seeks to portray India as a violator.

India has emerged as a responsible nuclear weapons State within the international system. Dr. Sheel Kant Sharma notes that India's "systematic diplomatic engagement" with key partners has significantly elevated its standing. The policy of restraint and responsibility, coupled with a commitment to security, has defined nuclear India. India has developed robust legal and institutional frameworks to regulate its nuclear commerce and fostered a strategic, normative and politically responsible culture.

As a responsible nuclear power, India has also sought confidence-building measures with its nuclear neighbours. It signed the 1988 Agreement on the Prohibition of Attack against Nuclear Installations and Facilities, with Pakistan, which became operational in January 1991. Although the Agreement predates India's nuclear weapons test, its spirit was reaffirmed upon India becoming a nuclear power. The 1999 Lahore Declaration further solidified this approach, and India has continued to pursue nuclear confidence-building measures with both Pakistan and China. China however, has shown little interest in genuine engagement on this front. Ms. Kanica Rakhra details various proposed measures– both governmental and non-governmental– pertinent to nuclear India. Additionally, India actively participates in international organizations like the UN to mitigate global nuclear risks.

Indian diplomacy has adeptly navigated various phases of its nuclear journey. Following the 1998 nuclear tests, India faced a brief period of international isolation. Ambassador D. Bala Venkatesh Varma indicates that, even during this time, the international community largely acknowledged India's rationale. Pakistan's subsequent nuclear tests shifted the focus, allowing Indian diplomacy to engage with significant global players, ultimately leading to India's integration into the global nuclear framework, exemplified by the 2005 India-US civil nuclear energy initiative. The process is still on, seeking an accommodation with the global nuclear system.

This responsible approach has yielded benefits for India. A substantial segment of the global security community recognizes that the 2005 initiative has mainstreamed India within the global non-proliferation regime, particularly following the clean exemptions granted by the NSG in 2008. Although all the NSG members except China supported India's membership bid, consensus principles hindered accession. Nevertheless, India has joined other multilateral export control regimes, including the MTCR, the Australia Group, and the Wassenaar Arrangement.

India's status as a responsible nuclear weapons State is further reinforced by its nuclear doctrine. After becoming a nuclear power, India worked to convey that its intentions are defensive, and it developed its arsenal solely for national security. Prime Ministers from Atal Bihari Vajpayee to his successors have consistently emphasized the non-aggressive nature of India's nuclear policy. The cornerstone of this doctrine is the principle of NFU, a stance shared only by China, albeit under increasing internal scrutiny.

However, the existing collaborations between China and Pakistan are enhancing both nations' strategic arsenals, which complicates India's nuclear calculus. Now the relationship between the two countries is also expected to enter into the realm of nuclear doctrine collaborations. The scenario of the partnership between Pakistan with the first-use policy and China with its NFU policy may complicate the Indian nuclear conundrum. As already discussed, China may not stick to its NFU policy, and to complicate the matter further, it is also rapidly modernising its nuclear arsenals. As discussed by Professor Rajesh Rajagopalan, these dynamics have significant implications for India's NFU doctrine.

To maintain credible deterrence, India has adopted a robust minimum nuclear deterrent tailored to its NFU policy. Key considerations include survivability and a rapid, massive response capability, ensuring the force structure remains effective without becoming excessive. While India has not disclosed the size of its nuclear stockpile, AVM Rajesh Kumar highlights the triad component of India's evolving nuclear force structure.

Nuclear India firmly believes that its nuclear force structure should enhance deterrence rather than facilitate warfighting. India advocates for a conventional battlefield, asserting that introducing nuclear weapons – even tactical ones– could provoke a devastating retaliation. To further this goal, India promotes an international no-first-use treaty, requiring the signature and ratification of all NWS notwithstanding their NPT membership.

A vital aspect of nuclear India is its unwavering commitment to nuclear disarmament. Despite becoming a nuclear weapons State, India has consistently championed the cause of disarmament. As Dr. Manpreet Sethi argues, India's national security is strengthened in a world free of nuclear weapons, and India actively pursues its long-standing disarmament vision and policy. The country has participated in discussions on the humanitarian impact of nuclear weapons and has taken a leading role in international forums advocating for disarmament.

India regards nuclear disarmament as critical for general disarmament, and has vocally supported the complete abolition of nuclear weapons. It has proposed practical steps towards this goal, arguing that a reduction in the military significance of nuclear arsenals could positively influence the disarmament agenda. India's vision includes a global, verifiable, and non-discriminatory nuclear disarmament treaty, termed the Nuclear Weapons Convention, aimed at eliminating nuclear weapons in a time-bound, legally binding universal framework.

However, India does not support the TPNW or regional disarmament measures, believing that the treaty, not negotiated within the CD, is inoperable and violates customary international law. India stayed away from its negotiations, and maintains that its provisions are not operable to it. As for regional disarmament, it maintains that nuclear weapons have the global reach and any regional solution is merely deceptive. India has also opposed the notion of South Asia as a nuclear weapons-free zone, though it maintains that any country is free to join any regional arrangements of its choice.

Significantly, India has adopted a proactive stance towards the non-proliferation regime. Its nuclearisation marked a new chapter in Indian policy concerning non-proliferation, enabling India to find its place within the global nuclear framework. The evolution of India's relationship with the non-proliferation regime, as detailed by Niranjan C. Oak and Abhishek Verma, illustrates the challenges India faced during the Cold War, post-Cold War and the post-nuclearisation eras.

The contradictions inherent in the NPT have led to the recurring crisis in the treaty. The non-compliance of the nuclear disarmament provision is primarily responsible for the perpetual crisis. India remains detached from the internal struggles of the NPT community. While India rejected the initial draft of the CTBT, it has since signalled a more favourable stance towards the treaty after its 1998 nuclear tests.

As the CTBT remains unratified 26 years after India's nuclearisation, the Indian government has adapted its policy to reflect changing strategic realities. The lack of disarmament provisions in the CTBT, combined with the ongoing modernisation of nuclear arsenals among nuclear-armed States, has further complicated the disarmament landscape. The debate surrounding operationalizing the CTBT often appears as strategic posturing rather than a genuine commitment to disarmament. Since these countries are not opting for nuclear disarmament, quite obviously, they have to refurbish and resuscitate their aging arsenals. The reason for the continued dormancy is the test requirement of old nuclear weapons countries. The internal debate in some of the countries reveals that they are concerned about their aging nuclear arsenals and uncertainty about the technology of laboratory simulation.

India's nuclear weapons development should not be misconstrued as an end to its peaceful use of nuclear energy. The country has actively engaged in nuclear energy projects domestically and internationally, without abandoning Dr. Homi Bhabha's three-stage nuclear power plan. Initiatives like SMR and Light Water Reactor Programmes are designed to complement this original plan.

As Dr. K.N. Vyas and Dr. M. Ramanamurthi emphasize, India's commitment to the peaceful use of nuclear energy aligns with the philosophy of *Vasudhaiv Kutumbakam*, positioning nuclear energy as a low-carbon energy source. Dr. R.B. Grover opines that nuclear power can also facilitate the generation of low-carbon hydrogen.

India has actively participated in global efforts to promote peaceful nuclear uses, receiving significant support for the Atoms for Peace initiative. Dr. Vyas and Dr. Ramanamurthi note that Bhabha was instrumental in the first international conference to promote the Peaceful Uses of Atomic Energy at Geneva in 1955. India's ongoing commitment to benefit humanity is evident in its nuclear science and technology programmes, which have led to advancements in areas such as medicine and agriculture. India has made substantial contributions through international organizations like the IAEA and various global projects. The GCNEP developed as a Centre of Excellence is considered a unique contribution of India's nuclear establishment to the world. This also demonstrates that India is seriously involved in global governance of nuclear issues.

In the Indian perspective, the IAEA serves as the nodal agency for global nuclear governance. Dr. Roshan Khaneijo outlines India's significant contributions to this governance framework. India has participated in all NSSs and is a signatory to relevant international laws regarding nuclear safety and security. The country has engaged in numerous forums to develop guidelines and codes of conduct for nuclear governance, supports initiatives like UN Security Council Resolution 1540 for preventing nuclear proliferation, and has implemented safeguards for its nuclear facilities, including an additional protocol to the IAEA.

As a responsible nuclear State, India is gradually being integrated into the global nuclear system, emerging as a net security provider not only for itself but also for the world. Until global nuclear disarmament is achieved, nuclear India will continue to play a vital role in ensuring its security and contribute to global peace.

Index